SUSTAINABLE PRODUCT INNOVATION

Entrepreneurship for Human Well-Being

Dariush Rafinejad, Ph.D.

Copyright © 2017 by Dariush Rafinejad

ISBN-13: 978-1-60427-147-8

Printed and bound in the U.S.A. Printed on acid-free paper.

10 9 8 7 6 5 4 3 2 1

Library of Congress Cataloging-in-Publication Data can be found in the WAV section of the publisher's website at www.jrosspub.com/wav.

Phone: (954) 727-9333
Fax: (561) 892-0700
Web: www.jrosspub.com

CONTENTS

CHAPTER 4: LIFE-CYCLE ASSESSMENT   75

CHAPTER 5: TECHNOLOGY AND PRODUCT STRATEGY   93

CHAPTER 6: THE PRODUCT CONCEPT AND
DEVELOPMENT PROCESS   113

CHAPTER 11: SUSTAINABILITY STANDARDS AND PRODUCT RATINGS — 193

CHAPTER 12: DECISION ANALYSIS AND MODELING IN PRODUCT DEVELOPMENT: SYSTEM DYNAMICS MODELING — 203

CHAPTER 13: RETURN ON INVESTMENT: INTELLECTUAL PROPERTY PROTECTION — 223

PROLOGUE

In spite of humankind's technological ingenuity and accomplishments, our current economic system has created severely undesirable consequences. We are ruled by our quest for material possessions, despite such desires being at the bottom of the hierarchy of needs for the actualization of human potential.[1] We have reframed art, spirituality, community bonding, and relationships with people and nature as monetized commodities. We have championed material wealth generation and technological advancement but have failed to offer most humans a minimal degree of equitable access to food, shelter, and healthcare. Finally, our current economic model has led us to the brink of an environmental and resource calamity that threatens to destroy our world and extinguish humanity's collective accomplishments.

Sadly, the individualism, alienation, and breakdown of interdependence caused by this system have left many material-rich people feeling insecure about the future and frightened about being without support from neighbors, communities, and society as a whole. In order to make an important and necessary shift and begin to reverse this dangerous process, we need to critically examine several currently unquestioned assumptions:

- Growth as the overarching objective of business
- A win-lose approach toward nature and other people
- Survival of the fittest as the best (and unavoidable) mechanism for development
- A focus on and prioritizing of short-term gains
- Globalization for the exploitation of resources (earth and labor) without globalization of equity
- Detachment from local and community issues
- Consolidation and centralization of the control of resources in a zero-sum game[2]

Human wellbeing—not customers' unmet needs or highest shareholder returns—*must* become the overarching goal of new technology and product development. The essentials of sustainable product development are innovation, challenging the status quo, thinking critically and in systems, and visioning sustainable development as the purpose of new products. This holistic approach to product innovation and commercialization represents a radical departure from the status quo. It requires bold leadership and managerial decision optimization on a global space-time framework that prioritizes sustainable development on both local and global scales. Most important, sustainable product development should be seen as a vast, untapped, limitless world of opportunity—the *blue ocean* or *white space* of a better future—and not as a constraint on innovation.

This book is informed by three decades of experiential leadership in product innovation in the semiconductor and solar energy industries. The ideas contained herein are based on a decade of teaching and research on sustainable innovation in products and manufacturing processes at Stanford University and Presidio Graduate School in San Francisco, California. I am grateful to the many colleagues and students who have inspired this work.

Endnotes

1. Abraham Maslow and K. J. Lewis, "Maslow's hierarchy of needs." Salenger Incorporated (1987): 14.
2. Robert C. Carlson and Dariush Rafinejad, "The Transition to Sustainable Production Development and Manufacturing," in Karl G. Kempf, Pinar Keskinocak, and Reha Uzsoy, (Eds.), Planning Production and Inventories in the Extended Enterprise: A State-of-the-Art Handbook, vol. 1, pp. 45–82 (New York: Springer, 2011).

INTRODUCTION

Product Innovation and Human Well-being:
A Historical Perspective

Products aim to improve the quality of life and human well-being. Since the Industrial Revolution and through multiple business cycles, the realization of new products has accelerated and significantly improved human productivity, mobility, and communication. New energy sources have been harnessed, and automation technologies have been substituted for manual labor. Products of mobility such as cars and jet planes have enabled previously unattainable economic activities on a global scale. Communication products such as phones and the Internet have lowered transactional costs and provided ubiquitous access to low-cost information. In addition, innovation in making new materials—such as textiles, steel, petrochemicals, plastics, and emerging bio-based materials—have been instrumental in shaping the modern way of life.

Every product has a life cycle, which consists of four steps—production, transportation, use, and end-of-life disposal. Each step of the product life cycle requires consumption of resources such as material, energy, and water. These resources are provisioned by the earth and include both renewable and nonrenewable entities. They are referred to as *sources*. Furthermore, each product life-cycle step generates and disposes waste to land, water, or air, which the earth then stores or processes. These functions are referred to as *sinks*. Both the extraction and utilization of the resources and the disposal of waste affect the earth's ecological systems and people, directly or indirectly.

The total ecological and human impact of a product is determined by multiplying the unit product's impact by the total number of units that are produced and used in the market. The unit product impact is proportional to the efficiency of the technologies and designs that are deployed during each of the four steps in the product life cycle. This efficiency determines the portion of input resources that is converted to useful functional output and the remainder that turns into waste. On the other hand, the total quantity of product units that are produced, consumed, and discarded is proportional to the population in the served market and the consumption intensity or consumption per capita.

Inefficiency and waste generation in converting input to output stem from the laws of physics (and the limitations of the second law of thermodynamics), nonoptimal product design, and wastefulness in consumer behavior. Waste is generated across the product life cycle and is discarded into the earth in gaseous, solid, and liquid phases. Examples of such waste include greenhouse gas (GHG) emissions from automobiles, municipal solid waste in landfills, and liquid wastes in industrial production or runoff in farming food.

The growth in global population since the beginning of the twentieth century has been astounding. In 1900, the world population was 1.8 billion. By 1950, it had increased to 2.5 billion, and in 2015, it was 7.3 billion. The consumption intensity or consumption per capita of the world population has also increased dramatically since the mid-twentieth century, in lockstep with rising living standards and improvements in hygiene.

To calculate the total ecological impact of a product, we turn to the so-called IPAT equation: $I = P \times A \times T$,[1] where I represents the ecological impact (the ecological footprint of human activities), P is population, A represents affluence or consumption intensity (the gross domestic product or GDP per capita), and T is technological efficiency (the ecological impact per unit of GDP). According to this model, sustainability requires *constant* or *declining* impact (I).

Marian R. Chertow[2] notes that increases in population and affluence can be balanced by improving the efficiency of technological systems. We can examine the implication of this hypothesis by looking ahead to 2050, when the world population is expected to reach 9 billion from 7.3 billion in 2015. In order to raise the living standard of the world to today's level of GDP per capita in the Organization for Economic Cooperation and Development (OECD) countries, the global GDP per capita must go up by 3.5 times.[3] The OECD per capita GDP in 2015 was $36,000, and the world GDP per capita was $10,600. If the 2050 impact (I_{2050}) is to remain at the 2015 level (I_{2015}), the ecological impact per GDP of 2050 can be calculated as follows:

$$I_{2015} = P_{2015} \times A_{2015} \times T_{2015} = 7.3 \times 10,600 \times T_{2015}$$

$$I_{2050} = P_{2050} \times A_{2050} \times T_{2050} = 9 \times 36,000 \times T_{2050}$$

If we set $I_{2050} = I_{2015}$, we get $T_{2050} = 0.24 \times T_{2015}$.

That is, we have to reduce the impact of global economic activities by $1/0.24 = 4$ times between 2015 and 2050 to just keep ecological impacts at the 2015 level. If we wish to avert catastrophic climate change effects as the result of global warming above 2°C, we need to reduce the impact significantly below the 2015 level.

The IPAT equation might be used to assess the necessary climate change strategy for the U.S. The U.S. must reduce its GHG emissions from fossil fuels by 80% over the next 40 years to stabilize GHGs at a safe level.[4] If the U.S. population grows by 1%

per year and the GDP grows 3% per year in the next 40 years, then according to the IPAT equation, we have to reduce GHG emissions by 7.7% per year. Achieving this goal requires an aggressive program of replacement and conservation of fossil fuels—converting all energy sources to solar, wind, and other renewables and improving efficiency in product designs, operational activities, and consumption habits.

The environmental impact of our products has led to an unsustainable situation that threatens both development and improvement of life quality. In other words, we are hindering and, in some cases, even reversing the quality-of-life improvements that are the objective utility of man-made products. The symptoms of this unsustainable situation are ubiquitous. Global demand for natural resources and environmental services has exceeded earth's carrying capacity. Adverse environmental impacts like global warming and toxic pollution pose severe and unprecedented threats to human well-being and biodiversity. Furthermore, the uneven distribution of benefits and harm (the externalities) from the production, use, and disposal of products has created severe spatial (transboundary) and temporal (intergenerational) inequities in the quality of people's lives across the globe.

Our prevalent economic system and legal framework are the contextual drivers of the business strategies and product life-cycle decisions that are responsible for the current unsustainable state. In this economic system, per capita GDP has become the most important indicator of a nation's living standard and quality of life. Consumption level is synonymous with economic health and social well-being and is tracked diligently by economists and governments.[5]

Another key feature of the prevailing economic paradigm is how natural resources and societal commonwealth (the common property) are treated. The value of a *common* property (including clean air, fresh water, oil, minerals, and most ecosystem services) is determined by the cost of access to the resource rather than by its contributed value in comparison with alternate means of producing the resource. Only the creation and depreciation of private and corporate wealth are accounted for in the economic models. The commonwealth is left out of business decision metrics. In other words, natural resources and sinks (otherwise known as nature's capital) that have been available at relatively low cost are not treated as assets. More important, they are assumed to be boundless.[6]

A NEW PATH FORWARD

We have the technological and financial means to make a course correction toward a sustainable future. This path forward in product innovation, entrepreneurship, business strategy, and public policy can be one of sustainable development that addresses the above symptoms and their consequences. Yet big questions remain. Do we have the wisdom, courage, and determination to make this step? Are we willing to see our current crisis as an *opportunity* for innovation in new technologies and products that support sustainable development?

This book offers a path toward seizing that opportunity. It is about strategies and techniques for the development and commercialization of sustainable products and services.[7] Such products serve the well-being of consumers without limiting that of others—both *here and now* and *elsewhere and later*. Sustainable products are produced in a way that is mindful of cross-generational and cross-boundary impacts on other people and on nature. The aim here is to explore product sustainability issues and their relationship to natural, economic, human, and social capitals. As part of this exploration, we examine sustainability indicators in design, manufacturing, operations, and supply chain management and discuss systems thinking and life-cycle optimization methodologies in product development and manufacturing.

It should be noted that although consumer well-being and positive societal contributions are the *purpose* of a product, the product's *commercial viability* for sustained business operation is also of vital importance. The commercial success of a sustainable product depends on three sets of factors:

1. Firm-level factors, such as the company's vision, strategy, technology, and operational processes;
2. Market conditions, including customer needs and preferences and the competitive landscape; and
3. Contextual factors, including the economic system, government policy, and regulations.

THE IMPLICATIONS OF A HOLISTIC SYSTEM

What is unique about our approach in product development? First, we take a systems approach and make multistakeholder optimization in product life-cycle design in order to meet the firm's objectives and the investors' return-on-investment expectations and to comply with regulatory requirements. Second, we consider global society and the earth as important stakeholders whose well-being must be included in product and technology development strategies, techniques, and decisions. Figure I.1 depicts the elements of a holistic product system from concept generation to end-of-life disposal of the product after use.

In the holistic system optimization model, the return on investment (ROI) in technology and product development is measured as the return in sustainable development (ROI-SD). In addition to traditional ROI models, we account for factors that are considered as externalities in the current prevailing economic frameworks. These externalities include earth ecological services (both their value and cost), nonrenewable resource rent, renewable resource replenishment cost, life-cycle-analysis (LCA) impacts on the environment and on life (both human and animal), and the product's societal benefits in the creation of jobs, sense of community, esthetics, and happiness.

This book is intended to offer a new paradigm. It is written for the general manager, senior-level executive, or entrepreneur who has the primary responsibility

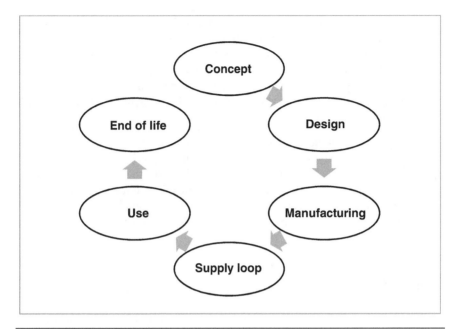

Figure I.1   Product life cycle as a holistic system

for creation, development, and commercialization of the product. The book is also designed as a textbook for the educators in degree and certificate programs, as well as in professional training. The objective is to help the reader understand why sustainable product development is essential, how it works within a start-up or an established company, and how to organize and lead the process of integrating sustainability effectively across a product life cycle, including research and development (R&D), design, production, use, and end-of-life disposal.

Using case studies to examine strategic decisions and best practices, we illuminate many key components of a new product development process, including the following:

- Perceiving market opportunity, conducting user-need research, developing a concept, building prototypes, and developing and framing a sustainable product's differentiated value in customer experience
- Establishing the technical feasibility and commercial viability of the concept
- Planning full design development and commercialization of the sustainable product
- Assessing the product's sustainability impact on a firm's competitive advantage and entrepreneurial opportunities
- Studying various sustainability frameworks in industrial ecology, LCA techniques, and design for sustainability

- Modeling techniques for integrating the environment and societal impacts into the traditional product design process
- Examining the evolution of environmental sustainability concepts and associated governmental regulations, business responses on a global scale, and the ways compliance with regulations and voluntary requirements for sustainable development affect a firm's ability to achieve its business and corporate objectives

This book offers a thorough review of the general management issues that managers and firms encounter when addressing sustainability in product development (and a product can include or be entirely a service). It offers the most effective decision-making tools for the development of sustainable products for commercial success, thereby helping you appreciate and navigate the complexities encountered when making this essential change in the way products are created, dispensed, used, and discarded.

Endnotes

1. John P. Holdren and Paul R. Ehrlich, "American Population and the Global Environment," *American Scientist* 62(3) (1974): 62.
2. Marian R. Chertow, "The IPAT Equation and Its Variants: Changing Views of Technology and Environmental Impact," Journal of Industrial Ecology 4(4) (2001): 13–29.
3. "Five to tenfold increase in manufacturing output will be needed just to raise developing world consumption of manufactured goods to industrialized world levels by the time population growth rates level off next century." United Nations World Commission on Environment and Development, "Industry: Producing More with Less," in Our Common Future ("Brundtland Report"), Gro Harlem Bruntland, (Ed.), sec. 5, p. 31 (New York: United Nations, 1987).
4. http://eere.energy.gov/news/ December 02, 2009. President Obama Sets a Target for Cutting U.S. Greenhouse Gas Emissions.
5. Two-thirds of all economic activities in the United States are in the consumer sector.
6. Robert C. Carlson and Dariush Rafinejad, "The Transition to Sustainable Production Development and Manufacturing," in Karl G. Kempf, Pinar Keskinocak, and Reha Uzsoy, (Eds.), Planning Production and Inventories in the Extended Enterprise: A State-of-the-Art Handbook, vol. 1, pp. 45–82 (New York: Springer, 2011).
7. The word product is used here in its most general sense. Service may be an important component of a product, or the product might be entirely a service. For example, a software product may have no other function than to provide a service, sometimes referred to as software as a service.

ABOUT THE AUTHOR

 Dariush Rafinejad, Ph.D., has over 30 years of executive leadership experience in product innovation, development, and commercialization at global high-technology companies in the semiconductor and solar energy industries. Dr. Rafinejad served as Corporate Vice President at Applied Materials Corporation and Lam Research Corporation, where he led the development and commercialization of numerous successful products, and was General Manager of several large business units.

Dr. Rafinejad also has experience with several start-up companies, serving as an investor and a member of their boards of directors. In 2004, he founded Blue Dome Consulting, a business consulting firm. He lists Novellus, SanDisk, Brewer Science, Aviza Tech, MKS, AMEC (China), and SoloPower among his corporate clients.

Dr. Rafinejad is a widely published author of articles and case studies and of research conducted at Stanford University. In 2007, he authored *Innovation, Product Development and Commercialization: Case Studies and Key Practices for Market Leadership*. His current research interests include innovation for sustainable development, sustainable product development, manufacturing and supply chain management, and renewable energy systems. He is a core faculty member at Presidio Graduate School in San Francisco, where he teaches Master of Business Administration and Master of Public Administration courses on Sustainable Products and Services: Innovation for Human Well-being and Sustainable Energy Management—CleanTech Management Series. He was previously an Associate Professor—Consulting at Stanford University, an adjunct professor at the Haas Business School of the University of California, Berkeley, and the Dean of Management at Menlo College in Atherton, California.

Dr. Rafinejad holds M.Sc. and Ph.D. degrees in Mechanical Engineering from the University of California, Berkeley, and has conducted post-doctoral research at Imperial College in London, England. His professional education at Stanford University includes an Executive Engineering Management Certificate and several continuing education courses.

He resides in Los Altos Hills, California.

 Web Added Value™

This book has free material available for download from the
Web Added Value™ resource center at *www.jrosspub.com*

At J. Ross Publishing we are committed to providing today's professional with practical, hands-on tools that enhance the learning experience and give readers an opportunity to apply what they have learned. That is why we offer free ancillary materials available for download on this book and all participating Web Added Value™ publications. These online resources may include interactive versions of material that appears in the book or supplemental templates, worksheets, models, plans, case studies, proposals, spreadsheets and assessment tools, among other things. Whenever you see the WAV™ symbol in any of our publications, it means bonus materials accompany the book and are available from the Web Added Value Download Resource Center at www.jrosspub.com.

Downloads for *Sustainable Product Innovation: Entrepreneurship for Human Well-being* include book support and teaching materials for use by instructors of college courses, continuing education programs, and professional training.

DEDICATION

I dedicate this book to my wife, Shanaz, and my son, Danny—
the sources of my inspiration.

CHAPTER 1

THE SUSTAINABILITY CHALLENGE

This chapter defines and explores the intricate linkages among the topics of business, environmental, and social sustainability. It introduces the concept of sustainable products as a radical departure from the traditional way of conceiving, designing, manufacturing, and marketing new products and services. Throughout, the need for systems thinking is emphasized in order to achieve optimal outcomes that benefit all stakeholders in business, the environment, and society. The approach includes three main steps:

- Provide an overview of the prevalent interpretations of sustainability in business and the corresponding strategies and methods in new product innovation and commercialization.
- Examine the effects of current economic activities on people and the planet and the ways they have created an untenable situation with present harm and long-term systemic risk.
- Define the term *social and environmental sustainability*, and posit that the root cause of the present sustainability risks is a lack of tight integration of environmental and social sustainability factors in business, technology, and product strategies.

Traditional product innovation and commercialization methods must be amended to deploy holistic systems thinking and decision optimization that achieve integrated business, social, and environmental sustainability. The new business and sustainable innovation practices can be successful only if they are reinforced by supporting public policies and informed citizens. Sustainable products are the outcome of the amended practices that are examined in-depth throughout this book.

The Prevalent Interpretation
of Business Sustainability

Traditionally, sustainability in business has meant continued success in attaining the firm's financial objectives, which is achieved by adopting effective marketing and operational strategies and by investing in technologies that strengthen the firm's competitive advantage and increase market opportunities. New products are developed and commercialized to grow revenues, market share, profitability, and shareholder value. Revenue is enhanced by products that expand the total available market and the served available market. The firm's product portfolio also is enhanced through horizontal and vertical mergers and acquisitions. To grow market share, new technologies and products are developed that create a compelling competitive advantage and help control the basis of competition and market assets in favor of the firm. Increased profitability is achieved through differentiated products that can demand higher prices, have lower cost of goods sold, and enhance the power position of the firm in the supply chain compared to other actors.

Growth and scalability are highly desirable for new products because they ensure shareholder value growth and an attractive return on equity throughout the product's life cycle. Figure 1.1 shows the steps in a new product's life cycle, from development and commercialization to the end of its useful life.

In addition to the firm's strategies and operational practices, business success depends on external factors like access to capital and efficient functioning of the supply chain. Start-ups might need venture capitalists to fund the development of high-risk new technologies, and established firms might need investment banks to provide the working capital to sustain their operation. Other capital market players enable companies to sell bonds and acquire capital for building new factories and growing their business. In addition, the sustainability of a business depends on the underlying contextual factors of a political economy, such as contract and intellectual property (IP) laws and regulatory regimes that influence risk assessment and decision optimization within a firm. In short, a business functions within an ecosystem comprised of the firm and its suppliers, investors, customers, and regulatory agents.

Today, the ecosystem of most businesses does not extend to include the environment or society. Furthermore, the outlook of business is limited to the investment-planning horizon without considering the long-term environmental and social effects of its activities. Only in recent decades have people become concerned about the availability of raw materials—the fossil fuels, water, food, and other resources we extract from the planet—or about the harmful health and societal effects of the waste that is generated throughout the life cycle of products that we produce and consume. This is reflected in standard business attitudes toward production. The principal resource issue of concern to a firm is affordability—that is, acquisition of resources and disposal of waste at the lowest cost in compliance with governmental regulations.

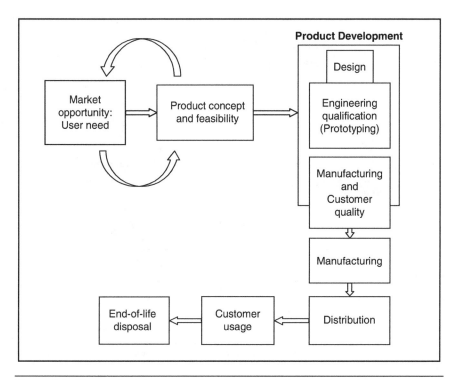

Figure 1.1   The product development and commercialization life cycle

The life cycle of every product involves a flow of material, energy, and waste (effluent); starting with extraction from the earth, continuing through production, and ending with consumption and disposal (Figure 1.2). Firms design products or devise operational strategies based on only a few steps in this life cycle—those adjacent to the production of their product. They strive to produce and deliver products at the lowest cost, to ensure continuity of material and resource supplies for their production, to fulfill demand with on-time delivery, and to meet their customers' quality requirements. Concern for the effluents (gaseous, liquid, and solid) is limited to the production steps directly under the firm's control and to those effluents that are obtained from the product in use and must comply with applicable regulatory requirements. This limited outlook ignores many steps of the actual product life cycle, thus failing to consider the holistic impact of a product on the earth's ecosystems and society. Each step of the product life cycle requires consumption of resources such as material, energy, and water. These resources are provisioned by the earth and include both renewable and nonrenewable entities. They are referred to as *sources*. Furthermore, each product life-cycle step generates and disposes waste to land, water, or air, which the earth stores or processes. These functions are referred to as *sinks*.

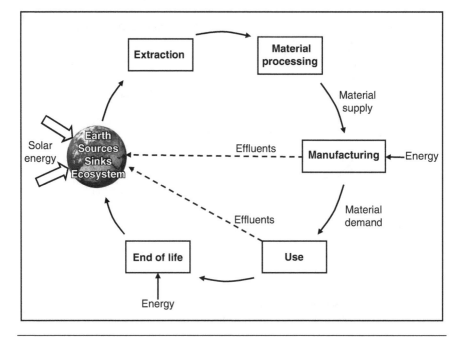

Figure 1.2   A holistic view of the flow of materials, energy, and effluents in a product's life cycle

Businesses are beginning to realize that global economic activities in aggregate affect the availability of resources for the manufacturing and consumption of our products and the capacity of the earth to store and process the waste. Since the Industrial Revolution, the impact of the human production-consumption system has grown exponentially relative to the earth's ability to supply the sources and to provide the ecofunctions of the sinks. As a result, the ratio of the human footprint to the earth's carrying capacity has risen exponentially (Figure 1.3). Can the current dominant growth strategy in business be sustained, at either the firm level or at the aggregate global system level? Unlimited growth in a limited system such as the earth is not feasible.

At the firm level, businesses argue that a single entity has only a small effect on the global system, and therefore they ignore the global system aggregation as they pursue their business growth strategies. Furthermore, the limits on this growth scenario are not universally accepted. Scarcity in global sources and sinks is believed to be resolvable by innovations in technology and free-market price mechanisms. Adverse impacts on the environment and society are also perceived to create entrepreneurial market opportunities for new product solutions.

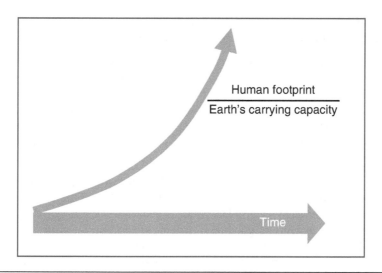

Figure 1.3 The rising human footprint relative to earth's carrying capacity

The lack of sustainability of the prevalent growth strategy is nevertheless gradually appearing on the list of business challenges and strategic considerations. *MIT Sloan Management Review* and Boston Consulting Group surveyed 4,700 executives, managers, and thought leaders from a range of worldwide industries about the primary business challenges facing their organizations over the next two years.[1] In the 2010 and 2011 surveys, only 14% and 16% of the respondents, respectively, considered the *threats and opportunities of sustainability* as a primary business challenge.

What Do Environmental Sustainability and Social Sustainability Mean?

The sources and sinks of the earth sustain our livelihoods and our economies. Some sources (like fossil fuels) are nonrenewable, and others (like air, land, fresh water, oil, minerals, plants, fish, and other animals) are renewable. The sinks absorb and process the effluents or wastes of living species and human technological activities, and provide ecofunctions (services) that sustain life. For example, the atmospheric ozone layer absorbs harmful ultraviolet (UV) radiation from the sun, trees and oceans sequester carbon dioxide (CO_2) emitted by transportation vehicles and industrial processes, fallen leaves turn into fertilizer to sustain the plant life cycle, coral reefs provide habitats to thousands of species, and soil among other things purifies water. There are many other ecofunctions that we might not yet know about.

The earth's capacity for sources, sinks, and ecofunctions are referred to as natural capital. The following is a list of services provided by the earth's ecosystem:

- Provisioning services, such as seafood, crops, livestock, and forest products
- Regulating services, including climate stabilization, water supply, fire prevention, flood control, sedimentation control, pest control, and pollination
- Cultural services, such as aesthetic values, knowledge systems, educational values, sense of place, spiritual values, inspiration, recreation, and ecotourism
- Supporting services and preservation of options through biodiversity and resilience

Figure 1.4 illustrates how ecosystem services affect human well-being according to the model developed by the United Nations Millennium Ecosystem Assessment.[2]

The word *sustainable* means able to last or continue for a long time. The association of sustainability to goodness—such as environmental protection or social well-being, which often is implied in sustainability circles—came about as the risks to human development and its sustainability over future generations were examined. In the United Nations report on *Our Common Future*, Gro Harlem

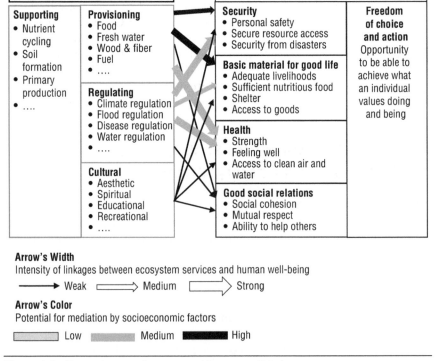

Figure 1.4   Ecosystem services support human well-being

Brundtland defines *sustainable development* as "development that meets the needs of the present without compromising the ability of future generations to meet their own needs."[3] As is discussed later in this chapter, this definition is unclear. It neither defines the meaning of *development* nor includes the important concept of equitable development. Traditionally, *human development* has been defined as the creation of economic surplus by exploiting natural resources and producing innovative products. This development has been mostly unconstrained and has resulted in excessive environmental degradation and social harm. Therefore, we need to be explicit when relating development to well-being and to state the importance of equity in social welfare. In this book, *sustainable development* is defined as equitable human well-being that continues for a long time.

Sustainability means a high-quality life (well-being) for all people in perpetuity through the preservation of earth sources, sinks, and ecofunctions (environmental sustainability). Well-being for all underscores an additional requirement—equity and social justice, which is social sustainability. Human economic and social activities that improve human well-being without harm to others—here and elsewhere, now and later—are sustainable development. The word *harm* means a limitation on opportunities for others to have a high-quality life (well-being).

Sustainable development often is depicted by the triple-bottom-line framework shown in Figure 1.5 at the intersection of economic, social, and environmental sustainability.

When the earth, society, and the economy are seen holistically as an integrated system, two types of variables can be distinguished—stocks and flows. Stock variables or capital provide the capacity for the functions of the system, and flows represent the rate at which services and activities take place. These economic, social, and environmental factors form a dynamic and complex system that functions through multiple feedback loops and nonlinear interactions over time.

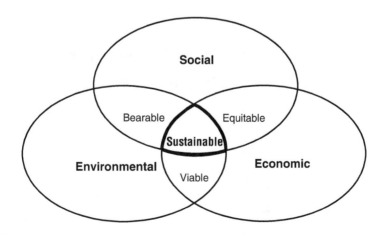

Figure 1.5   A triple-bottom-line framework for sustainable development

Four types of capital are needed to support sustainable development—natural capital (earth's capacity to provide sources, sinks, and ecofunctions), economic capital (physical infrastructure, means of production, and financial investments), social capital (trust and institutions that establish the rules that enable an optimal functioning of society), and human capital (education, health, and empowerment of citizens).

In applying the triple-bottom-line model to new product development, we must take a holistic systems view of a product's life cycle. We must consider all the steps and players in the supply loop shown in Figure 1.2, including the earth as the provider of the sources and sinks that support the entire system. The material inputs that support the supply chain start from the earth and the extraction of raw materials, and the effluents from various process steps are discharged to air, water, and land. At the end of their life, products also end up in landfills or in the atmosphere if incinerated.

This definition of sustainable development has both temporal and spatial dimensions. The well-being of present and future generations is considered on the temporal scale. On the spatial scale, sustainability is an equity and social justice issue: no one in the world should be denied the opportunity to have a high-quality life. Figure 1.6 illustrates the time and space scales in sustainable development.[4] Economic development and product development must consider the impact of human activities on the environment and society in both transgenerational (time) and transboundary global (space) scales. We must maximize benefits and minimize harm here and elsewhere, now and later.

The meaning of *well-being* that appears in our definition of sustainability and the meaning of *satisfaction of needs* that appears in Brundtland's definition of sustainable development need to be expanded. These concepts are critical in the development of sustainable products and technologies because products aim to satisfy users' needs and improve their well-being. Several questions need to be asked: What is *development*? Do we mean economic growth or developments in science, technology, health, art, leisure, and human relationships? What do we mean by *needs*?

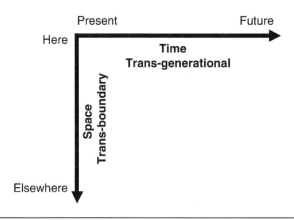

Figure 1.6   Time and space scales of sustainable development

Material needs or feel-good and spiritual needs? Is there a universal and trans-generational definition of needs, or do they vary and evolve across space and over time? Is there a floor for needs and need-satisfaction? Is there a ceiling? We also must ask whose needs should be satisfied and what geographic, race, social stratum, and class considerations are to be included in a definition of needs and their satisfaction. Well-being might be equated to satisfaction of a complex set of needs and aspirations[5]—existential needs for survival, needs for a healthy and meaningful life, and needs for community, love, and happiness. Perceptions of well-being and need-satisfaction are highly variable among people across space and over time. What is important is the freedom to choose and the opportunity to realize one's own well-being and need-satisfaction.

Another important issue in the definition of sustainable development is not compromising the ability of future generations to satisfy their needs. The question is: How would the *ability of future generations* be compromised by our products and economic activities? Would our activities deprive future generations of earth's resources (both sources and sinks), diminish biodiversity, cause genetic health damage, and create long-term ecosystem degradation?

We also should ask: How is the ability of *others* around the globe to satisfy their needs compromised? How do our production outsourcing practices and the life-cycle management of our products affect the well-being of the have-nots—often the workers in poor countries and neighborhoods where polluting factories are situated? Are we contributing to the privatization of common goods and the globalization of earth's resources and labor? The latter results in the virtual transfer of earth resources from poor regions to the rich and exploits workers by lowering wages across the globe.

Figure 1.7 illustrates a normative model of business decision making for sustainable development.[6] Human and natural constraints are shown as the driving potentials, and human technologies are a dynamic and formative force that affects

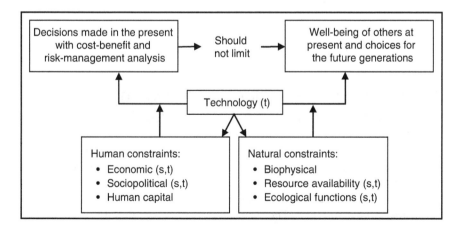

Figure 1.7   A model of business decision making for sustainable development

both human and natural constraints in space (s) and time (t). Note that human technology is an outcome of business decisions and its effects are manifest in every phase of a product's life cycle.

Karl-Göran Mäler, Sara Aniyar, and Åsa Jansson[7] have developed a mathematical model of sustainability in which sustainability means that human well-being ($W_{t,x}$) increases (or is constant) over time (t):

$$\frac{\partial W_{t,x}}{\partial t} \geq 0,$$

where well-being, $W_{t,x}$, is a function of both time (t) and space (x).

Social sustainability requires that inequality in well-being among people must be reduced over time:

$$\frac{\partial}{\partial t}\left[\frac{\partial W_{t,x}}{\partial x}\right] \leq 0,$$

where x is the space coordinate vector.

Well-being is the sum of the utilities that contribute to need-satisfaction (for example, according to Maslow's hierarchy of needs, existential, community, and potential needs). Well-being and production of the utilities are enabled through the underlying capital assets, including technological capital stock (human-made), natural capital stock (ecosystems for supporting, provisioning, and regulating services and other resources), and human and social capital stock (institutions, norms and mores, education).

According to Mäler et al., the accounting (shadow) price of capital stock (i) at time (t) is defined as (marginal utility as a result of change in increase/decrease in the capital asset, K_i):

$$p_{i,t} = \sum_{i=1}^{n} \frac{\partial W_{t,x}}{\partial K_i}.$$

For all assets, $i = 1, n$.

The Scorecard: The Effects of Prevalent Practices on People and the Planet

In this section, we examine the sustainability scorecard of human economic activities, technologies, and products, using the sustainability standards that are discussed in previous sections. The framework of Figure 1.6 is used to review the effects of human-made products on the *economic, natural, social, and human capitals—here and elsewhere, now and later*. The sustainability lens (according to our definition and the triple-bottom-line model) also is used to assess present trends in human development. The discussion focuses on selected sustainability indicators on the global scale in order to arrive at guidelines for sustainable product development. However, as pointed out elsewhere,[8] sustainable products must support sustainable development on a local scale.

Sustainability Rubrics

Michelle Greymore, Neil G. Sipe, and R. E. Rickson[9] reviewed several methods and their usefulness as tools for sustainability assessment on the regional scale (Table 1.1). The authors found none of the five methods listed was fully effective on the regional scale, primarily because of data limitations and also because they could not be easily understood and used to direct policy and decision making. However, the authors noted well-being as the most effective method. As discussed in later sections, we adopt *well-being* as the primary metric in the definition of a sustainable product.

Table 1.1   Sustainability assessment methods

Method	Description
Ecological footprint	This method calculates the integral index based on determining the amount of land required to support the population's activities (Wackernagel et al., 1993[i]). The method used for the ecological footprint evaluation is described by Simpson et al. (1998)[ii].
Well-being assessment	This method was developed by the World Conservation Union (Guijt and Moiseev, 2001; Prescott-Allen, 2001[iii]). This method of assessing sustainability gives equal weight to people and the ecosystem. The well-being assessment can be used at any level, from municipality to the world.
Quality of life	Quality of life is measured in a variety of contexts, including indicators like crime, participation in cultural and recreational activities, health, education, income, housing affordability, unemployment, water quality, air quality, and amount of open space.
Ecosystem health	This method of assessing sustainability is similar to quality-of-life assessment, where conditions and trends measured by environmental indicators (air, land, inland water, coastal and marine systems, and ecosystem services) are used to measure ecosystem health.
Natural resource availability	This approach uses a group of single indicators that measure the amount of selected resources available in a region.

[i] Wackernagel, Mathis. How big is our ecological footprint?: a handbook for estimating a community's appropriated carrying capacity, 1993.

[ii] Rod Simpson, Ian Lowe, and Anna Petroeschevsky. The Ecological Footprint of Australia with a Focus on the South-east Queensland Region. School of Public Health, Griffith University, 1998.

[iii] I. Guijt, and A. Moiseev. "Resource kit for sustainability assessment." IUCN, Gland, Switzerland and Cambridge, UK (2001).

Planetary Boundaries

The planetary boundaries framework was first introduced in 2009, when an international group of scientists identified and quantified the first set of nine planetary boundaries within which humanity can continue to develop and thrive for generations to come. Crossing these boundaries could generate abrupt or irreversible environmental changes.[10] Jonathan Foley and his colleagues[11] discuss the nine environmental processes that could disrupt the planet's ability to support human life and then set boundaries for these processes—limits within which humankind can operate safely. They also propose solutions to environmental threats.

The planetary boundaries framework was updated and published in *Science* by Will Steffen and his colleagues in 2015.[12] This article outlines the current status of the control variables for seven of the nine planetary boundaries. Figure 1.8 identifies three zones using different colors: safe operating space, zone of uncertainty (increasing risk), and the high-risk zone. The planetary boundary analysis shows that three processes—biodiversity loss, nitrogen pollution, and climate change—already exceed their boundaries, and all the others are moving toward the unsafe thresholds.

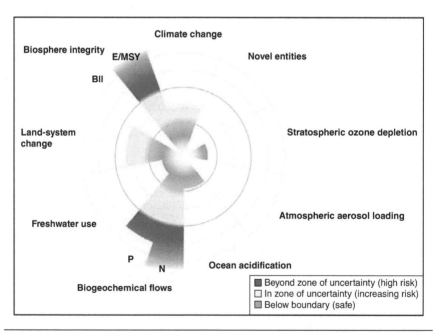

Figure 1.8 The planetary boundaries framework

Rules for a Sustainable Economy

Herman Daly and Joshua Farley[13] have established the following three rules for a sustainable economy:

1. For a renewable resource, the sustainable rate of use is less than the rate of regeneration of its source;
2. For a nonrenewable resource, the sustainable rate of use is less than the rate at which a renewable resource (used sustainably) can be substituted for it; and
3. For a pollutant, the sustainable rate of emission is less than the rate at which the pollutant can be recycled, absorbed, or rendered harmless in nature.

Ecological Footprint

Conceived by Mathis Wackernagel and William Rees at the University of British Columbia, the ecological footprint is now widely used to monitor ecological resource use and advance sustainable development.[14] The ecological footprint measures how much land and water area a human population requires to produce the resources it consumes and to absorb its wastes, using prevailing technology.

According to Mathis Wackernagel and William Rees, "If the entire population of the world had the same standard of living as the U.S., three earths would be needed."[15] According to the Global Footprint Network, the ecological overshoot day for 2015 occurred on August 13—the day when the human demand for resources exceeded earth's annual provisioning capacity. Under the business-as-usual scenario, the overshoot day for 2050 is expected to occur shortly after January 1.[16]

The Global Footprint Network[17] tracks the two sustainability indicators for having a fulfilling life without degrading the planet—the human development index (HDI) and the ecological footprint per person. The United Nations' HDI is a summary measure of average achievement in key dimensions of human development—enjoying a long and healthy life, being knowledgeable, and having a decent standard of living. The HDI is the geometric mean of normalized indices for each of the three dimensions.[18]

According to the Global Footprint Network, the sustainable biocapacity per person is 2 hectares and the sustainable HDI is larger than 0.8. Sustainable development means achieving both of these criteria. Despite increasing awareness and commitment to sustainable development, most countries today fail to meet both of these criteria.

Inclusive Wealth Index

Another index of sustainability developed by the United Nations is the inclusive wealth index (IWI).[19] IWI is an aggregate measure of a society's natural, human, and manufactured capital assets. IWI is an improvement over the gross domestic product (GDP) and the HDI as indexes of sustainability because it is a more comprehensive measurement of a country's capital assets.

Human Well-Being

Pamela Matson, William C. Clark, and Krister Andersson[20] propose a sustainability framework based on human well-being that is determined by five capital assets, including human capital, natural capital, manufactured capital, knowledge capital, and social capital.

For the Commission on the Measurement of Economic Performance and Social Progress,[21] well-being is multidimensional and has many aspects that should be considered simultaneously—including material living standards (income, consumption, and wealth), health, education, personal activities (including work), political voice and governance, social connections and relationships, the environment (present and future conditions), and insecurity (both economic and physical).

The Sustainability Hierarchy

The sustainability hierarchy (Figure 1.9) establishes the relative impact of human actions and their associated consequences according to the authors, from reducing the quality of life to endangering human survival.[22] This framework can be used to set weights when ranking alternate decision parameters in product design or operational strategies.

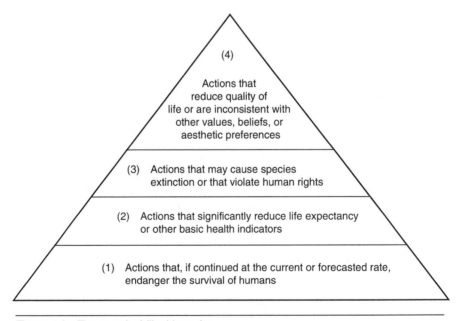

Figure 1.9 The sustainability hierarchy

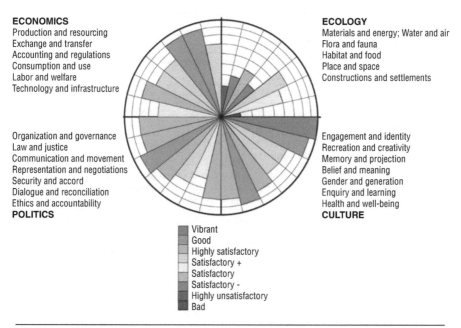

ECONOMICS
Production and resourcing
Exchange and transfer
Accounting and regulations
Consumption and use
Labor and welfare
Technology and infrastructure

ECOLOGY
Materials and energy; Water and air
Flora and fauna
Habitat and food
Place and space
Constructions and settlements

Organization and governance
Law and justice
Communication and movement
Representation and negotiations
Security and accord
Dialogue and reconciliation
Ethics and accountability
POLITICS

Engagement and identity
Recreation and creativity
Memory and projection
Belief and meaning
Gender and generation
Enquiry and learning
Health and well-being
CULTURE

Vibrant
Good
Highly satisfactory
Satisfactory +
Satisfactory
Satisfactory -
Highly unsatisfactory
Bad

Figure 1.10   Circles of sustainability

Circles of Sustainability

Another model used by the United Nations frames sustainable development progress according to the circles of sustainability (Figure 1.10).[23] For each of the four categories—economics, ecology, politics, and culture—the state of development is assessed on a nine-point scale from critical to vibrant.

What Is the Sustainability Scorecard of Human Economic Activities?

The biosphere is a narrow, fragile band—five miles above and five miles below the surface of the earth—where life exists. The adverse impact of human-made products and economic activities is felt across the environmental, social, and economic dimensions of sustainability. Anthropogenic greenhouse gas (GHG) emissions have accelerated global warming and risks of climate change; hazardous toxins have adversely affected human, animal, and plant life and the biodiversity of species; and economic inequity and a lack of social justice persist in both industrially developed and less developed countries. Table 1.2 summarizes the global-scale anthropogenic problems as reported by James Gustave Speth.[24]

Table 1.2 Global-scale environmental problems

	Problems	Symptoms
1	Depleting the ozone layer	Most of the stratospheric ozone layer was depleted before it was discovered.
2	Losing the forests	The rate of tropical deforestation is 1 acre per second.
3	Losing the land (desertification)	Half of agricultural land in drier regions suffers from desertification.
		Half of the world's wetlands and two-thirds of its mangroves are gone.
4	Losing freshwater	Freshwater withdrawals doubled globally from 1960 to 2000. The Colorado, Yellow, Ganges, and Nile rivers no longer reach the oceans in dry seasons.
5	Disrupting the climate	Greenhouse gas emissions have exceeded the equilibrium level (350 ppm CO_2).
6	Losing marine fisheries	Nearly 90% of large predatory fish are gone, and 75% of marine fisheries are now overfished.
7	Ingesting toxic pollutants	Dozens of persistent toxic chemicals can be found in every person.
8	Losing biodiversity	Species are disappearing at rates 1,000 times faster than normal.
9	Overfertilizing with nitrogen (such as eutrophication)	Overfertilization is causing hundreds of dead zones in oceans.
10	Acidifying the oceans	Nearly 20% of corals are gone, and another 20% are severely threatened.

In 2009, the White House Office of Science and Technology Policy stated that of all the challenges we face as a nation and as a planet, none is as pressing as the three-pronged challenge of climate change, sustainable development, and the need to foster new and cleaner sources of energy. According to the 2007 United Nations Intergovernmental Panel on Climate Change (UN IPCC), climate change refers to *a change in the state of the climate that can be identified by changes in the mean and/ or the variability of its properties and that persists for an extended period, typically decades or longer.*[25] The Natural Resources Defense Council (NRDC) reported in 2014 that *an acre of wetland is destroyed every minute in the U.S. and tropical forests are being destroyed at the rate of one acre per second.*[26]

Global Warming

Increases in anthropogenic GHG concentrations have caused most of the increases in global average temperatures since the mid-twentieth century. GHG emissions are the result of fossil fuel combustion and other industrial processes (such as cement manufacturing). The following GHGs were identified in the United Nations Kyoto

Protocol as the most potent contributors to global warming—CO_2, CH_4, N_2O, hydrofluorocarbons (HFCs), perfluorocarbons (PFCs), and sulfur hexafluoride (SF_6).[27] GHGs trap heat in the atmosphere and thereby cause global warming and climate change. The global warming potential (GWP) of these gases usually is measured in reference to that of CO_2 and referred to as CO_2-equivalent. The relative GWPs of the primary GHGs are shown in Figure 1.11.[28]

The major sources of GHG emissions are fossil fuel-based electricity generation plants, transportation vehicles, heating and cooling in residential and commercial buildings, and industrial processes. GHG emissions from agriculture include nitrous oxide (N_2O) from cultivation and methane (CH_4) from livestock.[29] Deforestation also is a significant contributor to the increase in carbon emissions because emissions that otherwise would have been captured by plants are released to the atmosphere.

CO_2 emissions from the use of fossil fuels represent approximately 60% of the total GHG emissions from all sources.[30] National Oceanic and Atmospheric Administration (NOAA) data collected at Mauna Loa Observatory in Hawaii demonstrate a steady rise of CO_2 concentration in the atmosphere since 1960 (Figure 1.12).[31]

A carbon concentration threshold of 450 parts per million (ppm) is predicted to produce a 2°C rise in the global average surface temperature above the preindustrial level, and avoiding 2°C is considered to be the target for precluding dangerous climate change impacts: "The linear relationship between cumulative carbon emissions and global climate warming implies that as mitigation is delayed, climate targets become unachievable."[32] By 2012, the global average temperature had risen

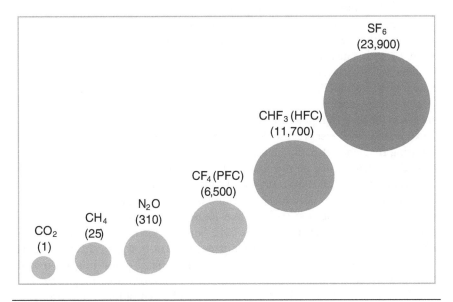

Figure 1.11   The global warming potential of greenhouse gases

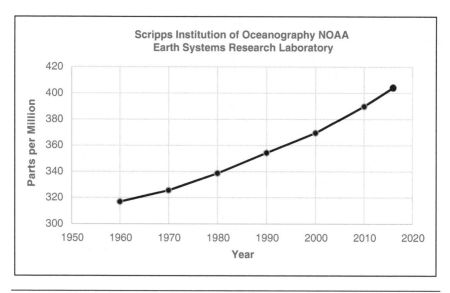

Figure 1.12   The steady rise of atmospheric CO_2 at Mauna Loa Observatory

by 1.5°C over the 1900 level, and by 2100, the planet's average temperature could be between 1.1°C to 5.4°C warmer than 2012. Figure 1.13 shows the rising trend in global temperatures since 1880.[33]

July 2016 was the hottest month on record for the globe. It was 0.87°C above the twentieth-century average, according to scientists from the NOAA's National Centers for Environmental Information.[34] This was the fifteenth month in a row to break a monthly heat record, surpassing July 2015 as the warmest month ever on record. Records date back 137 years to 1880.

Global warming is having a devastating impact on glaciers, as can be seen in two photographs of Muir Glacier in Alaska (Figure 1.14).[35]

Figure 1.15 shows how the changes in the extreme weather events scale with changes in the mean temperature.[36]

Extreme weather events cause floods, fires, and droughts, which now occur with increasing frequency at many places around the world. In 2012, the United States endured its warmest year on record, and the 13 warmest years for the entire planet have occurred since 1998, according to data that stretches back to 1880. The first six months of 2012 accounted for the warmest January-through-June period on record for the 48 contiguous states.[37] NOAA found that 170 American cities met or broke record-high temperatures in June 2012. South Carolina's 45°C high and Georgia's 44°C high could be the highest temperature records ever in their respective states. Conditions also had been very dry; it was the tenth-driest June on record. More than half the contiguous states had drought conditions, according to the *U.S. Drought Monitor*.[38] On the other hand, Florida had its wettest June on record (with more than 20 inches of rain in one weekend), and Washington state, Oregon, and

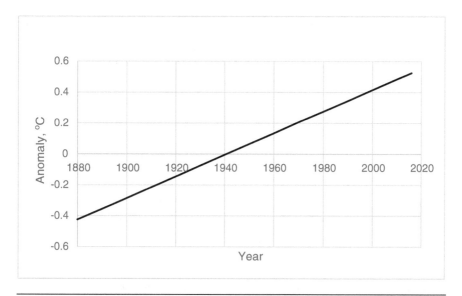

Figure 1.13   Trend in global land and ocean temperature anomalies with respect to the twentieth-century average, +0.07°C/decade

Figure 1.14   Muir Glacier, Alaska, September 2, 1892 and August 11, 2005

Maine each saw a top-ten wet June. At the same time, it rained in Mecca, Saudi Arabia, despite a temperature of 43°C, the hottest downpour in the planet's history.

Vulnerability to the effects of climate change is concentrated, especially in communities that are poor, lack advanced infrastructure, or have ineffective governance. From 1970 to 2008, over 95% of deaths related to natural disasters occurred in developing countries. When commenting on Somalia's 2011 drought, United Nations humanitarian relief coordinator Valerie Amos said, "We used to have drought every ten years, then it became every five years and now it's every two years"; the world

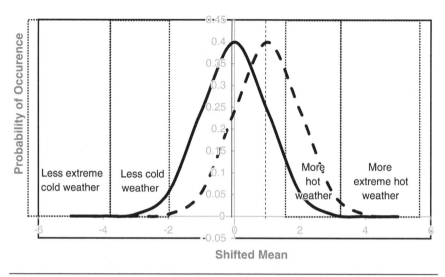

Figure 1.15   The probability of occurrences of extreme weather temperatures

"must take the impact of climate change more seriously."[39] In 2011, IRIN (formerly the Integrated Regional Information Network)[40] reported that Abdikadir Hirsi Shekhdon, a member of the government drought committee, said in Mogadishu that "some 11,000 people have died due to drought in the past 45 days, 9,000 of them in the Bay, Bakool, and Lower Shabelle regions, the rest in other regions in south-central Somalia." With nearly half of the Somali population (3.7 million people) in crisis—an estimated 2.8 million of whom are in the south—the scale of the crisis is huge.[41]

In Pakistan, the increasing exposure of people and assets has been the major cause of disaster losses. In 2010, six million people were left homeless by floods. Deforestation was reported to be the root cause of these floods:

> This year's monsoon lashing northern Pakistan with unusual intensity would historically have been absorbed by extensive forests, much like multiple layers of blotting paper, allowing the rains to run off more sedately than in modern times.
>
> But this month the mud and water deluge cascaded off the tree-bare mountains and hills with exceptional force and barreled down towards the plains in mammoth fury . . . engulfing an area of more than 60,000 square miles, more than twice the land area of Scotland. . . .
>
> *Dawn*, Pakistan's most widely circulated English language daily newspaper, said 80 million trees had been chopped down in the 'protected' Khebrani and Rais Mureed Forest in the three years before the floods inundated the plains this month.[42]

Extreme rains—like those that led to flooding and a cholera outbreak that killed hundreds in Pakistan in 2010—are happening 12% more often globally and 56% more frequently in Southeast Asia than if the world was not warming, according to a 2015 study by the Potsdam Institute for Climate Impact Research.[43]

Climate change will lead to massive conflicts, according to Nicholas Stern[44] and the U.S. National Security Agency. The potential for climate change to cause civil conflict seems quite likely when farmers' resources become critically scarce and governments' tax revenues diminish as a result of a drop in agricultural exports and they lose their capacity to mitigate risk.

The IPCC's *Climate Change 2014* report emphasizes risk management and calls for treating climate change as a threat multiplier: "We must implement strategies for adaptation and mitigation. Cost of mitigation is a 0.06% reduction in the global GDP growth rate (which is expected to be 1% per year). Socioeconomic development interacts with natural climate variations and human-caused climate change to influence disaster risk."[45] Figure 1.16, adopted from the IPCC report, depicts a model of disaster risk, causes, and management strategies.

In this model, disaster risk is the likelihood of severe adverse effects on a community that is exposed to weather or climate events and has vulnerable social and living conditions. Vulnerability is the tendency of a community to be adversely affected because of its poor infrastructure, inadequate building structures, and lack of recovery services. Figure 1.16 shows two strategies for dealing with the disaster risk— disaster risk management and climate change adaptation. Risk management refers to improving preparedness and response to extreme events for rapid recovery, and

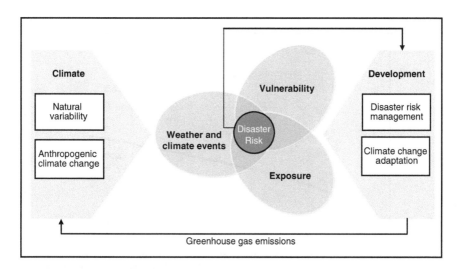

Figure 1.16 A disaster risk model: climate change and socioeconomic development

adaptation means reducing exposure and vulnerability and increasing the resilience of communities in managing extreme climate events. Building effective risk management capacity and adaptation strategies for preventing or reducing disaster risks requires significant investment in improving economic, social, and human capitals.

The implementation of adaptation strategies and of building risk management capacity costs money. Because financial resources often are limited, corrective actions must be prioritized. Figure 1.17 schematically depicts an approach to identifying the optimal strategy of investment in disaster preparedness and adaptation.[46] The cost on the vertical axis represents loss of property and post-disaster suffering because of diminished capacity for social services. The disaster cost at low preparation levels (low levels of adaptation and risk management capacity) is very high and decreases as people build capacity to withstand extreme events. On the other hand, the cost of building risk management capacity and adaptation resilience increases at higher levels of protective capacity. The optimal level of protection is at the lowest cost point on the total cost curve. Note that this cost-minimization model is constrained by *no loss of human life*. *Cost of life* is not incorporated into the optimization model because it is not appropriate to represent the value of life in monetary terms (even though this is done in some economic models). Hence, *no loss of life* is treated as a constraint in developing the optimal strategy.

These risk management and adaptation strategies favor the wealthy and advanced industrial regions. Although extreme climate events are likely to occur everywhere, the less industrially developed societies are likely to suffer the most.

In addition to causing climate change events, GHG emissions cause increasing ocean surface temperatures, rising sea levels, and acidification of the ocean—which

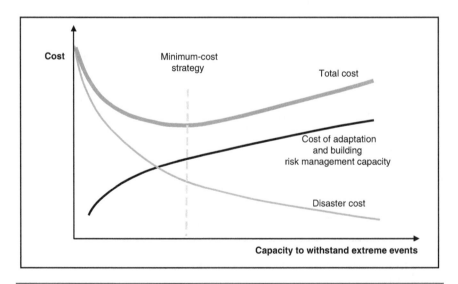

Figure 1.17   A cost-minimization model constrained by no loss of human life

are severely threatening reef-building corals. The ecosystems of coral reefs have immense biodiversity and contain a quarter of all marine species.

Environmental Justice and Equity

The harmful effects of our current unsustainable economic activities on human well-being and inequity in the world are staggering. Hazardous waste dumps and heavily polluting industries are situated near neighborhoods where minorities and the poor live. Migrant agriculture laborers are regularly exposed to high concentrations of pesticides. Globalization of production to low-cost regions and export of hazardous waste to poor countries (for reprocessing or landfill) cause those countries to shoulder disproportionately more of the environmental heavy burdens, even though most of their production outputs are exported. There is a deep link between ecosystem degradation and the persistence of rural poverty.

According to the United Nations Children's Fund (UNICEF), nearly five million people a year and 4,000 children die every day due to the lack of safe drinking water and sanitation.[47] The United Nations Environment Program (UNEP) reported on the devastating environmental and social impacts of the oil industry in Nigeria in 2011.[48] Prior to the discovery of oil in the 1950s, agriculture was the mainstay of Nigeria's economy, and the environment of Tai, a local government area of Rivers State in Nigeria was pristine. Oil exploration and production by the Shell Petroleum Development Company over the subsequent 60 years caused severe degradation of the environment and created serious health hazards for the local population. UNEP found that surface water in the creeks in and around Ogoniland contained hydrocarbons and floating layers of black oil varying from thin to thick. Air pollution related to oil industry operations affected the quality of life of close to one million people. UNEP observed hydrocarbons in the soil at depths of at least five meters. The UNEP report's *Recommendations for Government* asks for an initial capital injection of US$1 billion contributed by the oil industry and for the government to cover the first five years of the clean-up project. Individual contaminated land areas in Ogoniland can be cleaned up within five years, while the restoration of heavily damaged mangrove stands and swamplands will take up to 30 years.

Globalization of the production of products and services to low-cost regions, excessive consumption (particularly in the industrially developed countries), and profit maximization and growth as the principal business objectives have resulted in excessive social and economic inequity across the world. The wealth of the top 1% of American society is the same as that of the bottom 95%. In other words, three million people have the same wealth as the bottom 285 million people in the United States.[49] Robert Reich, professor at the University of California at Berkeley and U.S. Secretary of Labor in the Bill Clinton administration, has reported that *between 1962 and 2001, the wealth of the top 1% went up 2.5 times (in real dollars), while the wealth of the bottom 90% hardly increased.*[50] According to a report by Credit Suisse,[51] 0.7% of the world's adult population owns almost half of the world's wealth, as shown in Figure 1.18.

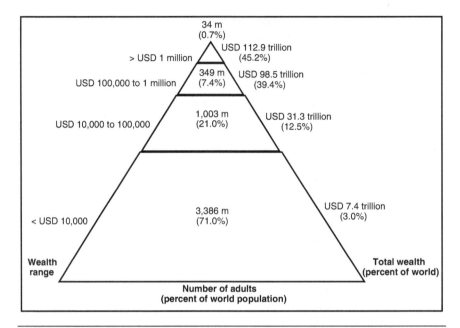

Figure 1.18   The global wealth pyramid

In 2015, the world's 62 wealthiest individuals owned as much as the poorest half of the global population, roughly 3.6 billion people. In fact, the wealth of the poorest half has fallen by US$1 trillion since 2010, while the wealth of the richest 62 people has risen by 44% to total US$1.76 trillion.[52]

The Temporal Dimension of Sustainability

In addition to the present and short-term effects of excessive demand for the earth's resources and its ecological services, there is a cross-generational or temporal dimension to the sustainability challenge. GHG accumulation in the atmosphere has a long life of one or two centuries and an enduring effect on rising temperatures and climate change. The adverse impact of global warming caused by GHGs that are emitted from our industrial and consumption activities will limit the choices of future generations for a high-quality life. Similarly, many hazardous chemicals contain biocumulative toxins, and exposure shapes the inheritance via genetic *memory*, which carries the environmental impact from one generation to the next.

The Effects of Industrial Systems

Injuries to workers or members of the public can occur from product designs, manufacturing processes, mishaps in plants and facilities operations, and unsafe chemicals. These safety issues present organizations with important economic, political, and moral challenges. The Center for Chemical Process Safety[53] has stated that *safety culture is the combination of group values and behaviors that determines the manner in which process safety is managed.* What can society do to improve the safety culture of an industry where there is evidence of systemic inattention to risk? A few proposals to alleviate industrial safety risks include transparency requirements, audits, fines, benchmarking, tax breaks, more inspections, outreach and training, and community advisory boards. With the appropriate frame of reference, safety problems can be solved in ways that also improve sustainability. Mike Wilson's case study of the California oil refinery sector, which has experienced catastrophic incidents, has become the focus of groundbreaking regulatory changes in California and the development of concepts that can be applied to solving safety problems in organizations while also improving sustainability and security.[54]

Industrialization and Globalization

Industrialization of life necessities (like food), globalization of production, and increasing consumption intensity have resulted in severe environmental, social, and economic sustainability risks. In the following sections, some of these risks—including loss of cultural diversity and virtual transfer of earth resources across the globe at the expense of the poor—are reviewed.

Losing Cultural Diversity

An important social sustainability challenge is the loss of cultural diversity caused by homogenization of products and consumption patterns and globalization of communication through the Internet. Globally ubiquitous McDonald's food, Starbucks coffee, and packaged processed food are just a few examples. The consumption preferences and lifestyles of the industrially developed and economically dominant nations cause homogenization of norms and mores and result in the loss of cultural diversity.

The Industrialization and Globalization of Food Production

Food production—from agriculture to livestock—has industrialized on a massive scale. Industrialization of plant and animal products is decoupling production from local consumption. For example, soy beans are grown in one country, they are fed to pigs and chicken in another country, animals are slaughtered and processed in a third, and meat products are shipped to a fourth country for consumption. Changes in consumption in one country affect the production patterns and environment in another country halfway across the globe. This practice transfers natural resources like water and nitrogen away from the people at the location of production.

Irreversible Effects on Sources and Sinks

Both the excessive exploitation of natural resources for production and the mindless generation and disposal of waste overshoot the source and sink capacities of the earth at local, regional, and global scales beyond repair. The irreversible destruction of the Aral Sea and the widespread damage of global marine fisheries are two examples.

In the 1960s, the Soviet Union undertook a major water diversion project in central Asia around the Aral Sea, one of the four largest lakes in the world. The region's two major rivers fed the lake and were used to transform the desert into farms for cotton and other crops. The diversion of river flow and the runoff of toxic fertilizers and pesticides from the cotton farms devastated the beautiful Aral Sea. It has shrunk steadily since the 1960s, and by 2007, it had declined to 10% of its original size. Figure 1.19 shows a map of the location of the sea and three photographs

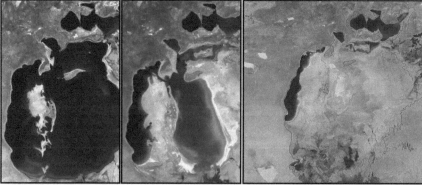

July - September, 1989   August 12, 2003   August 19, 2014

Figure 1.19   The irreversible tragedy of the Aral Sea

showing the sea in 1989, 2003, and 2014. The destruction of the region's fishing industry and heavy pollution have created serious economic and health problems for the people of the region.[55]

Global marine fisheries are in peril. Excessive farming from natural fisheries has resulted in the depletion of this natural capital close to extinction. Figure 1.20 shows the trends in the fishing industry from 1970 to 2005, demonstrating that although the fleet capacity (fishing power) of vessels has steadily increased, the catch per vessel has leveled, and the catch per unit of capacity has declined.[56] The Economics of Ecosystems and Biodiversity (TEEB) organization has called this trend *a tragedy caused by an economic race to the sea-bottom in a ruthless competition between fishing companies.*[57]

Waste: Generation and Management

The waste generated and disposed of by consumers and industrial processes has serious adverse effects on the earth's ecosystem. A few examples of waste are municipal solid waste, disposal of consumer products at their end of life, effluents from the production activities across the life cycle of products, and effluents from the products in use (such as tailpipe exhausts from transportation vehicles). The rising world population and increasing consumption intensity (and hence waste generation) in developing countries are intensifying the environmental, social, and economic impacts of waste.

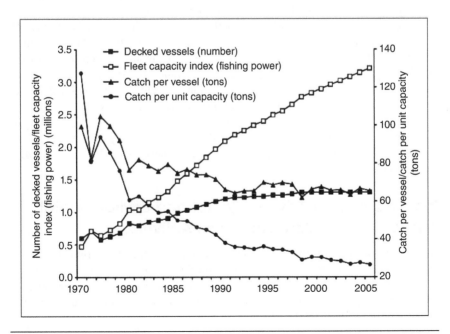

Figure 1.20   The depletion of global marine fisheries

According to the World Bank, world cities generated about 1.3 billion tons of solid waste in 2012,[58] and this volume is estimated to increase to 2.2 billion tons per year by 2025, a compound annual growth of 4%. Nearly 1 trillion plastic bags are discarded each year, and a significant portion of them end up in a *plastic soup* of waste that is floating in the Pacific Ocean. This soup is growing at an alarming rate and now covers an area twice the size of the continental United States. Plastic is believed to constitute 90% of all rubbish floating in the oceans. UNEP has estimated that in 2006 every square mile of ocean contained 46,000 pieces of floating plastic.[59] A third of the fish sampled by oceanographer Charles Moore's foundation contained plastic pellets in their stomachs, and human garbage was found inside the bellies of albatross chicks.

Human Well-Being versus Gross Domestic Product

The previous sections reviewed some of the serious harms that anthropogenic economic activities have inflicted on people and the environment. On the other hand, however, the rapid growth in the economic activities and GDPs of industrialized countries in the twentieth century significantly improved the material possessions and economic well-being of many people. GDP growth often is cited to validate the prevalent economic system and rationalize its harmful impacts. But the question we should ask is this: To what extent does human quality of life and well-being improve with growth in the GDP? A 2006 study by Deutsche Bank Research found that happiness does not completely depend on the GDP (Figure 1.21).[60]

The Institute for Innovation in Social Policy uses the index of social health (ISH) to measure social well-being.[61] The ISH combines 16 indicators: infant mortality, child abuse, child poverty, teenage suicide, teenage drug abuse, high school dropouts, unemployment, weekly wages, health insurance coverage, poverty among the elderly, out-of-pocket healthcare costs among the elderly, homicides, alcohol-related traffic fatalities, food insecurity, affordable housing, and income inequality. Figure 1.22 shows that over the 38 years from 1970 to 2011 when U.S. GDP per capita grew by a factor of two, the ISH remained stagnant or even declined slightly over the same period. The analysis demonstrates the weak linkage between the GDP and social well-being.

The Causes and Adverse Social and Environmental Impacts of Prevalent Economic Activities

The causes of the current unsustainable anthropogenic development can be grouped into two broad categories—(1) the production and consumption patterns of products and services and (2) the economic and sociopolitical frameworks that define the rules of economic activities and pose constraints on production and consumption.

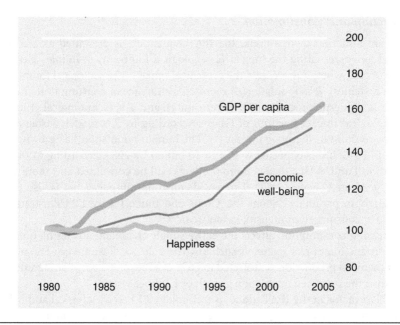

Figure 1.21   Trends in gross domestic product, economic well-being, and happiness in the United States (scale: 1980 = 100)

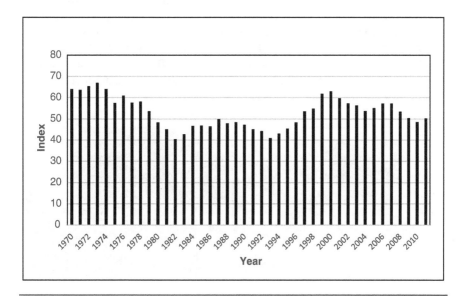

Figure 1.22   Index of social health in the United States, 1970 to 2011

Production and Consumption

In the introduction to this book, the IPAT equation[62] is presented as a concise method for representing the impact (or ecological footprint) of human activities: $I = P \times A \times T$, where I represents the ecological impact (the ecological footprint of human activities), P is population, A represents affluence or consumption intensity (the gross domestic product or GDP per capita), and T is technological efficiency (the ecological impact per unit of GDP). According to this model, sustainability requires *constant* or *declining* impact (I). The human population has grown to 7.3 billion in 2015 and is expected to rise to 10 billion by 2055, according to the UN Population Fund.[63] This means more products will be consumed and more waste will be generated (Figure 1.23). The world consumption per capita is also rising, particularly in populous regions like China and India. Figure 1.24 illustrates the increase in consumption intensity in footwear.[64]

Increasing consumption affects the entire supply chain and creates high growth in the production of raw materials such as chemicals. As illustrated in Figure 1.25, global chemical production is projected to grow at a rate of 3% per year, significantly faster than the projected population growth of 1.1% per year.[65]

The last factor in the IPAT model is technology (T). Technological and behavioral inefficiencies are creating excessive waste in the production and use of products and services that are discarded to air, water, and land. The inefficiencies come about because of the laws of physics, product and production design, and behavior. The efficiencies of production processes and the operation of products are limited by the laws of physics. Power plants, cars, and other products cannot operate at 100% efficiency. This means that significant amounts of primary resources are wasted. However, products and production processes can be designed for the maximum efficiency allowable by the laws of physics. Most of our products fail to meet this criterion. The tank-to-wheel efficiency of most automobiles on the road is less than 20%, and incandescent light bulbs are only 5% efficient. In contrast, the efficiency of hybrid electric vehicles exceeds 30% and light-emitting diode (LED) light

Figure 1.23   The rising world population increases consumption and waste

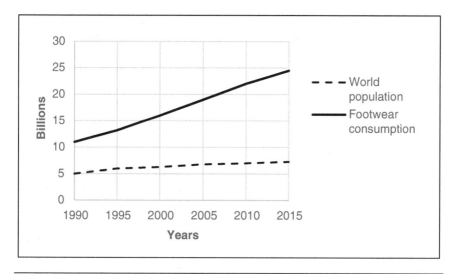

Figure 1.24   Consumption is rising faster than world population

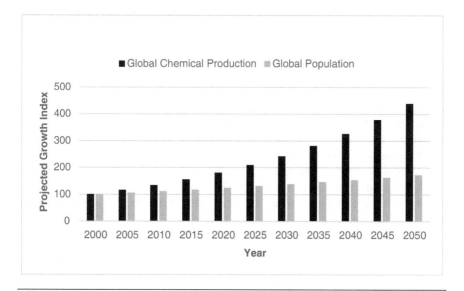

Figure 1.25   Global chemical production is rising faster than world population

bulbs are 80% efficient. Many products are designed to have a short life to promote consumption and increase the supplier's income.

Consumption behavior is another important factor in wastefulness and inefficiency—buying more than we need, equating material possessions with social stature and happiness, and simply not caring about wasting energy, food, water, and any other resources. The United States in 2007 consumed about 21 million barrels of oil a day, about the same as Japan, Germany, Russia, China, and India combined.[66] U.S. GHG emissions per dollar of GDP are twice that of Japan.[67] According to the United Nations Development Program (UNDP), the U.S. economy could do everything it now does, with currently available technologies and at current or lower costs, using half as much energy, if it operated at the present efficiency levels of Western Europe.

Economic and Sociopolitical Frameworks

Today, GDP and the level of consumption are believed to indicate human development and welfare. However, as previously mentioned, GDP is an inadequate measure for social health, and its growth is a misleading representation of social progress and sustainable development. GDP accounting does not distinguish between the types of economic activities and their levels of sustainability. Creating pollution undermines health but also increases economic activities (such as medical care and funeral services) and contributes to GDP growth. However, the production of pollution itself does not reduce the GDP. Furthermore, GDP does not account for inequity in the distribution of wealth generated by economic activities. Finally, GDP does not measure social values that are crucial to quality of life and happiness (like human relationships, love, the arts, and enjoyment of nature) but are not manifest in economic activities.

Currently, economic growth is the holy grail of our economy, and it is pursued by private businesses[68] and by governments in public policies, tax regimes, and other instruments. In the current capitalist system, self-interest and present-value maximization are considered to be rational human behaviors, economic surplus is the sole measure of value and expected utility, and surpluses and utility should be maximized. It is further assumed that cost-benefit calculations drive all human actions and that costs and benefits can be measured in monetary units—that is, life, happiness, self-actualization, and spirituality are interchangeable with monetary gains. Finally, all products and services are fungible with money. For the Nobel laureate economist Ronald Coase: "If we assume that the harmful effect of the pollution is that it kills the fish (in a stream), the question to be decided is: is the value of the fish lost greater or less than the value of the product which the contamination of the stream makes possible. It goes almost without saying that this problem has to be looked at in total *and* at the margin."[69] According to Coase, the product of the plant is fungible with the fish, and their respective worth is measured by the market price—even if the fish in the stream is the staple of local people's livelihood and the product of the factory is exported to distant markets. The local people lose their food source and are harmed by the pollution while the owners of the plant profit in overseas markets.

Another ground rule in our economic system is to discount future values and costs and to optimize decisions based on net present values in cost-benefit analysis. As a result, the potential harm of present externalities on future generations is considered much less consequential than it really is. Also, in the dominant capitalist economic system, government intervention to regulate business operations for the protection of the common good is considered harmful to economic growth—because of a belief that an unfettered free-market economy creates Pareto optimal results for society. As a result, the development of social and human capital and the protection of natural capital are hindered, giving rise to social injustice and ecological degradation.

It has long been explicitly and implicitly assumed that anthropogenic activities have a negligible effect on the earth's sources and sinks and that nature's resources and ecological sinks are inexhaustible. The assumptions are that even though we harm nature and create social injustice, these economic activities provide market opportunities for entrepreneurs to offer new products and services to mitigate the harm. Technology is widely believed to solve sustainability problems. Scarcity in global sources and sinks is believed to be resolvable by technology and market price mechanisms. For example, multiple geoengineering solutions have been proposed to solve some of the problems caused by climate change, and genetically modified crops are considered to be the solution to the use of harmful fossil-fuel based fertilizers in agriculture. According to Robert M. Solow, a Nobel laureate economist: "There is really no reason why we should not think of the productivity of natural resources as increasing more or less exponentially over time."[70]

We have developed a human-centric belief system in our interactions with nature. We believe that natural endowments are ours to exploit irrespective of the adverse effects on animals, plants, and the biodiversity of life on earth. Because humans consider themselves apart from nature and its ecological systems, they optimize business and policy decisions within a system that excludes nonhuman elements and that is confined to the short term. System dynamics and nonlinearities of interactions within the system often are not seriously considered, and decision models exclude time-integrated impacts in a generational timescale.

Why Sustainable Production Development Is Not Pervasive

The root causes of unsustainability enumerated in the previous section discourage investment in sustainable products and technologies that contribute to human well-being here and now, without adversely affecting the well-being of people elsewhere and without limiting the choices of future generations. In other words, the economic, environmental, and social requirements for sustainable development are not aligned with the contextual factors of the prevalent economic system. These contextual factors include institutions, social structures, operational rules, and laws of physics:

- Institutions are the organizations that make up the social order governing people's behavior and values, including the family, religion, education, the criminal justice system, the military, and the media.

- Social structures include economic systems, financial markets, systems of government, and regulatory bodies.
- Operational rules are laws (property rights, contract laws), environmental regulations, common pool resources management rules, accounting standards, models and metrics of valuation and assessment of costs and benefits, and decision rules based on objective utility.
- The laws of physics are a model of how nature works and are the basis of technological innovations and the creation of products and services.

Our value system affects everything—our relationships with nature and other people, our perceptions of technology and its strengths and shortcomings, our views of consumption, our definitions of well-being and the meaning of life, and even our philosophical views of the human condition.

The dominant neoclassical economic system has established the rules of economic activities and the constraints within which they can operate. It is based on the belief that the free-market (capitalist) economic system allocates resources efficiently and grows the economic pie. It assumes that actors are rational and seek self-interest and makes resources excludable (through property rights). This economic system is built on the assumptions that resources are rival (that is, consumption of a specific good by one consumer reduces its availability to others) and that information is equally available to everyone (there is symmetry). Future effects (both value and harm) are discounted, and products are treated as fungible (one good can be replaced by another of equal monetary value).

The neoclassical economic system seeks to maximize efficiency and assumes that efficiency is maximized if economic activities are undertaken by those who have the comparative advantage. This has led to consolidation of capital, the production system, the distribution network, and hence, market power. Consolidation leads to inequity in the distribution of wealth, loss of diversity, and diminished local self-sufficiency. Consumer preference often is cited as a justification for the behavior of producers in promoting consumerism. Efficiency is cited as a justification for the consolidation of capital and the means of production. The fallacy in this argument is that consumer preference is not innate but is manufactured by advertisements in the media (radio, television, and the Internet), the built environment (billboards and elevators), and modes of transportation (buses, taxis, and trains). Many traditional cultural occasions like Christmas and birthdays are turned into opportunities to purchase products, and other occasions are turned into marketing opportunities to encourage high levels of consumption throughout the year. In his last book before his death, the Harvard University economist John Kenneth Galbraith stated: "Belief in a market economy in which the consumer is sovereign is one of our most pervasive forms of fraud. Let no one try to sell without consumer management or control."[71]

The contextual economic, social, business, and public policy factors by and large support maintenance of the status quo. And changing the status quo is complex and difficult because in order to do so, many actors must align themselves with the realities and uncertainties of a new world. Coal miners and their elected representatives fear that they will lose their jobs and livelihoods if we shut down all coal power plants and switch to solar and wind energy. Even though the coal miners are exposed to the health hazards of coal mining and even if they are sympathetic to the need for climate change action, a future without coal looks uncertain and risky to them. The near instantaneous availability of information that is enabled by technology has broken the boundaries of space and time. There is no time to measure or analyze the sustainability consequences of our products and production choices. Market conditions are changing too fast, and decisions are optimized for short-term profit and loss.

Another factor hindering the development and commercialization of sustainable products is globalization, which has increased the physical distance between consumers and harm and has decreased the urgency for remedial action in spite of almost instantaneous information availability. A consumer electronic company that underpays assembly workers in China and pollutes the water and land near the factory does not feel any pressure from its customers in the United States. Although its consumers might be aware of the harm being done (since information is available instantaneously), the factory is not in their backyard. They might sympathize with the plight of the communities near the factory but would not change their buying behaviors and therefore would indirectly support the company's practices.

The development of sustainable products requires a new outlook toward nature and society by both producers and consumers. A sense of unity with nature is needed, and responsibility for the well-being of society and the common good must be assumed—here and now, and elsewhere and later. Even if we conceptually adopt this outlook, change is hard. We cannot solve problems with the same tools and optimization models that created them in the first place. We need to establish new tools for decision making in business and new metrics for assessing micro- and macroeconomic conditions.

Because such new systems thinking is not easy, and because it carries multiple risks and uncertainties, many firms shy away from taking decisive actions to change. And they rationalize their maintenance of the status quo by arguing that the impact of a single company is too small to make a material difference. The prevalent business environment is a barrier for transitioning to sustainable product development and operations, too. Businesses argue that sustainability creates competitive disadvantages. It increases their cost base, dissuades investors, and does not attract new or more customers. Customers often do not state their preference for sustainable products. Even though consumer preference in most cases is manufactured by industry, changing consumer choices is costly and time consuming. Finally, the regulatory regime is a force of inertia and a maintainer of the status quo. Elected officials in a democratic society are representatives of the people, and they usually are the followers rather than leaders of change. Therefore, there is a strong linkage between consumer preferences and the regulatory regime.

When businesses are conceiving of new products and services, they need to consider both *utility* and *meaningfulness* aspects by distinguishing between *in order to* and *for the sake of.*[72] Traditional product development focuses only on the utility of the product and aims to promote consumerism as the purpose of a product. Developing a product *for the sake of* human well-being requires a different perspective and a holistic view of people and their place in nature. Sustainable product development considers both the *how* and *what* of product development—how to develop a commercially successful product and what kind of product to develop. *How* is about methods of product design, manufacturing, use, and after-life disposal (which often is referred to as the process of design for sustainability). *What* is the essence of the product and establishes the direction of innovation for improving human well-being, for making positive contributions to the society, and for minimizing harmful natural and social externalities. *How* applies sustainability criteria and metrics of quality and sustainability and adopts efficient design development and commercialization tools and processes. *What* informs business objectives and strategies: what market opportunity should the firm create or pursue, what technology should it invest in, and what operational choices should the firm make in the globalization versus localization decisions?

There are choices to be made in business and product development strategies. Developing a gigantic shovel for coal mining or a technologically sophisticated deep-sea oil production device might be rewarding engineering endeavors and profitable commercial undertakings in the energy sector, but these products enable low-cost coal mining for electricity generation and sustain oil production for transportation vehicles—both of which severely affect people's health and contribute to global warming. Contrast those product strategies with the development of solar and wind energy products to generate electricity and electrify transportation. In the auto industry, innovators can design a Hummer for transportation or a Prius that consumes five times less fuel. In the software game market, innovative programmers and artists can be directed to develop a Grand Theft Auto–type of video game or educational games and games that promote love and peace rather than teach violence and crime. Integrating safety and performance efficiency can be set as the overarching requirements for a product, or managers can direct engineers to design a low-cost product that merely complies with minimal regulatory requirements for safety and efficiency.

Questions and Exercises

1. Map out the holistic supply chain system of a product of your choice (hint: use sources on the Internet). How would you characterize the system? Consider factors such as distance traveled by materials, complexity, number of suppliers, open and closed loop interactions, etc.
2. Should the ecological footprint of our economic activities be assessed against the carrying capacity of the earth on a national or global level? Why? What is the implication of your response?

3. In this chapter, we argue that human well-being rather than profit maximization should be the overarching goal in new product development. Is this a realistic goal? Why?

Endnotes

1. "First Look: Highlights from the Third Annual Sustainability Global Executive Survey," MIT Sloan Management Review 53(1) (Fall 2011).
2. Source: United Nations Millennium Ecosystem Assessment, "Ecosystems and Human Well-Being," in *Ecosystems and Human Well-Being: A Framework for Assessment*, pp. 71–84 (Washington, DC: Island Press, 2005), http://millenniumassessment.org/en/Framework .html, http://millenniumassessment.org/documents/document.301.aspx.pdf.
3. United Nations World Commission on Environment and Development, Our Common Future ("Brundtland Report"), Gro Harlem Bruntland, (Ed.), (New York: United Nations, 1987), p. 10.
4. Source: "Report of the United Nations Conference on Sustainable Development" (Rio +20), Rio De Janeiro, Brazil, June 20–22, 2012, The Future We Want, p. 1.
5. Abraham Maslow and K. J. Lewis, "Maslow's Hierarchy of Needs." Salenger Incorporated (1987): 14.
6. Ni-Bin Chang, *Systems Analysis for Sustainable Engineering: Theory and Applications* (New York: McGraw Hill Professional, 2010).
7. Karl-Göran Mäler, Sara Aniyar, and Åsa Jansson, "Accounting for Ecosystem Services as a Way to Understand the Requirements for Sustainable Development," Proceedings of the National Academy of Sciences 105(28) (2008): 9501–9506, www.pnas.org.
8. Robert C. Carlson and Dariush Rafinejad, "The Transition to Sustainable Production Development and Manufacturing," in Karl G. Kempf, Pinar Keskinocak, and Reha Uzsoy, (Eds.), *Planning Production and Inventories in the Extended Enterprise: A State-of-the-Art Handbook*, vol. 1, pp. 45–82 (New York: Springer, 2011).
9. Michelle L. Graymore, Neil G. Sipe, and R. E. Rickson, "Regional Sustainability: How Useful Are Current Tools of Sustainability Assessment at the Regional Scale?" Ecological Economics 67(3) (2008): 362–372.
10. Stockholm Resilience Centre, Stockholm University, Stockholm, Sweden, http://www .stockholmresilience.org/21/research/research-programmes/planetary-boundaries.html.
11. Jonathan Foley et al., "Boundaries for a Healthy Planet," Scientific American Magazine, March 19, 2010.
12. Will Steffen et al., "Planetary Boundaries: Guiding Human Development on a Changing Planet," Science 347(6223) (February 13, 2015).
13. Herman E. Daly and Joshua Farley, *Ecological Economics: Principles and Applications* (Washington, DC: Island Press, 2011).
14. Mathis Wackemagel and William Rees, *Our Ecological Footprint: Reducing Human Impact on the Earth* (Gabriola Island, BC: New Society Publishers, 1996).
15. Ibid.
16. Global Footprint Network, "Earth Overshoot Day: in Less than Eight Months, Humanity Has Exhausted Earth's Budget for the Year." http://www.footprintnetwork.org/en/index.php/ GFN/page/earth_overshoot_day.
17. Global Footprint Network, http://www.footprintnetwork.org/en/index.php/GFN/page/ fighting_poverty_our_human_development_initiative.

18. United Nations Development Program, Human Development Reports (UNDP, UDP), "Human Development Index (HDI)," http://hdr.undp.org/en/content/human-development-index-hdi.

19. United Nations University—International Human Dimensions Program and United Nations Environment Program (UNU-IHDP and UNEP), *Inclusive Wealth Report 2014: Measuring Progress toward Sustainability* (Cambridge: Cambridge University Press, 2014).

20. Pamela Matson, William C. Clark, and Krister Andersson, *Pursuing Sustainability: A Guide to the Science and Practice* (Princeton, NJ: Princeton University Press, 2016).

21. Joseph E. Stiglitz, Amartya Sen, and Jean-Paul Fitoussi, Report by the Commission on the Measurement of Economic Performance and Social Progress (Paris: Commission on the Measurement of Economic Performance and Social Progress, 2009).

22. Julian D. Marshall and Michael W. Toffel, "Framing the Elusive Concept of Sustainability: A Sustainability Hierarchy," Environmental Science and Technology 39(3) (2005): 673–682, p. 675.

23. Paul James, with Liam Magee, Andy Scerri, and Manfred Steger, *Urban Sustainability in Theory and Practice: Circles of Sustainability* (Abington, UK: Routledge, 2015).

24. James Gustave Speth, *The Bridge at the Edge of the World: Capitalism, the Environment, and Crossing from Crisis to Sustainability* (New Haven, CT: Yale University Press, 2009).

25. United Nations Intergovernmental Panel on Climate Change (UN IPCC), Climate Change 2007: Synthesis Report. Contribution of Working Groups I, II, and III to the Fourth Assessment Report of the Intergovernmental Panel on Climate Change (Geneva: UN IPCC, 2007).

26. Allen Hershkowitz, personal communications, Natural Resources Defense Council (NRDC), New York, 2014.

27. United Nations, "Kyoto Protocol to the United Nations Framework Convention on Climate Change," 1998, Annex A, page 19, http://unfccc.int/resource/docs/convkp/kpeng.pdf.

28. Source: IPCC Fourth Assessment Report, Table 2.14, Chapter 2, p. 212, http://www.ipcc.ch/pdf/assessment-report/ar4/wg1/ar4-wg1-chapter2.pdf. According to the U.S. EPA, methane (CH_4) is estimated to have a GWP of 28–36 over 100 years: https://www.epa.gov/ghgemissions/understanding-global-warming-potentials.

29. United States Environmental Protection Agency, "Sources of Greenhouse Gases: Agriculture Sector Emissions," 2014, https://www3.epa.gov/climatechange/ghgemissions/sources/agriculture.html.

30. UN IPCC, Climate Change 2007.

31. National Oceanic and Atmospheric Administration (NOAA), Earth System Research Laboratory, "Recent Monthly Average Mauna Loa CO_2," Mauna Loa Observatory, Hawaii, September 2016, http://www.esrl.noaa.gov/gmd/ccgg/trends/full.html.

32. Thomas F. Stocker, "The Closing Door of Climate Targets," Science 339 (January 18, 2013): 280–282. The IPCC is calling for a reduction of greenhouse gases compared to 2000 by 24 to 40% by 2020 and 80 to 95% by 2050.

33. National Oceanic and Atmospheric Administration (NOAA), National Centers for Environmental Information, https://www.ncdc.noaa.gov/cag/time-series/global/globe/land_ocean/1/1/1880-2017?trend=true&trend_base=10&firsttrendyear=1880&lasttrendyear=2016.

34. National Oceanic and Atmospheric Administration (NOAA), "July Was Hottest Month on Record for the Globe," August 17, 2016, http://www.noaa.gov/news/july-was-hottest-month-on-record-for-globe.

35. USGS, Glacier and Landscape Change in Response to Changing Climate https://www2.usgs.gov/climate_landuse/glaciers/repeat_photography.asp.

36. Adapted from Christopher B. Field, Vicente Barros, Thomas F. Stocker, and Qin Dahe, "Managing the Risks of Extreme Events and Disasters to Advance Climate Change Adaptation: Special Report of the Intergovernmental Panel on Climate Change" (New York: Cambridge University Press, 2012).

37. National Oceanic and Atmospheric Administration (NOAA), "NCDC Announces Warmest Year on Record for Contiguous U.S.," https://www.ncdc.noaa.gov/news/ncdc-announces-warmest-year-record-contiguous-us.

38. United States Drought Monitor: http://droughtmonitor.unl.edu/.

39. Alastair Good, "Climate Change Is Cause of Ethiopian Draught," The Telegraph, July 10, 2011, http://www.telegraph.co.uk/news/worldnews/africaandindianocean/ethiopia/8628735/Climate-change-is-cause-of-Ethiopian-drought.html.

40. IRIN (formerly the Integrated Regional Information Network), "Time for Immediate Action on Famine—UN," July 20, 2011, http://www.irinnews.org/report.aspx?reportid=93280.

41. Ibid.

42. "Pakistan: A Land Left to Drown by the 'Timber Mafia,'" Sunday Herald (Scotland), August 29, 2010.

43. Potsdam Institute for Climate Impact Research, "Record-Breaking Heavy Rainfall Events Increased under Global Warming," July 8, 2015.

44. Nicholas Stern, The Economics of Climate Change: The Stern Review (Cambridge: Cambridge University Press, 2007), http://webarchive.nationalarchives.gov.uk/20070108124733/http://www.hm-treasury.gov.uk/independent_reviews/stern_review_economics_climate_change/stern_review_report.cfm.

45. Intergovernmental Panel on Climate Change (IPCC), "Summary for Policymakers," in Climate Change 2014: Impacts, Adaptations, and Vulnerability. Part A: Global and Sectoral Aspects. Contribution of Working Group II to the Fifth Assessment Report of the Intergovernmental Panel on Climate Change (Cambridge: Cambridge University Press, 2014), fig. SPM.1; IPCC, (Cambridge: Cambridge University, 2014), 1.1.2.1 (pp. 9–10), 1.1.2.3 (pp. 12–13).

46. Adapted from Jimmy Y. Jia and Jason Crabtree, Driven by Demand: How Energy Gets Its Power (Cambridge: Cambridge University Press, 2015), p. 231.

47. UNICEF, Water, Sanitation and Hygiene, https://www.unicef.org/wash/index_25637.html.

48. United Nations Environment Program (UNEP), Environmental Assessment of Ogoniland (Nairobi: UNEP, 2011), http://web.unep.org/disastersandconflicts/where-we-work/nigeria.

49. Edward N. Wolff, "Recent Trends in Household Wealth in the United States: Rising Debt and the Middle-Class Squeeze. An Update to 2007," Working Paper No. 589, Levy Economics Institute of Bard College, March 2010.

50. Robert Reich, http://inequalityforall.com/.

51. Anthony Shorrocks, James Davies, and Rodrigo Lluberas, Global Wealth Databook 2015 (Zurich: Credit Suisse, 2015).

52. Oxfam, "An Economy for the 1%: How Privilege and Power in the Economy Drive Extreme Inequality and How This Can Be Stopped," Oxfam Briefing Paper 210, Oxfam International, January 18, 2016, http://policy-practice.oxfam.org.uk/publications/an-economy-for-the-1-how-privilege-and-power-in-the-economy-drive-extreme-inequ-592643.

53. Center for Chemical Process Safety (CCPS) of the American Institute of Chemical Engineers (AIChE), 2012. The CCPS is a not-for-profit, corporate membership organization that identifies and addresses process safety needs within the chemical, pharmaceutical, and petroleum industries (http://www.aiche.org/ccps).

54. Mike Wilson, "Case Study: The Richmond, Chevron Refinery Fire. Chemical Facility Safety in an Era of Climate Change: Training for Worker Participation and Community Engagement," Department of Industrial Relations, State of California, April 8, 2013, pp. 1–39; State of California, Department of Industrial Relations, Division of Occupational Safety and Health, Proposed General Industry Safety Order (GISO) §5189.1, Process Safety Management for Petroleum Refineries, Version 5.0, September 14, 2015.

55. Rebecca Lindsay, "Shrinking Aral Sea," Earth Observatory, National Aeronautics and Space Administration (NASA), August 25, 2000, http://earthobservatory.nasa.gov/Features/WorldOfChange/aral_sea.php.

56. World Bank and Food and Agriculture Organization (FAO) of the United Nations, *The Sunken Billions: The Economic Justification for Fisheries Reform* (Washington, DC: World Bank, 2008), p. 21 (Figure 2.11, The evolution of global fleet productivity, decked vessels).

57. Pavan Sukhdev and Pushpam Kumar, "The Economics of Ecosystems and Biodiversity (TEEB)." Wesseling, Germany, European Communities (2008), http://www.teebweb.org.

58. Daniel Hoornweg and Perinaz Bhada-Tata, "What a Waste: A Global Review of Solid Waste Management," No. 15, (Washington, DC: World Bank, March 2012).

59. Kathy Marks, "The World's Rubbish Dump: A Garbage Tip That Stretches from Hawaii to Japan," The Independent (UK), August 6, 2009.

60. Deutsche Bank Research, "Measures of Well-being: There Is More to It than GDP," Frankfurt-am-Main, September 8, 2006, http://www.dbresearch.com/PROD/DBR_INTERNET _DE-PROD/PROD0000000000202587.PDF.

61. Institute for Innovation in Social Policy (IISP), "The Index of Social Health," IISP, Vassar College, Poughkeepsie, NY, http://iisp.vassar.edu.

62. John P. Holdren and Paul R. Ehrlich, "American Population and the Global Environment," American Scientist 62(3) (1974): 62.

63. UN Population Division, World Population Prospects: The 2015 Revision, online July 29, 2015, http://www.unfpa.org/world-population-trends.

64. Shahin Rahimifard, Theodoros Staikos, and Gareth Coates, "Recycling of Footwear Products," Centre for Sustainable Manufacturing and Reuse/Recycling Technologies (SMART), Loughborough University, UK, December 2007.

65. Michael P. Wilson and Megan R. Schwarzman, "Toward a New U.S. Chemicals Policy: Rebuilding the Foundation to Advance New Science, Green Chemistry, and Environmental Health," Environmental Health Perspectives 177(8) (2009): 1203.

66. James Gustave Speth, *The Bridge at the Edge of the World: Capitalism, the Environment, and Crossing from Crisis to Sustainability.* Yale University Press, 2008.

67. Joseph E. Stiglitz, "A New Agenda for Global Warming," in Joseph E. Stiglitz, Aaron S. Edlin, and J. Bradford DeLong, (Eds.), *The Economists' Voice: Top Economists Take on Today's Problems*, pp. 22–27 (New York: Columbia University Press, 2008).

68. Business strategies are based on growth in revenue, market share, profitability, and shareholder value.

69. Ronald H. Coase, "The Problem of Social Cost" (1960), in Chennat Gopalakrishnan, (Ed.), Classic Papers in Natural Resource Economics, pp. 87–137 (London: Palgrave Macmillan UK, 2000).

70. Robert M. Solow, "Growth Theory and After," American Economic Review 78(3) (1988): 307–317.

71. John Kenneth Galbraith, *The Economics of Innocent Fraud: Truth for Our Time* (New York: Houghton Mifflin, 2004), 14.

72. Hannah Arendt, *The Human Condition* (Chicago: University of Chicago Press, 1958).

CHAPTER 2

TRANSITION TOWARD SUSTAINABLE DEVELOPMENT AND BUSINESS STRATEGY

Excessive exploitation of the earth's sources and sinks, and degradation of its carrying capacity are continuing unabated in the second decade of the twenty-first century. Two major trends—consolidation of global markets and capital assets, and the centralized control of increasingly larger and more complex financial and business enterprises—have resulted in loss of diversity and heightened global inequities in human development. As William E. Rees has stated: "The enormous purchasing power of the world's richest nations enables them to finance their ecological deficits by extending their ecofootprints deeply into exporting nations and throughout the open ecosphere. Wealthy and powerful nations can now achieve through global commerce what used to require territorial occupation."[1]

Furthermore, this consolidated capitalism has resulted in escalating economic uncertainties and recurring "irrational exuberance" of markets followed by "unexpected and prolonged contractions."[2] The current unsustainable patterns of production and consumption are likely to increase competition over limited resources and consequential local and regional violence. Sustainable development and war are irreconcilable. Unfortunately, war and violence are considered justifiable instruments of conflict resolution by civil society, and therefore, a large portion of global wealth across the globe is spent on military hardware and warfare at the expense of investment in sustainable development that improves human welfare at the local level. Even President Barack Obama, in his speech accepting the Nobel Peace Prize, resorted to Orwellian doublespeak when he said, "So yes, the instruments of war do have a role to play in preserving the peace."[3] He acknowledged his debt to the ideals of Mahatma Gandhi and Martin Luther King Jr., but went on to defend war as, at times, being *morally justified*. On the other hand, Gandhi also said, "I object to violence because, when it appears to do good, the good is only temporary; the evil it does is permanent."[4]

We must change course and establish new social and economic systems that are in harmony with nature and are conducive to sustainable development. We must innovate products and adopt consumption patterns that enable sustainable development. However, transition to sustainable development is as much about reexamining underlying virtues and ethics as it is about transforming our economic system, business models, and methods for new product development. "In a sense, sustainability requires letting go of the story of the supremacy of the human in nature, the story that the natural world exists as mere resources to serve human progress."[5] Innovation is needed in cultural renewal as much as in public policy, economic models, and technology development. Vaclav Havel, the former president of the Czech Republic, stated: "I'm skeptical that a problem as complex as climate change can be solved by any single branch of science. Technological measures and regulations are important, but equally important is support for education, ecological training, and ethics—a consciousness of the commonality of all living beings and an emphasis on shared responsibility."[6]

Opportunities for cultural renewal and systemic innovation in technology, finance, and policy abound. We must start with transforming personal values and redefining the objective utilities that we aim to optimize in policy, finance, and technology decisions. We must seek freedom from material wants and ask "not how much, but how good; not only how to create wealth, but how to use it; not only how fast we are going, but where we are headed. . . . We do not intend to live in the midst of abundance, isolated from neighbors and nature, confined by blighted cities and bleak suburbs, stunted by a poverty of learning and an emptiness of leisure."[7] We need a social redesign to seek human development rather than economic development and seek social justice across geographic and trans-generational scales rather than fulfillment of self-interest. Current systems of political economy and approaches to technological innovation must be redesigned. The path to sustainable development requires a reexamination of many deterring human constructs, such as national borders and a zero-sum game approach toward other people and nature.

The desired alternative economic system for sustainable development is a distributed and circular economic system of distributed economic units that are globally linked, shared intellectual property, and self-managed commonly pooled resources in harmony with local natural resources. A distributed economic system is a transparent system, and sources of negative externalities are known to society because of their short latency in feedback loops. In a distributed economic system, corporations are small, and their workers and managers are part of the community within which production and consumption take place. Because corporations are small, they cannot wield undue power over markets and society. Furthermore, a circular economy uses local and renewable materials and energy. In this system, supply chains are short, and there is no virtual transfer of natural resources over long distances. The waste management system becomes a resource recovery system that enables the production of clean water, energy, nutrients, and materials from waste. This water offsets a demand for imported fresh water, the energy helps eliminate a demand for fossil fuels, the nutrients offset a demand for petroleum-based fertilizers, and the new materials offset a demand for imported materials made from nonrenewable feedstock. A distributed circular economy enables technological innovations in new methods of resource recovery, such as chemical recycling and use of feedstock derived from the local waste stream.

Sustainable product development applies transformative innovations in design and a commercialization approach to achieve triple-bottom-line—economic, environmental, and social—performance. Sustainable development requires a holistic system approach to problem solving, where spatial and temporal feedback loops are considered in decision optimizations. In sustainable product development, we must integrate three strategies—a strategy for creating a prosperous business, a strategy for supporting ecological systems (sources and sinks), and a strategy for contributing to consumer well-being and social justice. We must change the basis of competition to triple-bottom-line performance. In risk management and decision optimization, we must include how people are affected by environmental risks and the harmful impacts of externalities. These requirements open opportunities for a different type of innovation in technology, marketing, and business models—innovation in the sustainability space that is driven by opportunities for economic prosperity and for the common good. Sustainable products support renewal and growth of all four types of capital that are needed for sustainable development:

- Natural capital (with thriving ecological systems),
- Economic capital (both physical and financial),
- Social capital (including trust and effective institutions), and
- Human capital (created through education, health, empowerment, and social justice).

The development of sustainable products needs new methodologies and tools, including new decision rules and metrics of performance. The inclusion of economic, environmental, and social costs and benefits in both space and time requires systems thinking and dynamic system analysis. This system includes traditional elements (such as technology, marketing, operations, and finance) but also ecological sustainability and social justice. It is complex and has myriad feedback loops with nonlinear dependencies and time delays. The new methodologies and tools cannot be successfully implemented without a supporting societal, economic, and regulatory (policy) infrastructure.

A successful transition to sustainability requires vision in both the private and public sectors, shared global ethics, innovation in technology and in contextual structures, commitment to change, and perseverance throughout the change process. In the next sections, the focus is on implementing strategic and organizational initiatives in business to enable the necessary transformational changes.

The Business Case for Sustainable Products and Processes

Because the development, production, and delivery of products and services are central to most business enterprises, sustainable product design and manufacturing are integral to the core strategy of a corporation that adopts sustainability as its principle operational imperative. In other words, the case for sustainable products and processes is also the case for sustainable business strategy, which can be supported through the following arguments:[8]

- **Social and environmental responsibility:** More than ever before, large multinational corporations are integrating social and environmental responsibility into their core strategies. They express support for striving toward the overarching goal of sustainability to achieve economic prosperity while protecting the natural systems of the planet to ensure a high quality of life for current and future generations across the globe. The drivers for the current trend include the changing preferences of customers and investors, government regulations, and the advocacy of the media and nongovernmental organizations. Nearly fifty years ago, the economist Milton Friedman offered a counterargument that absolved corporations of social responsibility beyond legal compliance. Friedman argued that social welfare is the business of governments, which safeguard the commons by enacting laws and regulations.[9] This minimalist view is workable only if governments are not subjugated to corporations and if they assume ownership of the commonwealth and responsibility for its protection.
- **Maximizing the efficiency of the resource value chain for short-term business benefits by reducing operating costs:** Improving energy efficiency, reducing manufacturing waste, and taking other resource efficiency measures translate directly to a reduction in operating costs and increased profits. At the same time, these efficiency-improvement measures are good for the environment and for reducing the depletion of nonrenewable resources.
- **Business opportunities in meeting the market demand and market preference for sustainable products and services:** The Prius hybrid car is a good example of how new business opportunities arise from changing market preferences for sustainable products. Acting against the conventional marketing wisdom of the early to mid-1990s, Toyota Motor Corporation envisioned that the basis of competitive advantage in the future would be fuel efficiency—and thus, invested in hybrid technology.
- **Entrepreneurial business opportunities in environmental protection (practicing *envirocapitalism* or *doing well by doing good*):**[10] For example, entrepreneurial opportunities might arise in promoting tourism through environmental protection, in turning the by-products (waste) of one industrial process into marketable products in another sector and thereby reducing environmental damage, and in developing and improving property value through environmental revitalization and enhanced aesthetics.

- **Sustained business leadership for long-term shareholder value growth:** The motivation in this category is to circumvent medium- to long-term threats of resource scarcity and environmental management costs, and the resulting jeopardy to business sustainability. There are several counterarguments against this motivation. First, one firm (no matter how large) can have only a limited impact on the global scale, and long-term measures can be effective only if adopted by all producers. Second, voluntary strategies might be self-discriminatory in the fiercely competitive global landscape. And third, the overarching business objective of sustained growth in return on equity is achieved through growth in market opportunities and the maximization of people and capital productivity (that is, the maximization of output per unit of labor cost and the deployed capital). This objective encourages continuous growth in production and corresponding consumption, reduction in worker value (lower wages and benefits and longer working hours), and increased production output capability (through automation, economies of scale, and centralization of production)—all of which tend to be counter to sustainable utilization of resources. In other words, the goal of continuous business growth is irreconcilable with the objective of environmental and resource sustainability.
- **Government regulations:** Increasingly, governments around the world are enacting tighter environmental, health, and safety regulations. Some of these regulations are in the form of global agreements through the United Nations to address climate change, atmospheric ozone depletion, and hazardous chemical production and use. Although there is significant variability between or even within different countries, stringent environmental regulations are on the rise, posing future risks to business. The proactive adoption of sustainable strategies in product and manufacturing development reduces this systemic risk.

Over the past decade, some business leaders have become increasingly aware of these sustainability imperatives and potential business opportunities. Figure 2.1 depicts the four areas in which leading businesses have responded to sustainability needs. These areas only partially address the previously listed opportunities. Although these four dimensions of response are helpful, they are generally reactive, opportunistic, and short-term market-focused. A proactive commitment to sustainable development is mostly lacking in business. The United Nations Global Compact reported in 2014 that 84% of the 1,000 global CEOs surveyed agreed that business should lead efforts to define and deliver new goals on global priority issues, but only a third said that business is doing enough to address global sustainability challenges. And only one in twelve companies links executive remuneration to sustainability performance.[11]

The apparent dichotomy between business and environmental and social sustainability might be reconciled with a change in underlying conceptual frameworks. For example, an alternative to the business strategy of sustained shareholder value

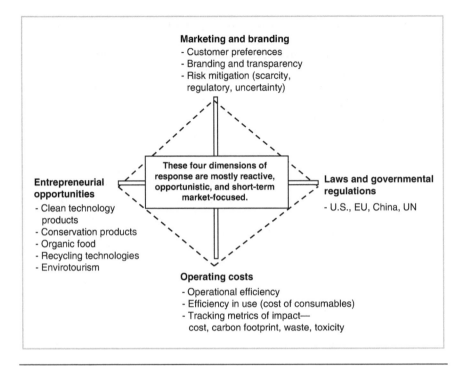

Figure 2.1   Business responses to sustainable product innovation, development, and commercialization

growth might be sustained stakeholder value growth—where stakeholders are shareholders, employees, the community, and the environment where the firm's economic activities take place across the entire supply chain. In this revised strategic viewpoint, *value* is redefined and takes a broader meaning beyond the mere financial metrics. The revised definition of *value* might be *quality of life and well-being*. Although definitions of *quality of life* are appropriately vague and subjective, the term has many universally shared dimensions, such as satisfaction of physical needs, security, happiness, liberty, equity, opportunity, and community.

Sustainability Is an Opportunity for Transformative Innovation

Although sustainable products are not pervasive, significant environmental, health, and safety (EHS) standards are in place in industrially developed countries like the U.S. These standards regulate manufacturing operations and impose constraints on product design. Many of the standards were established by industry associations like the American Society of Mechanical Engineers (ASME) and the National Fire

Protection Association (NFPA). Other standards have evolved through regulations enacted by governments in response to the social costs of externalities created by industrial activities. Excessive air pollution in major metropolitan areas like the city of Los Angeles contributed to the passage of the 1970 amendments to the Clean Air Act of 1963, which greatly expanded federal enforcement in the U.S. The depletion of the atmospheric ozone layer led the United Nations in 1987 to enact the Montreal Protocol on Substances That Deplete the Ozone Layer, which banned the production of chlorofluorocarbons (CFCs), beginning in 1989. The Chinese government also is imposing strict air pollution standards in response to excessive air pollution in Beijing and Shanghai. The EHS standards for the production, distribution, use, and end-of-life management of products vary widely around the world and even within a country. Many suppliers have taken advantage of this variability and strategically selected low-cost locations for the production, use, and end-of-life waste management of their products. These strategies have contributed to the profitability of these companies at the expense of the well-being of humans and nature. By our definition, these products and practices are not sustainable.

Opportunities for innovation and the development of sustainable products are abundant. The following is a short list of opportunities for innovation in developing sustainable products and services:

- Grow food, purify water, and generate renewable energy in harmony with local natural endowments
- Develop materials and pharmaceutical products based on green chemistry principles[12]
- Develop entertainment products that promote community, peace, love, diversity, and harmony as opposed to aggression, violence, and domination
- Invest in technologies that help prevent health and environmental degradation over technologies of mitigation and management
- Refrain from developing products that are intended for violence and war
- Develop products that have the potential to be regenerative or restorative of social or environmental capital

In the following sections, a few examples of sustainable product innovation are presented. By reducing carbon emissions to mitigate global warming and the high risks of climate change, businesses in multiple sectors can create many opportunities for technology and product innovation.

Consider the following equation, which accounts for total carbon emissions in the energy sector of the economy as the product of population by three ratios— gross domestic product (GDP) per capita, energy intensity of the economy, and carbon emission of energy production and use:

$$\text{Total carbon emissions} = Population \cdot \frac{GDP}{Person} \cdot \frac{Energy\ consumption}{GDP} \cdot \frac{Carbon\ emission}{Energy\ consumption}$$

To reduce total carbon emissions, we can adopt strategies to reduce every term (or factor) on the right-hand side of the aforementioned equation, as shown in Table 2.1.

Table 2.1 Products that reduce carbon emissions in the energy sector

Factor	Strategy and product opportunity to reduce the factor
Population	• Products that improve the standard of living (hygiene and nutrition)
GDP per capita	• Products that have longer life spans to reduce consumption • Products that lack harmful health externalities (for example, by using green chemistry, not petroleum, in daily staple products) and that improve health (leading to less drug consumption and fewer hospital visits)
Energy per GDP	• Energy-efficient products and manufacturing processes (such as LED (light-emitting diode) lights and regenerative hybrid cars) • Products that improve consumer behaviors for efficient energy utilization (for example, motion-sensitive lights that turn off when no one is in the room and a reward app that encourages the use of public transportation)
Carbon emission per unit of consumed energy	• Products that produce energy from non-carbon sources such as solar and wind

In countries where the standard of living is high (with good hygiene, nutrition, education, and employment for men and women), birth and mortality rates are often in equilibrium, resulting in a stable (or even declining) population.

Efficiency is an important enabler of sustainable development. Efficiency means accomplishing the desired benefits with fewer resources such as material and energy. When a car is painted in a manufacturing plant, a 100% efficient paint process is achieved when the total amount of paint consumed is the same as the amount coated on the car. Energy efficiency has been the biggest contributor to balancing the energy supply and demand over the past 40 years in the United States. Figure 2.2 shows the U.S. energy consumption pattern over the past six decades, including sources of production and net imports as reported by James Sweeney.[13] The *limited energy efficiency energy consumption* line represents business-as-usual consumption at the prevailing rate in the early 1970s. Energy consumption patterns have changed significantly since the early 1970s because of behavioral changes and public policies that mandate energy efficiency in products. The bold downward arrow indicates the reduction in consumption because of improvements in efficiency.

U.S. refrigerators are a good example of efficiency improvement in products—for achieving more output for less input. Figure 2.3 shows that beginning in the mid-1970s, energy use in refrigerators in the U.S. declined in spite of the fact their size continued to increase.[14] What also is striking is that energy efficiency did not come at a cost: refrigerator prices declined significantly over the period of efficiency improvement and size increase. This impressive accomplishment is credited to public policy standards and technological improvements.

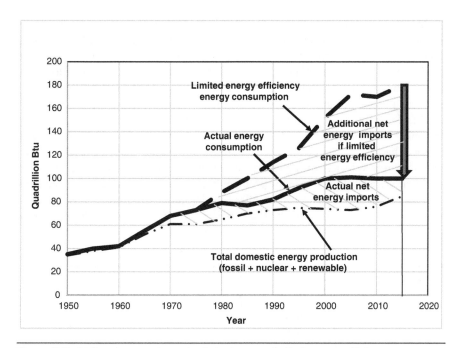

Figure 2.2   U.S. net energy imports: Actual versus limited energy efficiency

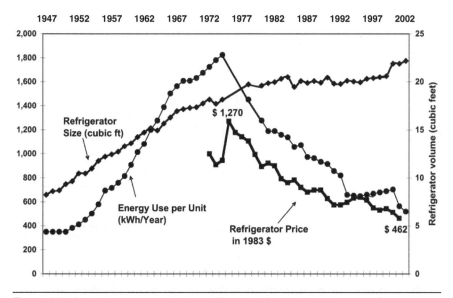

Figure 2.3   Improvement in the energy efficiency of refrigerators in the U.S.

One efficiency-improvement opportunity in the transportation sector is to reduce vehicles' tank-to-wheel energy losses. As shown in Figure 2.4, only 21.5% of consumed fuel energy is used for moving the average vehicle.[15] A substantial proportion of this useful output is lost. The figure shows the breakdown of the average losses of cars with internal combustion engines (this fleet is 70% petrol and 30% diesel).

As the previous examples demonstrate, there are ample opportunities to create sustainable products or improve the sustainability of existing products through strategies that redesign, reengineer, and redefine the product. We can redesign and improve the fuel efficiency of internal combustion engine (ICE) vehicles, and we can reengineer vehicles to implement regenerative hybrid drives in ICE cars and in electric vehicles. Redefining the problem in the transportation sector could help us move away from owning automobiles to using public transportation and redesigning cities that facilitate walking and using bikes. Opportunities for efficiency

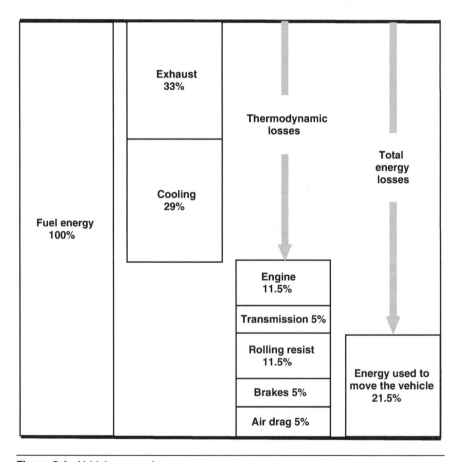

Figure 2.4 Vehicle energy losses

improvement exist in almost every product by using less material in design and less energy in manufacturing and use. New materials based on green chemistry can significantly reduce the environmental and health impacts of products. There are ample opportunities for inventing technologies and products to mine the waste, such as recycling technologies. We can design products for recyclability and reuse of recycled material. Batteries are used in electronic devices and increasingly in electric vehicles. There are ample opportunities to design new batteries that have a long life, are efficient, have high weight and volume density, and use green-chemistry materials. Solar and wind energy products have significantly improved over the past few decades, but their efficiencies can still be improved, and costs can be reduced.

The Life-Cycle Management (LCM) initiative of the United Nations Environmental Program (UNEP) recommends the following four sustainability strategies that companies can use:[16]

- **Innovation:** Use business processes and research and development (R&D) to develop new and improved products and services that maximize societal value and minimize environmental impacts.
- **Choice influencing:** Use marketing and awareness campaigns to enable and encourage customers and consumers to choose and use products and services more efficiently and sustainably. (Reducing consumption lowers the impact on the environment and also can improve happiness.)[17]
- **Choice editing:** Remove *unsustainable* products and services from the marketplace in partnership with other actors (such as retailers) or via market mechanisms.
- **Life-cycle tools:** Use life-cycle assessment, environmental life-cycle cost, ecodesign, and green outsourcing, procurement, and consumption. (These tools are discussed in Chapter 4.)

In addition to the above strategies, businesses should proactively promote public policies that create the necessary economic and social contexts that are conducive and supportive of sustainability strategies. A few high-priority policies include pricing harmful externalities (like carbon), making subsidies of fossil fuels and other unsustainable industries transparent,[18] creating a new economic metric beyond the GDP (to measure societal well-being), and empowering women to improve their education, health, and economic well-being.[19]

Management and Leadership for Sustainable Product Development

Sustainable product development and manufacturing require strong leadership and effective management practices. Sustainability and sustainable product development must become the standard operating process within each company. Leadership is needed to envision imperative sustainable development, to drive sustainable strategies, and to mainstream sustainability within the firm with a supportive corporate culture. The sustainable strategies must be operationalized at all management levels and within every functional unit of the firm.

Often companies create a corporate social responsibility group that reports corporate performance annually and informs stakeholders about the company's initiatives in one or more of the four areas that are highlighted in Figure 2.1. This approach is inadequate and often results in *green washing* rather than a serious commitment to sustainable development. The realization of sustainable products requires proactive and integrated participation by all functional building blocks of an organization that would incorporate sustainability in their daily functions. Figure 2.5 illustrates the building blocks of an organization and highlights the focus area within each as described later. The building blocks of sustainability in this figure are interlinked, and it is not possible to achieve the objectives of any block without the contributions of the other blocks. In other words, the firm must practice sustainability in every organizational unit with an orchestral harmony.

Leadership

Corporate leadership must establish the sustainability vision and promote a culture where triple-bottom-line performance and the well-being of the community within which the organization operates are the expected norms at all levels of the organization—starting at the top: "Sustainability leaders are system thinkers, have open minds, are deeply reflective and adaptive thinkers, are self-aware with deep empathy and compassion for the well-being of others, and finally they have a collaborative and strategic drive to create and implement new pathways to sustainable development."[20]

Strategy

A firm's strategy must pursue triple-bottom-line performance and consider environmental and social sustainability as high priorities in decision rules. Corporate strategies must be established using a systems-thinking approach and must be implemented consistently across all company operational units globally. Furthermore, firms must have a clear strategy in developing and sharing intellectual property (IP) pertaining to sustainability. Traditional strategies for protection of IP through patents and trade secrets must be amended. Technologies and know-how that reduce harmful environmental and health impacts of products and operations should be shared freely with customers, suppliers, and even competitors and players in adjacent markets.

Marketing

Marketing enables sustainable product development in several important ways. Marketing invents the product concept or establishes its specification based on customers' needs and preferences or based on opportunities for a new market creation.

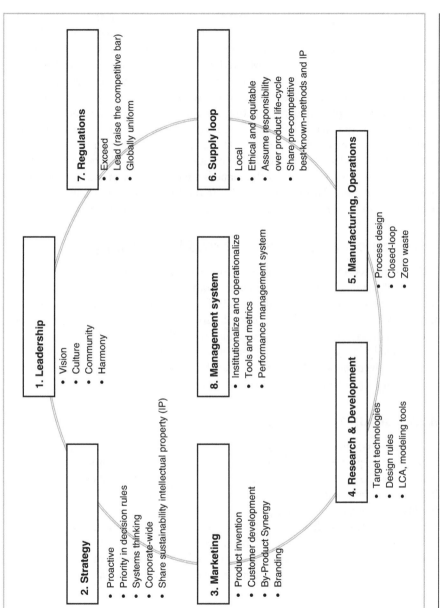

Figure 2.5   Building blocks of sustainable operations and product realization

It is therefore the responsibility of product marketers to invent a sustainable product that is commercially viable, contributes to human well-being, and does not harm the environment. Sustainability must be an integral part of the market requirements specification (MRS) of a product. Marketing, which often plays a central role in market development and branding, must inform customers about a product's sustainability advantages and create demand for sustainable products. In sustainable product management, product marketing should play an additional role that traditionally is not practiced. This new role is taking responsibility for the end-of-life (EOL) management of the product. At the end of their life, products often are treated as waste and sent to a landfill. We must divert EOL products from landfills and market them as feed stock for the manufacturing of other products inside and outside the company. This process that is often referred to as by-product synergy enables recycling and reuse and can be pivotal in creating a circular economy.

Research and Development and Engineering

R&D and engineering must focus on developing sustainable technologies and products following the design-for-sustainability guidelines that are described in Chapter 8. They must use systems analysis and life-cycle assessment methodologies to make holistic assessments of the economic, social, and environmental impacts of alternate technologies and product designs. Technologists and engineers must go beyond merely complying with MRSs and assume responsibility for the sustainability of their invention and design. They must be citizen engineers[21] who care about the social and environmental impacts of their creation.

Manufacturing and Operations

The design-for-sustainability approach (Chapter 8) must be utilized in designing manufacturing processes, too. For example, the manufacturing process must efficiently allow the least possible amount of waste and effluents to be delivered to the air, water, and land and must use safe chemicals based on green-chemistry principles. Furthermore, manufacturing processes should be designed for closed-loop and zero-waste operations where the waste from one cycle is used as feedstock for other manufacturing cycles. The zero-waste reuse and recyclability principles should apply to packaging design, too. Facilities managers must run an efficient operation and deploy sustainable resources such as renewable energy and recycled water.

Supply Loop

The supply-loop[22] approach must be adopted to replace the traditional linear supply chains where virgin materials are sourced. In supply-loop design, designers and manufacturing reuse materials and components and purchase recycled materials. Supplies also should be sourced locally. Suppliers must be treated ethically and with equitable compensation. Buyers must not take advantage of their market power to push down prices to the detriment of the safety and well-being of their suppliers' worker, particularly in poor countries where local labor laws are lax or not enforced. Firms must assume responsibility for the environmental and social impacts of their product over its entire life cycle and ensure that triple-bottom-line principals are applied throughout the supply loop. Firms must share precompetitive sustainable methods and IP with the suppliers and competitors if those methods and IP reduce waste, greenhouse gas emissions, and hazardous materials. The firm's objective must be triple-bottom-line performance by all players in the supply loop—a win-win approach for the firm, the suppliers, and nature.

Regulations

Often the EHS regulations that are set by local governments are the minimum requirements (the floor) for the safety of users and workers and the protection of the environment. Furthermore, EHS regulations are uneven among various countries or even regions of the same country. Responsible companies are the leaders on the sustainability maturity index, as defined in the following section. They exceed governmental EHS regulations and practice the most stringent requirements homogeneously across the globe, irrespective of lax local regulatory regimes.

Management System

Organizational units and individual employees will not adopt sustainability strategies and practice sustainability principles without an enforcing management system. The management system includes the tools and methodologies of performance management plus a supportive corporate culture that helps institutionalize and operationalize sustainable practices. The management system should institute key performance indicators (KPIs) and tools for achieving sustainability goals across the company and at every function. The management system must comprise both individual and team KPIs and rewards for attaining sustainability results.

The Sustainability Maturity Index in Business

The sustainability maturity index (SMI) is the measure of a firm's commitment to sustainability as manifest in its business strategy, operational processes, products, and services.[23] There are five maturity levels based on the company's rating score in the following six areas: (1) legal and contractual compliance, (2) employee awareness and education, (3) strategic outlook, (4) characteristics of products and processes, (5) proactive supply chain management, and (6) entrepreneurship.

1. **Compliant:** Adheres to minimum legal and regulatory requirements and customer specifications for environmental protection. May inadvertently harm the environment.

2. **Supportive:** Establishes policies in support of sustainability. Develops employee awareness and minimizes harm to the environment in operational practices.
3. **Active:** Develops operational efficiency plans to minimize waste and resource utilization with explicit consideration for sustainability. Establishes operational metrics (indicators) and targets for sustainability and monitors reductions in environmental impacts.
4. **Proactive:** Defines sustainability goals for products, services, manufacturing, and operations in conjunction with annual operating plans extending to the entire supply chain. Proactively implements the plans and monitors progress toward objectives. Educates the workforce (at all levels) in sustainability opportunities and best-known methods.
5. **Leader:** Develops sustainability as a strategic imperative and integrates it into the business strategy and model. Is far-sighted and innovative in implementing sustainability goals in conjunction with all other business objectives. Creatively resolves conflicts between meeting business requirements and sustainability leadership on a global scale. Demonstrates entrepreneurship in opportunities for sustainability and investments in sustainable technology and product and process development. Empowers employees and rewards sustainability initiatives at all levels (through kaizen, continuous improvement of business practices). Seeks holistic solutions through societal outreach and stakeholder engagement, including local and global communities and governments.

Who Are the Agents of Transition to Sustainable Development?

Sustainable development can be achieved only if everyone in society has a strong sense of global citizenship. There must be a strong sense of mutual interdependence and responsibility between individuals and the local and global society, where society cares for the individual and individuals care about the well-being of society and the environment. The agents of the transformational changes that are needed for sustainable development are everyone. They are CEOs, scientists, engineers, entrepreneurs, biologists, economists, policymakers, venture capitalists, teachers, pharmacologists—and you and I.

The path is not straightforward, and obstacles are abundant. But with a steadfast and optimistic outlook, the pursuit of sustainable development can be energized and achieved.

Questions and Exercises

1. What are the top three initiatives a business can take to establish sustainable product development as a standard operating practice?
2. Create a spreadsheet assessing the Sustainability Maturity Index (SMI) of a company of your choice in various dimensions of its operational building blocks shown in Figure 2.5. Can you develop an aggregate SMI score for the company?
3. What are the factors that constrain efficiency maximization in a product's life cycle (design, manufacturing, use, and end-of-life management)? Is a zero-waste strategy attainable?

Endnotes

1. William E. Rees, "Ecological Footprint and Biocapacity: Essential Elements in Sustainability Assessment," in Jo Dewulf and Herman van Langenhove, (Eds.), *Renewables-Based Technology Sustainability Assessment,* pp. 143–158 (Chichester, UK: Wiley, 2006).
2. Alan Greenspan, "The Challenge of Central Banking in a Democratic Society," remarks delivered at the American Enterprise Institute, Washington, DC, December 5, 1996. Greenspan was the chair of the Federal Reserve of the United States from 1987 to 2006.
3. Barack H. Obama, "A Just and Lasting Peace," Nobel Lecture, Oslo, Norway, December 10, 2009.
4. Mahatma Gandhi, "On the Verge of It," in Gandhi: Selected Political Writings, (Ed.), Dennis Dalton (Indianapolis, IN: Hackett, 1996), p. 43.
5. Peter M. Senge and Goran Carstedt, "Innovating Our Way to the Next Industrial Revolution," MIT Sloan Management Review 42(2) (Winter 2001).
6. Vaclav Havel, "Our Moral Footprint," New York Times, September 27, 2007, A31. Havel was the president of Czechoslovakia from 1989 to 1992 and president of the Czech Republic from 1993 to 2003.
7. Lyndon B. Johnson, Annual Message to the Congress on the State of the Union, January 4, 1965.
8. Robert C. Carlson and Dariush Rafinejad, "The Transition to Sustainable Product Development and Manufacturing," in Karl G. Kempf, Pinar Keskinocak, and Reha Uzsoy, (Eds.), Planning Production and Inventories in the Extended Enterprise: A State-of-the-Art Handbook, vol. 1, pp. 45–82 (New York: Springer, 2011).
9. Milton Friedman, "The Social Responsibility of Business Is to Increase Its Profits," New York Times Magazine, September 13, 1970, pp. 122–124.
10. Terry L. Anderson and Donald R. Leal, Enviro-capitalists: Doing Good While Doing Well (Lanham, MD: Rowman & Littlefield, 2000).
11. Sheila Bonini and Steven Swartz, "Bringing Discipline to Your Sustainability Initiatives," McKinney & Company, August 2014, http://www.mckinsey.com/insights/sustainability/bringing_discipline_to_your_sustainability_initiatives?cid=other-eml-alt-mip-mck-oth-1408.
12. Paul T. Anastas and John Charles Warner, *Green Chemistry: Theory and Practice* (New York: Oxford University Press, 1998).
13. James Sweeney, *Energy Efficiency: Building a Clean, Secure Economy.* Hoover Press, 2016, Fig. 1.

14. Arthur H. Rosenfeld, Commissioner, "Successes of Energy Efficiency: The United States and California National Environmental Trust," May 2, 2007, California Energy Commission, http://www.energy.ca.gov/2007publications/CEC-999-2007-023/CEC-999-2007-023.PDF.

15. Steven Chu and Arun Majumdar, "Opportunities and Challenges for a Sustainable Energy Future," Nature 488 (August 16, 2012): 294–303.

16. United Nations Environment Program (UNEP) and Society of Environmental Toxicology and Chemistry (SETAC), "Life Cycle Management: How Business Uses It to Decrease Footprint, Increase Opportunities and Make Value Chains More Sustainable," UNEP/SETAC, 2008.

17. Tim Jackson, "Live Better by Consuming Less? Is There a 'Double Dividend' in Sustainable Consumption?" Journal of Industrial Ecology 9(1–2) (2005): 19–36.

18. According to a 2011 UN panel report, the global fossil fuel subsidy is $350 billion to $500 billion per year. Gro Brundtland, "Climate Change and Our Common Future," paper presented at the Global Climate and Energy Project symposium, Stanford University, Stanford, CA, October 8, 2013.

19. For additional policies, see United Nations, "Sustainable Development Goals: Seventeen Goals to Transform Our World," September 25, 2015, http://www.un.org/sustainabledevelopment/sustainable-development-goals.

20. Pamela Matson, William C. Clark, and Krister Andersson, *Pursuing Sustainability: A Guide to the Science and Practice* (Princeton, NJ: Princeton University Press, 2016), p. 131.

21. Yvon Chouinard and Vincent Stanley, *The Responsible Company: What We've Learned from Patagonia's First Forty Years* (Ventura, CA: Patagonia Books, 2013).

22. Roland Geyer and Tim Jackson, "Supply Loops and Their Constraints: The Industrial Ecology of Recycling and Reuse," California Management Review 46(2) (Winter 2004): 55–73.

23. Robert C. Carlson and Dariush Rafinejad. "The Transition to Sustainable Product Development and Manufacturing," *Planning Production and Inventories in the Extended Enterprise*, pp. 45–82 (New York: Springer US, 2011).

CHAPTER 3

SUSTAINABILITY FRAMEWORKS AND INDUSTRIAL ECOLOGY

The state of the art in product innovation, development, and commercialization comprises many excellent strategies and tools.[1] However, these practices are optimized to serve the goal of maximizing return on investment in products within the framework of prevalent business practices. The state of the art must be amended for development of sustainable products. The purpose of this chapter is to review several guidelines and methodologies for designing sustainable products and services. Many of them are based on the principles of industrial ecology and systems approach in design, which are the foundation of the design-for-sustainability (DfS) methodology.

Industrial ecology (IE) is defined as: "the study of the flows of material and energy in industrial and consumer activities, of the effects of these flows on the environment, and of the influences of economic, political, regulatory and social factors on the flow, use, and transformation of resources."[2] This industrial ecology quest is how industrial systems can be restructured to make them compatible with the functioning of natural ecosystems. IE is systems thinking applied to the economy and the environment.[3] IE encompasses the design of industrial products and processes and also the overarching business strategies and the contextual institutions (and rules).

Today's prevalent industrial systems are incompatible with the functioning of natural ecosystems. For example, in the industrial global supply chain, animals are fed crops that are grown hundreds (or thousands) of miles away, transferring resources like nitrogen and water across the globe. In the case of nature's closed-loop ecosystem, animals are fed local crops, and their waste is returned to the soil as fertilizer, closing the nitrogen cycle.

Product development, manufacturing, and commercialization can be thought of as the activities within a corporate system. The input to this system is the flow of material (and other products) from the first-tier and second-tier suppliers, and the output of the system is a product or service that fulfills the market demand. In this model, the manufacturer optimizes system performance by ensuring that suppliers have adequate capacity to meet the demand, the product is manufactured at the lowest possible cost, and the quality of the output (that is, the product) satisfies customer expectations. System performance optimization is constrained by the desired commercial return on the investment and by the required compliance to laws and regulations. Concerns about the disposal of waste and effluents generated by the system are limited to compliance with the regulatory requirements within the facilities that the firm owns and directly controls. In this approach, the space-time impact of the design and manufacturing activities on the natural ecosystem and society is not considered.

In sustainable product development, however, the boundaries of the system must be expanded, and systems thinking must be applied in a whole new way. We must optimize the product design and supply chain strategy (that is, system performance), not only to maximize profits and minimize costs, but also to comply with the requirements that make a product sustainable (as is discussed in earlier chapters). As such, we must integrate the product's life-cycle ecological and social impacts in design decisions and supply chain strategies. In short, sustainable products must deliver optimal triple-bottom-line performance for economic, environmental, and social sustainability. This is the previously mentioned product-design approach called DfS, which is based on an expanded systems-thinking model and deploys the principles of IE.

In DfS, concerns for the sustainability of environmental and social capitals and for the optimal economic outcomes are included in the design decisions. And the environmental and social externalities (that is, the harms that are imposed on others) are minimized throughout the product's life cycle. Product life-cycle considerations extend beyond the activities that the firm controls directly and include all upstream and downstream steps in the production, use, and end-of-life of the product. This approach is often referred to as a cradle-to-grave approach.

In the next section, the systems-thinking concept for the development of sustainable products is discussed in more detail. Traditional product development deals with systems that are limited in both scope and time. System performance optimization is carried out over the product's life, which is often quite short and influenced by rapid changes in technology. Sustainable product systems are vastly different. Their spatial scale is global, and their temporal dimension is generational.

Systems Thinking

Sustainable product development requires dealing with complex systems. The functional design of the product or service must meet or exceed user expectations and return an acceptable return on development investment, and sustainable products must contribute to sustainable development and serve human well-being. Therefore, product concepts, technology choices, and manufacturing and supply-loop strategies must be based on decisions that are optimal in space and time in a system that is inclusive of the environment and the global society. The product must have minimal environmental impact (that is, unit impact times the quantity consumed) over its life cycle—from the extraction and processing of input material to the product's manufacturing, delivery, use, and finally disposal at the end of its life. The social impact of the product must also be considered by answering the *what* question: what is it for? We make a product *in order to* perform a function and, more important, *for the sake of* improving the well-being of its users.

The complex system that we must consider in sustainable product development comprises the firm, the economic context, the global society, and the environment. In Chapter 12, systems analysis methodology and system dynamic modeling tools and their application in sustainable product development are discussed. Here the focus is on the general concepts of systems thinking[4] that are imperative in sustainable product development.

A system is a set of interconnected elements (subsystems or components) that are organized in such a way that they produce the system's unique characteristics and dynamics behavior, and achieve something. The systems often are constrained by boundary conditions and driven by outside forces. The system's response to external forces is a function of its characteristics, which are shaped by the performance of individual components as well as their interaction through feedback signals.

Systems analysis is a methodical examination of the system's behavior and may include trade offs in the choice of system components to achieve a specified performance under the external constraints and boundary conditions. For example, a product as a system might comprise myriad components that collectively perform the functions of the product and create certain environmental and social externalities. Product development includes systems analysis, where product performance is optimized by designing components and subsystems that produce the desired outcome. Constraints on the system might include limits on production cost, on the life-cycle environmental impact (such as greenhouse gas [GHG] emissions) from production and use, and on the product's adverse social impacts. Often systems analysis is performed with a model of the stock and flow variables in the system (as discussed in Chapter 12).

In analyzing complex economic, social, and environmental systems, we must identify and model nonlinearities in system behavior. The behavior of complex systems is often nonlinear, and past trends cannot be extrapolated to predict the future state of stock variables such as financial, natural, human, and social capitals. Figure 3.1, adapted from John Ehrenfeld, depicts the nonlinear characteristic behavior of a complex system.[5] In this figure, the earth's carrying capacity (the capital stocks of sources and sinks) and the physical economy (such as the gross domestic product per capita) and population are plotted as a function of time.

In Case 1 in Figure 3.1, the exponential growth in demand is always met by a corresponding increase in the carrying capacity that is enabled by technology. For example, if we run out of easily recoverable oil, we develop new technologies to recover less accessible deep-sea or shale oil economically. The situation in Case 2 assumes that demand stabilizes in equilibrium with the constant carrying capacity

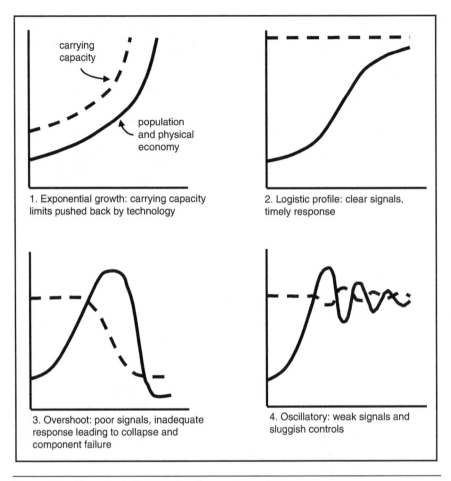

Figure 3.1   Characteristic behavior of complex systems

of the earth through controlled response and adaptation. In this case, signals are clear, feedback latency is short, and effective responses to future problems are rapidly deployed. Case 3 represents an overshoot situation where because of poor signals or lack of response, the system collapses. For example, the carrying capacity of many fisheries in the world has collapsed, and they have become extinct because of overfishing. The ecological system of the Aral Sea in Central Asia has collapsed because of excessive exploitation of its source and sink capacities for several decades (see Figure 1.13). In both examples, the feedback signals were clear, but the corrective response was lacking. Case 4 in Figure 3.1 is an oscillatory dynamic behavior caused by weak signals and delays in corrective response. Perhaps the atmospheric ozone concentration could be represented by this behavior. The depletion of the atmospheric ozone capacity was detected in the 1970s. The global corrective action was instituted a decade later through the Montreal Protocol (1987), which banned the production of ozone-depleting chlorofluorocarbons (CFCs) beginning in 1989. CFCs were mostly replaced with hydrochlorofluorocarbons (HCFCs), which are less harmful to the ozone layer. After the CFC ban, the ozone concentration recovered somewhat. However, after several decades, efforts are now underway to ban HCFCs, too, because they do not completely solve the ozone-depletion problem and, more important, are potent global warming agents.

Note that in all four cases in Figure 3.1, the demand curve represented by the physical economy and population has a similar initial trend indicating a gradual rise, well below the carrying capacity. We might incorrectly extrapolate this trend into the future and construe that the physical economy and population can grow exponentially and be supported by the earth's carrying capacity indefinitely. However, the system behavior is nonlinear, and past trends are not representative of the future state. Because of the interactive dependence of the system components, the physical economy adversely impacts the environment and diminishes its carrying capacity, and demand eventually overshoots the carrying capacity (as in Case 3 in Figure 3.1). Consequently, both carrying capacity and the physical economy collapse, and the earth's ecological system ceases to support the human population.

Another important aspect of thinking in systems is recognizing that the interconnectedness of the subsystems might cause cascades of unintended consequences. For example, as shown in Figure 3.2, energy generation and use (in buildings, transportation, and industry) produce GHGs and other pollutants, such as nitrogen oxide and sulfur oxide. Excessive GHG concentration in the atmosphere causes global warming, which causes sea-level rise, heavy rains, drought, species extinction, and other impacts. These consequences, in turn, impact the availability of food and drinking

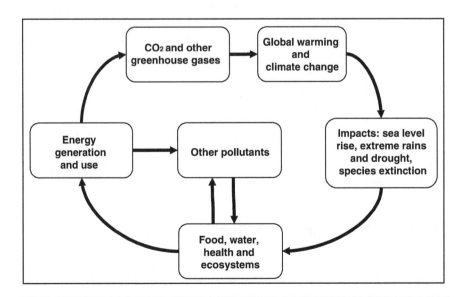

Figure 3.2 System interconnectedness and its unintended consequences

water, cause health issues, and change ecosystems. The latter changes in ecosystems affect energy-use and energy-generation patterns, completing the feedback loop. The other pollutants from energy production and use also impact the state of food, water, health, and ecosystems through another feedback loop, which is shown in Figure 3.2.

If problems are not solved holistically and systemically, solutions often solve one problem but create a new one. For example, to comply with the Clean Air Act, some polluters of volatile organic compounds (VOCs) have reduced VOCs by combusting them with natural gas. However, the natural gas combustion process produces carbon dioxide (CO_2), which is a GHG. As the result, the VOC problem is solved by aggravating the global warming problem. Also, as previously mentioned, the ozone-depletion problem was alleviated by replacing CFCs with HCFC and hydrofluorocarbon (HFC) compounds, which are potent GHGs and change the atmosphere's chemical dynamics.

We also should be warned against having a blind belief in the power of technology to solve all the environmental and social problems created by the production and use of products. The lack of understanding of the complexities of these issues—the economic-social-environmental system and the interconnectedness of its components and nonlinear characteristics of the system—has led some to revert to a persistent belief that technology can *fix* all problems. Consequently, we hear that geoengineering solutions will be able to fix environmental problems like global warming—for example, by manipulating the global climate directly and massively, either by injecting particles such as sulfur dioxide into the atmosphere to block sunlight or by scattering oceans with iron particles to encourage the growth of algae that consume carbon dioxide. Furthermore, geoengineering could turn to genetic science to engineer drought-resistant plants or trees that sequester more carbon dioxide. The proponents of geoengineering ignore the unintended consequences of the proposed solutions and solve one problem while creating many new ones. Sustainable products and technologies are different. They do not focus on only the utility of the product in addressing an unmet need but seek to offer holistic solutions through systems thinking. Mitigation of the problem is often the best solution. The best fix to the global warming problem is to avert it.

The unintended consequences of our technologies reflect our incomplete understanding of the system characteristics and inherent complexities of natural and human systems. A holistic approach requires many new engineering, environmental science, social, economic, political, and ethical tools. It is also important to develop economic and social systems that do not hamper the resiliency of natural ecosystems by pushing it to the tipping point of collapse.

System Dynamics and Resilience

A system is often represented by two types of variables—*stocks* and *flows*. Stock variables represent the state of the system at a given time, and flow variables are the inputs and outputs to the stock variables that cause changes in the state over time.

These variables are interconnected and in certain circumstances form feedback loops that can be reinforcing (positive) or balancing (negative). In feedback loops, the flows change the stocks, which, in turn, impact the flows. In a positive feedback loop, the increase (or decrease) in one variable causes a corresponding increase (or decrease) in another.

Resilience is a system's ability to tolerate perturbations in exogenous factors and variability in operating conditions (represented by flow variables). In a resilient (or robust) system, small changes in the external variables do not shift the system off its equilibrium state.

Social Considerations in Industrial Ecology

IE is concerned with consumer behavior in consumption and social ecology. Today, product design and marketing strategies are unsustainable because they seek to maximize consumption. Products are designed for obsolescence by having short platform and product lives, and perceived obsolescence is promoted by fashion. Furthermore, marketers establish *social meaning* for products by creating associations between consumption and satisfaction of human needs such as communal belonging, self-esteem, and actualization of one's potential.

We must reverse this course and move consumers away from excessive consumption and waste. Consumer behavior can be changed by economic incentives, emotional manipulation, education, and societal safeguards. The consumer culture and its values also need to be changed from *more is better* to a desire for *quality* products and services. Product design strategies must be amended to support this new consumer behavior by creating quality products that last a long time.

The social ecology perspective calls for social redesign that supports industrial ecology and personal values transformation for creating a new economy that is in harmony with nature:

> "Because money and economic systems, like politics, technology, and even religion, are human constructions (in a sense, merely 'tools') that enable us to act on our values, they should not be accorded similar status to the environment or personal well-being when considering sustainability. Like all tools, they must be regarded as *subject to change as needed*, and their appropriateness must be judged against a broad range of life-affirming values."[6]

Elements of Industrial Ecology: Eco-Efficiency and Eco-Effectiveness

The IE model institutes both eco-efficiency and eco-effectiveness in product design, manufacturing, and other operational activities of an enterprise. Eco-efficiency means a minimal use of resources, waste, and environmental impact (with less pollution). It often can be accomplished with incremental improvements to the current system to achieve more output, while using less resources. Eco-efficiency is calculated as the ratio of value of a product (or economic creation) to the environmental impact (or ecological destruction) caused by the product. Economic creation equals the product price minus the costs of manufacturing and environmental impact abatement. And ecological destruction is the cumulative normalized life-cycle impact of the product. The impact assessment is based on a life-cycle assessment (LCA) that accounts for energy and material consumption, emissions, toxicity potential, and risk potential (that is, the risk of manufacturing accidents or misuse of the product).

Eco-effectiveness calls for a new circular economy that does not deplete natural resources and that prevents the generation of waste and pollution in the first place. Eco-effectiveness includes *upcycling* in addition to the recycling of materials at the end of the product's life within virtuous closed loops.

Eco-efficiency and eco-effectiveness must be built into the design of industrial systems, the supply chain structure, and transportation logistics in order to achieve IE symbiosis. By-product synergy (BPS) is a methodology that connects manufacturing cycles and helps create supply loops. In BPS, instead of being discarded into landfills, manufacturing by-products that are considered waste are reused as feedstock in other manufacturing cycles, either within the same facility or in the manufacturing cycles of other companies. In the latter case, firms market their by-products as raw stock materials. Susan Mackenzie cites several BPS examples, including the following two:[7] Steel slag, which is waste residue produced in the steel manufacturing process, can be converted to raw material and used as input material for cement manufacturing. Wastewater from copper-impregnated graphite manufacturing could be sold to another company that extracts copper for commercial value. Figure 3.3 depicts a manufacturing product life cycle and the opportunities for reuse, recycling, and by-product synergy to create a closed-loop system. The product life cycle is comprised of the following six major steps:

- Extraction of virgin material,
- (Primary) material processing,
- Manufacturing (including component manufacturing, final assembly, and packaging),
- Distribution and sales,
- Use (including installation, consumption, service, and support), and finally
- End of life.

The logistics—including transportation, warehousing, and distribution—are shown by arrows. In each step of the process, energy is required as an input, and effluents are generated as output.

A well-known application of IE and BPS occurred in the municipality of Kalundborg in Denmark, as shown in Figure 3.4.[8] In this industrial symbiosis, there is a strong interconnectedness among various plants, where waste from one plant is used as input stock in another process or plant. This synergy was developed by

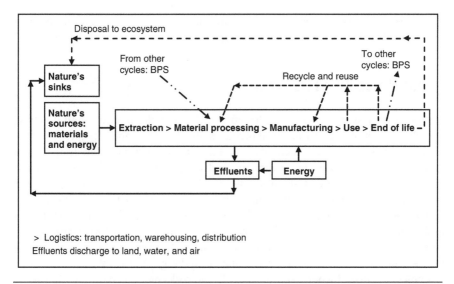

Figure 3.3   The manufacturing life cycle and opportunities for eco-effectiveness

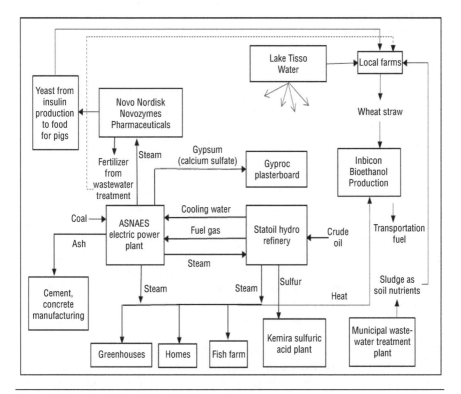

Figure 3.4   Industrial symbiosis in Denmark

design. For example, various plants were located near each other, and production processes were designed to maximize synergy.

Sustainability Frameworks

Sustainability frameworks attempt to reframe IE principles in usable and practical guidelines for sustainable industrial practices, including product design, manufacturing process design, and facilities operation. In this section, a few frameworks that have been proposed by researchers and nongovernmental organizations are reviewed. These include cradle to cradle (C2C), The Natural Step (TNS), natural capitalism, biomimicry, the total beauty of sustainable products, LCA, and cost of sustainability. These frameworks differ significantly in their specificity as design tools. Some state certain principles as overarching guidelines for formulating operational strategies, and others serve as tools that can be used in product design and in assessing the environmental impact of a given design. In the following sections, examples are cited of where some of these frameworks have been used in industry.[9]

The LCA methodology is the most comprehensive and holistic tool for analyzing a product and for quantifying the environmental impact of the product in its life cycle. The LCA methodology is introduced in this section, but because of its importance, all of Chapter 4 is dedicated to an in-depth exploration of LCA.

Cradle to Cradle

In their 1976 research report to the European Commission, "The Potential for Substituting Manpower for Energy," Walter Stahel and Genevieve Reday sketched the vision of an economy in loops (or a circular economy) and in 1980 used the term C2C.[10] The term C2C later was popularized by William McDonough and Michael Braungart.[11] C2C focuses on eco-effectiveness—that *less bad does not equal good*! The three underlying principles of the C2C protocol are designing for disassembly, designing industrial processes that do not generate pollution and waste in the first place, and using recycled and recyclable materials. C2C considers materials to be either biological nutrients (nature-made), technical nutrients (human-made), or *monstrous* hybrids of the two—and it classifies a material as green, yellow, orange, or red based on its life-cycle impact on human health and environment. The Cradle to Cradle Products Innovation Institute certifies designs according to the following five scoring categories[12]—material health, material reutilization, renewable energy and carbon management, water stewardship, and social fairness.

The application of the C2C protocol at the Herman Miller Corporation is reported in a Harvard Business School case study titled "Cradle-to-Cradle Design at Herman Miller: Moving toward Environmental Sustainability."[13] This case shows, in detail, the steps and resources used to implement C2C in the design decision to use an environmentally-friendly material, rather than a polyvinyl chloride material, in the Mirra chair product. The case study also shows that by scrutinizing its processes through an environmental lens, Herman Miller was able to make process and product improvements and effect change in the corporation.

The Natural Step (TNS)

TNS organization was founded in 1989 by Karl-Henrik Robèrt in Sweden.[14] TNS framework has four sustainability principles. In a *sustainable society*, nature is not subject to systematically increasing concentrations of substances extracted from the earth's crust—such as heavy metals and CO_2 from fossil fuels. It is not exposed to concentrations of substances produced by society—such as antibiotics and endocrine disruptors. Nature is not subject to excessive degradation by physical means— such as over-harvesting forests and paving over critical wildlife habitat. And in that society, people are not endangered by conditions that systemically undermine their capacity to meet their needs—such as unsafe working conditions, poor health, and not enough pay to live on.

TNS principles were deployed at Millipore Corporation in 2007 and helped the company to define sustainability within the organization and distinguish sustainability from conventional environmental, health, and safety (EHS) issues.[15] Millipore established GHG reduction targets and developed an implementation plan to achieve the targets, but realized that effective sustainability initiatives must be operationalized across the organization in product development, manufacturing, marketing, supply chains, investor relations, and government relations.

Natural Capitalism

The natural capitalism model espouses sustainability through increased resource efficiency, reduced waste, a shift to solution-oriented business, and investment in nature.[16] The following four major shifts must occur in current business practices to achieve *natural capitalism*:

- Dramatically increase the productivity of natural resources, and reduce the waste and destructive flow of resources.
- Shift to biologically inspired production models. Eliminate waste by using a closed-loop production system. This would require the formation of industry alliances—within and across sectors—and cooperatives to sell and service the by-products.
- Move to a solution-based business model. This results in providing *illumination, for example, instead of a light bulb* as manufacturers shift to a service-leasing business model and to life-cycle ownership of their products. (This approach works if the cost of local labor to service and repair a product is less than the manufacturing and carrying costs of the defective subsystem and the component that is sourced from a *low-cost region*.)
- Reinvest in natural capital (similar to the investment in the means of production) to restore, sustain, and expand the planet's ecosystems.

Biomimicry

Biomimicry is the examination of nature—its models, systems, processes, and elements—to emulate or take inspiration from to solve human problems. According to the Merriam-Webster dictionary, *biomimetics* is: "the study of the formation, structure, or function of biologically produced substances and materials (as enzymes or silk) and biological mechanisms and processes (as protein synthesis or photosynthesis) especially for the purpose of synthesizing similar products by artificial mechanisms which mimic natural ones."[17]

Biomimicry as a framework for product development strives to use nature as a model, measure, and mentor. With nature as a model, we study nature's systems and imitate its designs and processes to solve human problems; with nature as a measure, we use ecological standards to judge our product innovation; and with nature as a mentor, we view and value nature in a new way based on what we can learn and not what we can extract from it.[18]

The salient characteristics of nature's ecosystems that should inspire sustainable product development include survival over the long haul, diversity, a no-growth model, survival of the fittest (where *fittest* means not *strongest and domineering* but *most able to adapt and live in harmony with others*), resilience, and closed-loop processes where waste in one cycle is food for another.

The following biomimicry principles (adopted from the Biomimicry Institute's website)[19] can guide sustainable product and process development:

- Use waste as a resource; diversify and cooperate to use the habitat in symbiosis;
- Gather and use energy efficiently;
- Shift to solar and wind energy;
- Optimize rather than maximize;
- Choose quality not quantity;
- Use materials sparingly and dematerialize products;
- Don't foul the nests—reduce toxins;
- Don't draw down resources—use renewables;
- Remain in balance with the biosphere—don't disrupt natural cycles by pollutants;
- Run on information—reward sustainable behavior; and finally,
- Shop locally.

The Total Beauty of Sustainable Products

The founder of Biothinking: Consultancy & Training for Sustainable Design, Edwin Datschefski, describes sustainable products as having *total beauty* and promotes the following design guidelines.[20] Designs should be:

- Cyclic (products should be made from compostable organic materials or minerals that are recycled in a closed loop),

- Solar (in their manufacture and use, products should consume only renewable energy that is cyclic and safe),
- Safe (all releases to air, water, land, or space should be food for other systems),
- Efficient (in their manufacture and use, products should require 90% less materials, energy, and water than equivalent products providing equivalent utility did in 1990), and
- Social (the manufacture and use of products should support basic human rights and natural justice).

Life-Cycle Assessment

LCA is a quantitative tool for analyzing consumption of resources (both renewable and nonrenewable) and emission of waste to the environment (air, water, and land) in a system or subsystem. LCA allows inclusion of environmental externalities in making business decisions from a systems point of view. LCA can be used for product development and improvement, and for integrated system analysis to deliver a solution. Furthermore, LCA can benefit strategic planning, marketing, and public policy. For example, in evaluating alternate transportation strategies, LCA can help us make a holistic system analysis. Instead of assessing cars versus trains and then roads versus rails, the life-cycle impacts of cars plus roads are compared to the impacts of trains plus rails. (The LCA methodology is discussed in detail in Chapter 4.)

Cost of Sustainability

The concept for cost of sustainability (COS) is modeled after the cost-of-quality (COQ) model proposed by Joseph Juran in 1951. He defined COQ as the unavoidable cost minus the avoidable cost of quality. The avoidable cost includes the cost of reworking defects in manufacturing, the cost of repairing failures in the product warranty period, and the cost of dealing with customer dissatisfaction. The unavoidable cost of quality is the cost of preventive measures—including cost increases in product manufacturing because of quality improvements in product design, extra inspections, and statistical process control. In the decades following the inception of the COQ idea, the so-called quality movement led to new product development and manufacturing paradigms where quality was designed-in as a standard operating practice. Unlike what the terminology implied, quality did not *cost* anything. In fact, the COQ proved to be negative, and high-quality products delivered dividends in profitability and customer satisfaction.

COS would also be negative—and sustainable products can deliver triple-bottom-line dividends to business, the environment, and society. The COS for a product is the unavoidable cost minus the avoidable and opportunity costs of making a sustainable product. The unavoidable cost is the sum of the extra engineering costs for following the DfS rules, the manufacturing cost increase caused by DfS, and the opportunity cost for being late to market due to incremental research and development.[21] The avoidable cost is equal to the sum of the following gains attained through DfS: operational efficiency improvements (by using less water and nonrenewable energy), lowered manufacturing cost (by dematerialization and weight reduction), and reduced costs of consumables (COC). The opportunity cost is equal to the value of gain in market share because of sustainability plus the social value of reducing the ecological footprint of the product and creating positive externality. In summary:

$$\text{Cost of sustainability (COS)} =$$
$$\text{Unavoidable cost} - \text{Avoidable cost} - \text{Opportunity cost,}$$

where,

- Unavoidable cost = Incremental cost of DfS (in design and manufacturing) + Late-to-market cost;
- Avoidable cost = Savings in operational efficiency + Product manufacturing cost reduction by DfS + Reduction in nonrenewable consumption (in COC); and
- Opportunity cost = Value of market share gain + Social value of reducing the ecological footprint of the product.

Note that the terms in the COS equation reflect the incremental costs associated with making a product sustainable. The standard costs associated with developing a product that satisfies market requirements and complies with the EHS regulations are excluded. The COS might depend on the cost of compliance (to EHS regulations) because the global regulatory landscape is nonhomogeneous. This nonhomogeneity often leads to a global sourcing strategy where managers opt to manufacture products in *low-cost* regions with lax environmental restrictions. In these situations, the cost of sustainable manufacturing will be higher, and market share value might be lower than the baseline alternative.

Questions and Exercises

1. Can you identify additional IE frameworks beyond those listed in this chapter?
2. Which sustainability framework is most effective as a practical tool for developing a sustainable product?
3. What are the top three factors that enabled creation of the industrial symbiosis in Denmark (Figure 3.4)?

Endnotes

1. Dariush Rafinejad, *Innovation, Product Development and Commercialization: Case Studies and Key Practices for Market Leadership* (Plantation, FL: J. Ross Publishing, 2007).
2. Robert White, "Preface," in B. R. Allenby and R. J. Deanna, *The Greening of Industrial Ecosystems*, 5–6 (Washington, DC: National Academy Press, 1994).
3. T. E. Graedel and B. R. Allenby, *Industrial Ecology*, 2nd ed. (Upper Saddle River, NJ: Pearson Education, 2003).
4. Donella Meadows, Jorgen Randers, and Dennis Meadows, *Limits to Growth: The Thirty-Year Update* (White River Junction, VT: Chelsea Green Publishing, 2004); Donella H. Meadows and Diana Wright, *Thinking in Systems: A Primer* (White River Junction, VT: Chelsea Green Publishing, 2008).
5. John R. Ehrenfeld, "Industrial Ecology: Paradigm Shift or Normal Science?" American Behavioral Scientist 44(2) (October 2000): 229–244; John R. Ehrenfeld, "Industrial Ecology: A Framework for Product and Process Design," Journal of Cleaner Production 5(1) (1997): 87–95.
6. Stuart B. Hill, "Enabling Redesign for Deep Industrial Ecology and Personal Values Transformation: A Social Ecology Perspective," in Ken Green and Sally Randles, eds., Industrial Ecology and Spaces of Innovation, pp. 255–271 (London: Edward Elgar, 2006).
7. Susan Mackenzie, with Terry Anderson, "Applied Sustainability LLC: Making a Business Case for By-product Synergy," case number E-118, Graduate School of Business, Stanford University, February 2002.
8. Source: http://www.symbiosis.dk.
9. A critique of this model as the basis for an economy that supports sustainable development is provided in Robert C. Carlson and Dariush Rafinejad, "Economic Models for Environmental and Business Sustainability in Product Development and Manufacturing," International Journal of Environmental, Cultural, Economic and Social Sustainability 7(4) (2011): 199–210.
10. Walter R. Stahel and Geneviève Reday, "The Potential for Substituting Manpower for Energy," research study 76-13, V/343/78-EN, Program of Research and Actions on the Development of the Labor Market, DGV, Commission of the European Communities, Brussels, Batelle Geneva, final report July 30, 1977; published as Walter R. Stahel and Geneviève Reday, *Jobs for Tomorrow: The Potential for Substituting Manpower for Energy* (New York: Vantage Press, 1981).
11. William McDonough and Michael Braungart, *Cradle to Cradle: Remaking the Way We Make Things* (New York: North Point Press, 2002).
12. Cradle to Cradle Products Innovation Institute, "Cradle to Cradle Certified Product Scorecard," http://www.c2ccertified.org/get-certified/product-certification.
13. Lee Deishin and Lionel Bony, "Cradle-to-Cradle Design at Herman Miller: Moving toward Environmental Sustainability," Harvard Business School Case 607-003, May 2007, revised February 7, 2008, revised December 2009.
14. The Natural Step, Stockholm, Sweden, www.thenaturalstep.org.
15. Michael W. Toffel and Katharine Lee, "Sustainability at Millipore," Harvard Business School Case Study 610-012, July 2009, revised December 10, 2009, revised January 2014.
16. Amory B. Lovins, L. Hunter Lovins, and Paul Hawken, "A Road Map for Natural Capitalism," Harvard Business Review 85(7–8) (July–August 2007): 172.
17. https://www.merriam-webster.com/dictionary/biomimetics.

18. Janine M. Benyus, Biomimicry (New York: Morrow, 1997); Janine Benyus, "Biomimicry's Surprising Lessons from Nature's Engineers," talk delivered at the Technology, Entertainment, and Design (TED) conference, February 2005.

19. Biomimicry Institute, https://biomimicry.org.

20. Edwin Datschefski, Biothinking: Consultancy & Training on Sustainable Design, http://www.biothinking.com/slidenj.htm.

21. Robert C. Carlson and Dariush Rafinejad, "The Transition to Sustainable Product Development and Manufacturing," in Karl G. Kempf, Pinar Keskinocak, and Reha Uzsoy, (Eds.), *Planning Production and Inventories in the Extended Enterprise: A State-of-the-Art Handbook*, vol. 1, pp. 45–82 (New York: Springer, 2011).

CHAPTER 4

LIFE-CYCLE ASSESSMENT

Life-cycle assessment (or analysis) (LCA) methodology is a quantitative tool for analyzing the consumption of resources (renewable and nonrenewable) and emission of wastes to the environment (air, water, land) in a system or a subsystem. LCA characterizes the environmental and health impacts of resource consumption and emissions in a system.

LCA accounts for multiple impacts across the life cycle of a product or service and can be used as a decision-making tool in sustainable product design, sustainable manufacturing process design, supply-chain trade-offs, strategic planning, risk analysis, marketing, and public policymaking.

Let's consider a few examples in product design. In China, 45 billion pairs of chopsticks are produced a year, consuming millions of trees and bamboo plants. Would (reusable) steel or plastic chopsticks be better (that is, more sustainable) than the wooden (one-time use) design? Although tree and bamboo plants are renewable resources, their excessive consumption could result in deforestation. On the other hand, steel chopsticks have adverse environmental impacts, too, both in mining and manufacturing processes and later when they are washed after each use. Plastic chopsticks that are petroleum based consume a nonrenewable resource and cause many environmental and health impacts. Alternative chopstick designs can be assessed with the LCA tool to select the least impactful solution. Another example would be: which is better for the environment—a one-time-use paper coffee cup or a ceramic mug that can be washed and reused multiple times? Using LCA, studies have shown that the ceramic mug is better only after 70 uses.

LCA is also important to integrated system analysis in designing sustainable solutions. For example, in evaluating alternate transportation strategies, it is not enough simply to compare the environmental impacts of cars versus trains. We need to assess the environmental impacts of different transportation systems. LCA enables us to compare cars plus roads with trains plus rails.

LCA methodology has been used in the industry for many decades. The Coca-Cola Company is reported to have used LCA as early as 1969 to quantify the environmental and energy impacts of solid waste from packaging.[1] Robert Ayers reports on the early history and background of LCA methodology.[2] A 2006

Environmental Protection Agency (EPA) report presents the basics of LCA principles and practice.[3]

According to the International Organization for Standardization (ISO) standard 14040:2006, there are four phases in an LCA study, as shown in Figure 4.1.[4] The objective of the LCA study is to compile an inventory of system inputs and outputs, assess associated impacts on natural sources and sinks, and input the results into a business decision-making process for holistic system optimization.

In the first phase, the goal and scope are defined to identify the problem and define the objectives and range of the study. In this phase, the system function, its boundaries, and the functional unit (the unit that will be studied) are defined. In the second phase, the life-cycle inventory (LCI) analysis, the relevant inputs and outputs of the system throughout its life cycle are quantified. The full inventory of the required raw materials and the air, water, and soil emissions relative to the considered functional unit is analyzed.

In the third phase, the life-cycle impact assessment (LCIA) evaluates the magnitude and significance of the environmental impacts of the system using the LCI analysis results. The LCIA focuses on the relative environmental impacts rather than the absolute prediction of risk. In the fourth and final phase of the LCA study, the results from prior steps are interpreted to solve the stated problem and to meet the stated objectives of the study.

LCA is a cyclical process in which every phase is closely linked to the others. All results hang on the problem setting and the definition of the system function and functional unit. Usually, the LCA is carried out in two steps. In the first step, the order of magnitude of the material and emissions inventory and impacts is assessed, and in the second step, a detailed analysis is carried out to improve the assessment for the most significant impacts.

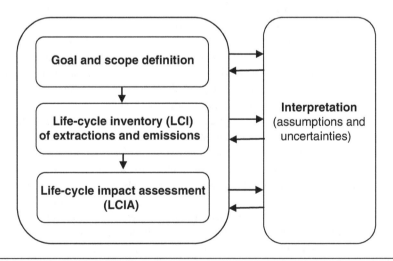

Figure 4.1   The LCA framework according to ISO 14040:2006

In the ISO 14041 standard, a product system has the following definition: "A product system is a collection of unit processes connected by flows of intermediate products which perform one or more defined functions. A product system description includes unit processes, elementary flows and product flows across the system boundaries and intermediate product flows within the system. The essential property of a product system is characterized by its function and cannot be defined solely in terms of the final products."[5]

LCA provides a method for collecting and managing materials and energy data for each process within the system boundaries and for assessing the potential adverse environmental and human impacts of materials and energy flows through the system boundaries.

Attributional and Consequential LCA

LCA can be performed to quantify the LCI of a system of products or processes (attributional) or to quantify the impact caused by a change in the system (consequential). The U.S. EPA gives the following definitions: "attributional life-cycle assessment: an LCA that accounts for flows/impacts of pollutants, resources, and exchanges among processes within a chosen temporal window"; "consequential life-cycle assessment: a cradle-to-grave approach for assessing industrial systems that evaluates all stages of a product's life. It provides a comprehensive view of the environmental aspects of the product or process."[6]

Before the above phases are discussed in more detail, the following case study is reviewed as an example of an LCA study.

Case Study: Beverage Containers

In this study of material choices for beverage containers, three types of containers are considered: a 16-ounce aluminum can, a 20-ounce polyethylene terephthalate (PET) bottle, and a 25.4-ounce glass bottle.[7] The objective in the case is to find out which container material has the lowest environmental impact based on LCA. First, the indicators of environmental impact for the analysis have to be established. For example, the primary energy demand might be used as an indicator of environmental impact, and a container material that requires the least energy in its life cycle might be selected. Other indicators—such as global warming potential (GWP) and terrestrial ecotoxicity potential (TETP)—of the effluents in the life cycle of the container might be included in the LCA study, too. In other words, the decision maker might choose to perform a single or multi-indicator LCA study.

Let's start with the primary energy demand as the only indicator of environmental impact—as illustrated in Figure 4.1. The next step is to define the scope of the LCA or the system boundary—that is, to define what parts of the container life cycle is included or excluded in the analysis. The system boundary is shown in Figure 4.2

and includes material production, container forming, transportation, and end-of-life management of the container. All other processes in the container's life cycle (such as container filling) are excluded.

For LCA analysis, we must define the function or the service that the system provides and the functional unit for quantifying the service. In this case, the function is holding and protecting the beverage, and the functional unit is the unit of volume—say, one liter of beverage. In Phase 2 of the LCA or the LCI phase, we determine the reference flows—the amount of material required for delivering the functional unit by each of the three container types. Because the containers under consideration have different volumes, we normalize their mass to one liter of beverage. The reference flows are 40 grams of aluminum can, 44 grams of PET bottle, and 433 grams of glass bottle.

The next step is to calculate the primary energy required to process the reference flows in each of the four life-cycle steps within the system boundary, as seen in Figure 4.2. The output of the analysis is the primary energy demand per liter of beverage, as shown in Figure 4.3. Note that container recycling is accounted for as an energy-saving step because the energy demand in material production is reduced if recycled materials (instead of virgin sources) are used as feed stock. According to the total energy results in Figure 4.3, the PET container has the lowest environmental impact and is the material of choice. Would the conclusion be the same if other environmental impact indicators in addition to energy were considered?

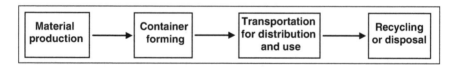

Figure 4.2   The system boundaries of the beverage container life cycle

Beverage container	Material production (MJ/liter)	Container manufacturing (MJ/liter)	Transportation* (MJ/liter)	Container recycling^ (MJ/liter)	Total life-cycle energy (MJ/liter)
Aluminum	8.5	0.4	0.05	-3.7	5.3
PET	3.6	0.7	0.05	-0.2	4.2
Glass	5.2	1.3	0.54	-0.5	6.5
* 500 km distance ^ saved energy					

Figure 4.3   Primary energy demand in megajoules per liter (MJ/liter)

	Energy (MJ)	Global warming potential – GWP* (kg CO$_2$ equivalent)	Terrestrial ecotoxicity potential – TETP (g DCB^ equivalent)
Aluminum	4.66	0.354	1.073
PET	3.94	0.205	0.553
Glass	6.88	0.426	0.430
All values are per liter of packaged beverage. *The global warming potential is for a 100-year time horizon. ^DCB is dichlorobenzene ($C_6H_4Cl_2$)			

Figure 4.4   Results of the LCA with multiple environmental indicators

Figure 4.4 shows the results of the multi-indicator LCA using GaBi[8] data sources. Note that although PET has the lowest environmental impact in the energy and GWP categories, it is not the best in the terrestrial ecotoxicity category. Therefore, to make the final decision about the material of choice for the beverage container, the decision maker must prioritize the relative importance of the impact indicators.

LCA Project Management

The LCA study should be conducted like any business project. A steering committee should be assigned to guide the study and validate the choices made in the definition of goals, scope, scenarios, functional unit, and assumptions. The stakeholders should be involved from the start of the study through the steering committee. Peer reviewers (or project reviews) are recommended to check the quality of the study and the consistency between final results and conclusions. Before the LCA study begins, a meeting should be held with the key stakeholders for a critical review of the goal, scope, and final report format.

Phase 1: Goal and Scope Definition

In this phase, the intended application of the LCA study is stated, and the intended audience and stakeholders who will use the results of the study are identified. In sustainable product development, the goal of LCA as a design-for-sustainability tool might be to gain information about an existing product, assess the product's life-cycle impact (in comparison with the competitor's product), assess alternate design approaches or materials, identify the highest-impact component or material used in the product, or identify the most energy-intensive life-cycle step. The audience and stakeholders of the study might be company managers, engineers, consumers, a governmental body, or nongovernmental organizations.

The scope of the study includes the system's function, functional unit, and boundaries. Everything that is included within the system boundary should be specified. The data requirements, assumptions, and limitations of the study also should be clarified. LCA relates the environmental impacts to a specific product function (function is the service provided by the system). Products or systems can be compared only on the basis of a similar function. Systems may have multiple functions. For example, the primary function of a bar of soap is to wash and clean, but a secondary function might be to moisturize the skin. If the secondary functions of two products differ significantly, then the validity of any comparison between the two products is questionable, so it is essential to include secondary functions in the study.

As an example, consider the LCA of a coffeemaker. The scope might be stated as the manufacturing of the coffee machine and the coffee filters and the energy used in operating the machine. We assume that the coffeemaker is used at half capacity, two times per day for five years, consuming 3,650 filters and 350 kilowatt hours of electricity. Another example is the LCA of a portable phone. The scope of the study would be the analysis of the manufacturing and use of the device, including battery charging and two replacements of the battery over the three-year life of the phone. The battery charger is also included in the study.

The functional unit is the quantitative value of the system function and serves as the basis for scenario comparison. For example, the functional unit for a telephone could be 1,000 hours of conversation, and for paint, the functional unit could be 1 square meter covered by the paint at a specified thickness. The functional unit of a bar of soap could be the number of showers a person takes, such as 20 standard showers per bar. The functional unit of an office chair might be seating for one person for 20 years. Let's consider the goal of comparing the environmental impacts of the packaging and delivery of two different milk containers—a cardboard carton that can be used only once and a glass bottle that can be used 10 or more times. The functional unit is set as 1,000 liters of milk. Therefore, the environmental impact of making 1,000 milk cartons is being compared with the environmental impact of making 100 glass bottles plus 900 washings (assuming nine return trips for each bottle). For a component of a product (such as phone batteries), the functional unit corresponds to the overall functional unit of the product. If the functional unit of a phone is 1,000 hours of communication, the functional unit of the battery is the number of batteries used for 1,000 hours of communication.

Reference Flows

Reference flows provide the product quantities in the bill of materials needed per functional unit. The reference flows in the paint example are the quantity of paint and the brushes necessary to cover 1 square meter, and in the soap example they are the mass of soap and the volume of hot water required to take 20 showers. For 1,000 hours of phone communication, the reference flow is one phone whose lifetime is 1,000 hours or two (lower-quality) phones whose lifetimes are 500 hours.

Let's compare an incandescent bulb with an LED (light-emitting diode) bulb. The primary function of these products is lighting, and their secondary functions are aesthetics, heating, and providing a warm (comfortable) light color. The functional unit is 1,000 lumens of light intensity for 10,000 hours. The lumen is the SI unit (published by the International System of Units) of luminous flux, which is a measure of the intensity of light perceived by the human eye. For 1,000 lumens, humans need a 75 watt (W) incandescent bulb or a 20 W LED bulb. The 75 W incandescent bulb has a lifetime of 1,000 hours and weighs 45 grams (g). The LED bulb has a 10,000-hour lifetime and weighs 200 g. Therefore, the reference flows for 10,000 hours of service at 1,000 lumens (1) for the incandescent bulb are 10 bulbs and 750 kilowatt hours (kWh) of energy and (2) for the LED bulb are 1 bulb and 200 kWh of energy. The LCIA for the two cases will be based on the weight and materials of construction of the two types of bulbs, plus the impact of producing and delivering the required energy.

Product System Boundary

The product system boundary specifies what is included in the LCA study and what is excluded. For example, in the LCA of paper, it should be decided if the impact of growing trees is included or not. Usually, the capital goods used in the manufacture and transport of materials are excluded from the LCA. The product LCA includes the fuel used by trucks transporting a product from the manufacturing site to the retailers, but it does not include the LCA of the trucks themselves. A typical system boundary is depicted in Figure 4.5.

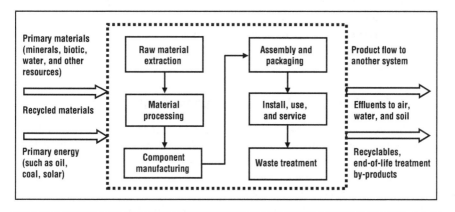

Figure 4.5   The system boundary of a product

Unit Processes

The product system can be disaggregated into unit processes (UPs). Flows of intermediate products connect these UPs together. Each unit can have extractions from the environment (resources and energy) and emissions to the environment (to water, air, and soil). The flows in and out of UPs are the elementary flows. In defining the UPs and elementary flows, one faces the problem of how far to extend the system boundary. For example, should the plant infrastructure needed to manufacture the product and the workers be included, too? Often the LCA is used for design purposes and for the selection of alternate materials or design concepts. In these cases, the UPs that are common between alternate concepts need not be considered in the comparative assessment.

Phase 2: Life-Cycle Inventory Database

In the LCI phase of an LCA study, we gather the inventory of the input and output materials and energy flows for all UPs within the system boundary. The National Renewable Energy Laboratory (NREL)[9] and its partners have created the U.S. LCI Database. This database provides individual gate-to-gate, cradle-to-gate, and cradle-to-grave accounting of the energy and material flows into and out of the environment that are associated with producing a material, component, or assembly in the United States. The NREL's LCI Database provides up-to-date, critically reviewed LCI data for commonly used materials, products, and processes in the United States. The database is compatible with international LCI databases. The data categories quantify the common UPs, including:

- Agricultural and biobased products (such as cotton and corn),
- Building products and assemblies (such as plywood and laminated veneer lumber),
- Plastics (like PET and PVC [polyvinyl chloride]),
- Energy and fuels (like coal and nuclear),
- Transportation (such as cold rolled sheet production),
- Metals (like primary aluminum production),
- Textiles, and
- Water.[10]

Phase 3: Life-Cycle Impact Assessment

The LCIA evaluates the magnitude and significance of the potential natural and human impacts of a product system using the LCI results. In the LCIA phase, both midpoint and endpoint impacts and their relevance are considered. Figure 4.6 illustrates sample midpoint and endpoint impact categories caused by the life-cycle emissions and resource utilization in the LCI database.[11] For example, as indicated by the arrows, CO_2 (carbon dioxide) emissions cause global warming, which in turn causes climate change and sea-level rise.

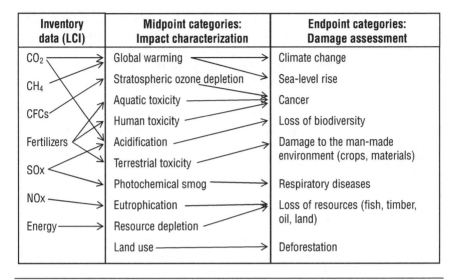

Figure 4.6   LCI data, impact characterizations, and damage assessments

Midpoint characterization scores are based on equivalency principles. That is, they are expressed in kilogram equivalents of a substance to a reference substance. For example, the global warming impact of x kilograms (x-kg) of CH_4 (methane) is represented as the equivalent y kilograms (y-kg) of CO_2 that have the same impact. In all impact categories, overall long-term effects are considered through the use of "infinite" time horizons (approximately 500 years).

The U.S. EPA's Tool for Reduction and Assessment of Chemicals and Other Environmental Impacts (TRACI) groups life-cycle impacts into 10 categories representing ecological damage, resource depletion, and human health damage, as shown in Table 4.1.

Table 4.1   Impact and damage categories per EPA's TRACI

	Impact categories	Damage categories
1	Acidification	
2	Ecotoxicity	
3	Global warming	Ecological
4	Ozone depletion	
5	Water eutrophication	
6	Fossil fuel depletion	Resource depletion
7	Human carcinogen	
8	Human respiratory	Human health
9	Human toxicity	
10	Photochemical smog	

The EPA impact categories are not exhaustive and do not include genetically modified organisms, biodiversity, radiation, nonrenewable resource depletion other than fossil fuels, rate of harvest of renewable resources (such as wetlands, forests, and fisheries), and human casualties due to accidents. The United Nations Environmental Program (UNEP) Life Cycle Initiative database includes more comprehensive impact categories, as shown in Figure 4.7.[12]

Table 4.2 lists more details about several impact categories, the contributing LCI data and characterization factors of midpoint impacts, and the reference substances in quantifying the impacts.[13]

The LCI and LCIA phases quantify the environmental and human impacts across all relevant impact categories and all relevant life-cycle stages, as illustrated in Figure 4.8.

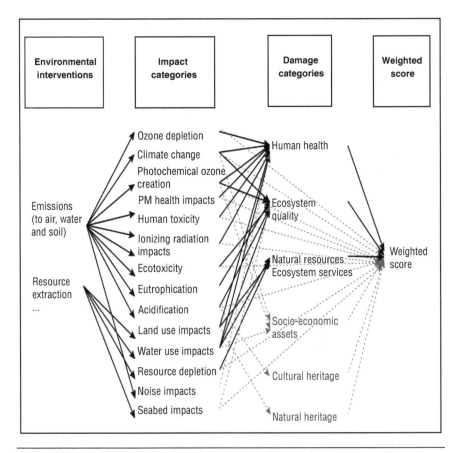

Figure 4.7   The UNEP Life Cycle Initiative's LCIA framework

Table 4.2 Impact categories and midpoint characterization factors

Impact category	Scale	Examples of LCI data	Midpoint characterization factor	Reference substance characterization factor
Global warming	Global	Carbon dioxide (CO_2) Nitrogen dioxide (NO_2) Methane (CH_4) Chlorofluorocarbons (CFCs) Hydrochlorofluorocarbons (HCFCs) Methyl bromide (CH_3Br)	Global warming potential	Converts LCI data to carbon dioxide (CO_2) equivalents *Note:* Global warming potentials can be 50-, 100-, or 500-year potentials.
Stratospheric ozone depletion	Global	Chlorofluorocarbons (CFCs) Hydrochlorofluorocarbons (HCFCs) Halons Methyl bromide (CH_3Br)	Ozone-depleting potential	Converts LCI data to trichlorofluoromethane (CFC-11) equivalents
Acidification	Regional Local	Sulfur oxides (SOx) Nitrogen oxides (NOx) Hydrochloric acid (HCL) Hydrofluoric acid (HF) Ammonia (NH_4)	Acidification potential	Converts LCI data to hydrogen (H+) ion equivalents
Eutrophication	Local	Phosphate (PO_4) Nitrogen oxide (NO) Nitrogen dioxide (NO_2) Nitrates Ammonia (NH_4)	Eutrophication potential (depletion of dissolved oxygen)	Converts LCI data to phosphate (PO_4) equivalents

Impact category	Scale	Examples of LCI data	Midpoint characterization factor	Reference substance characterization factor
Photochemical smog	Local	Nonmethane hydrocarbon (NMHC)	Photochemical oxidant-creation potential	Converts LCI data to ethane (C_2H_6) equivalents
Terrestrial toxicity	Local	Toxic chemicals with a reported lethal concentration to rodents	LC50[a]	Converts LC50 data to equivalents Uses multimedia modeling and exposure pathways
Aquatic toxicity	Local	Toxic chemicals with a reported lethal concentration to fish	LC50	Converts LC50 data to equivalents Uses multimedia modeling and exposure pathways
Human health	Global, regional, local	Total releases to air, water, and soil	LC50	Converts LC50 data to equivalents Uses multimedia modeling and exposure pathways
Resource depletion	Global, regional, local	Quantity of minerals used Quantity of fossil fuels used	Resource-depletion potential	Converts LCI data to a ratio of quantity of resource used versus quantity of resource left in reserve
Land use	Global, regional, local	Quantity disposed of in a landfill or other land modifications	Land availability	Converts mass of solid waste into volume using an estimated density
Water use	Regional, local	Water used or consumed	Water-shortage potential	Converts LCI data to a ratio of quantity of water used versus quantity of resource left in reserve

[a] LC50 is the lethal concentration (LC) capable of killing 50% of the exposed population (also called median lethal dose)

Life-cycle impact categories

	Global warming	Ecotoxicity	Photochemical smog	Ozone depletion	Etc.
Raw material extraction					
Material processing					
Component manufacturing					
Assembly and packaging					
Install, use, and service					
Waste treatment					
Total life-cycle impact					

(Left margin label spanning rows: **Life-cycle stages**)

Figure 4.8   Impacts across the life-cycle stages of a product

Phase 4: Interpretation and Analysis

The last phase of the LCA study is to interpret the LCIA data and make decisions to achieve the objectives of the study. There is no universally accepted interpretation method, but current methods employ two steps—normalization and evaluation or weighting to reduce the total impact to a single-figure score. As shown in Figure 4.8, by the end of the LCIA phase, the LCIs of the product in various impact categories have been determined. If the objective is to choose the best (least impactful) design among the alternatives, the impacts have to be compared and their importance has to be prioritized. For example, if a design option has a lower global warming impact but higher ecotoxicity impact than another competing design, then which design is optimal? Or, in other words, which is the least impactful? To answer this question, we have to make a value judgment and weigh the importance of different impacts— is global warming more or less harmful than ecotoxicity impact?

Normalization is a step that divides the impact in each category by the estimated impact from a reference. For example, the estimated impacts in each impact category can be normalized (scaled) to the impact produced by the average person in the United States in one year.[14]

Weighting assigns relative importance to the different impact categories based on their perceived importance, reflecting the study goals and stakeholder values.

For example, the National Institute of Standards and Technology (NIST)[15] has assigned weighting factors to different impact categories according to their relative importance, as shown in Figure 4.9.[16] The EPA's TRACI uses the weights that were assigned to 10 impact categories by the EPA Science Advisory Board, as shown in Table 4.3.

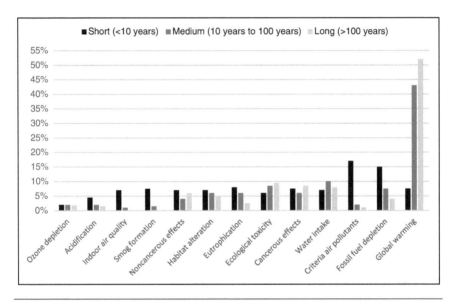

Figure 4.9 NIST's impact categories by relative importance and time horizon

Table 4.3 The EPA's impact categories and weights

Damage categories		Impact categories	Weights by EPA Science Advisory Board
Ecological	1	Acidification	0.07
	2	Ecotoxicity	0.15
	3	Global warming	0.22
	4	Ozone depletion	0.07
	5	Water eutrophication	0.07
Resource depletion	6	Fossil fuel depletion	0.07
Human health	7	Human carcinogen	0.09
	8	Human respiratory	0.09
	9	Human toxicity	0.07
	10	Photochemical smog	0.09

Weighting Methods

A number of approaches are used to arrive at appropriate weights for different impact categories, including the panel method, the distance-to-target method, and the economic evaluation method. In the panel method, a panel of experts is assembled, and the weights are decided by consensus. The key issues in this method are the criteria for selecting the panel members and the value system they represent in establishing the significance of different impact categories. The distance-to-target method prioritizes the impact categories by the ratio of annual fluxes to the target levels and gives a higher weight to the categories that are closer to exceeding the associated planetary boundary, according to the planetary boundary framework described in Chapter 1 (Figure 1.8). The economic evaluation method is based on the cost analysis of alternate impact categories, including the damage cost estimate and the cost to control or avoid the damage.

Integration of LCA and Life-Cycle Costing Methods

In order to make the LCA a useful decision-making tool in sustainable product and process design, it has to be integrated with financial and business models, such as the life-cycle costing (LCC) method. Such integration enables us to design a product that meets the triple-bottom-line objectives—a product that is economically viable, is environmentally sustainable, and adds value to social well-being.

Let's assume that we would like to select the optimal product among alternate design concepts based on the integrated LCA and LCC performance. The environmental or social performance of each product concept will be represented by the corresponding weighted LCA score shown in Figure 4.7. The LCC merit of a product concept is quantified by the net present value (NPV) of investing in that concept. The financial and environmental scores are then combined into a single overall score or figure of merit for the product concept as the NPV divided by the LCA score. The product concept that has the highest overall score is optimal.

Selected LCA Resources

This list of selected LCA resources was gathered from public and commercial sources. Additional LCA books and articles are referenced later in this chapter.

1. **U.S. Life Cycle Inventory Database** (http://www.nrel.gov/lci): The National Renewable Energy Laboratory (NREL) and its partners created the U.S. LCI database to help LCA experts answer their questions about environmental impact.
2. **BEES software**[17] (https://www.nist.gov/services-resources/software/bees): The BEES software is a technique for selecting cost-effective, environmentally preferable building products. Developed by NIST and the Fire Research Laboratory, the tool is designed to be practical, flexible,

and transparent and is based on consensus standards: Life-Cycle Costing (ASTM E917), ISO 14040, and Multi-Attribute Decision Analysis (ASTM E1765). Version 4.0 of the decision support software is aimed at designers, builders, and product manufacturers and includes actual environmental and economic performance data for 230 building products.

3. **Life Cycle Initiative** (http://www.lifecycleinitiative.org): The Life Cycle Initiative is a joint organization of the United Nations Environmental Program and the Society of Environmental Toxicology and Chemistry. It was established in 2002 to enable users around the world to put life-cycle thinking into effective practice. Many training tools and publications are available at the website.

4. **Commercial LCA software**:
   Sustainable Minds (http://www.sustainableminds.com)
   SimaPro (https://www.pre-sustainability.com/simapro)
   GaBi (http://www.gabi-software.com/international/software/gabi-software)

Current Shortcomings of LCA Tools

The LCA methodology is data- and time-intensive, which can deter some product development practitioners. The LCI data usually is an industry average or technology-specific and is not plant-specific for the product or process that is being analyzed. Some impact models (such as the toxicity model) are simplistic and have large error margins. For some environmental concerns, such as biodiversity and ecosystem services, there is currently no sound impact assessment approach. ISO 14040 requires uncertainty analysis in LCA, but uncertainty data is lacking.

Additional LCA Books and Articles

- Curran, Mary Ann. "Life Cycle Assessment: Principles and Practice." EPA/600/R-06/060. 2006.
- Geyer, Roland and Tim Jackson. "Supply Loops and Their Constraints: The Industrial Ecology of Recycling and Reuse." *California Management Review* 46(2) (2004): 55–73.
- Schenck, Rita and Philip White, (Eds.). *Environmental Life Cycle Assessment: Measuring the Environmental Performance of Products*. Washington, DC: American Center for Life Cycle Assessment, 2014.
- White, Philip, Louise St Pierre, and Steve Belletire. *Okala Practitioner: Integrating Ecological Design*. Herndon, VA: Industrial Designers Society of America (IDSA), 2013.

Questions and Exercises

1. A single-indicator environmental impact assessment simplifies the LCA project. In what circumstances would this approach be useful in product design?
2. What is the business justification for integrating LCA in computer aided design tools?
3. Is LCA more valuable in the design of a new product or in continuous improvement projects of existing products?

Endnotes

1. Robert G. Hunt, William E. Franklin, and R. G. Hunt, "LCA: How It Came About," International Journal of Life Cycle Assessment 1(1) (1996): 4–7.
2. Robert U. Ayres, "Life Cycle Analysis: A Critique," Resources, Conservation and Recycling 14(3) (1995): 199–223.
3. Scientific Applications International Corporation, "Life Cycle Assessment: Principles and Practice," EPA/600/R-06/060, U.S. Environmental Protection Administration, Washington, DC, May 2006.
4. International Organization of Standardization (ISO), "ISO 14040:2006: Environmental management—life cycle assessment—principles and framework," ISO, 2006.
5. ibid
6. U.S. Environmental Protection Agency, "Life Cycle Assessment Principles and Practices Glossary," Vocabulary Catalog, EPA, 2006.
7. Roland Geyer, University of California at Santa Barbara, GaBi life cycle inventory data, personal communication, 2012. GaBi is a commercial LCA software product (http://www.gabi-software.com).
8. Ibid.
9. National Renewable Energy Laboratory, http://www.nrel.gov/lci.
10. National Renewable Energy Laboratory, "U.S. Life Cycle Inventory Database," NREL, 2012, https://www.lcacommons.gov/nrel/search.
11. United Nations Environment Program (UNEP) and Society for Environment Toxicology and Chemistry (SETEC), "Life Cycle Initiative," UNEP/SETEC, 2003.
12. United Nations Environment Program (UNEP), Life Cycle Initiative, Global Guidance for Life Cycle Impact Assessment Indicators, vol. 1, UNEP, 2016, http://www.lifecycleinitiative.org/download/5746.
13. Ibid.
14. Jane Bare, Thomas Gloria, and Gregory Norris, "Development of the Method and U.S. Normalization Database for Life Cycle Impact Assessment and Sustainability Metrics," Environmental Science and Technology 40(16) (2006): 5108–5115.
15. National Institute of Standards and Technology (NIST), BEES software version 4.0, 2006; Bobbie Lippiatt, "Purchasing Environmentally-Preferable, Cost-Effective Products: The BEES Approach," May 13, 2002.

16. Thomas P. Gloria, Barbara C. Lippiatt, and Jennifer Cooper, "Life Cycle Impact Assessment Weights to Support Environmentally Preferable Purchasing in the United States," Environment, Science, and Technology 41(21) (2007): 7551–7557.

17. Barbara C. Lippiatt, BEES 4.0: Building for Environmental and Economic Sustainability Technical Manual and User Guide, National Institute of Standards and Technology and Building and Fire Research Laboratory, Gaithersburg, MD, August 1997.

CHAPTER 5

TECHNOLOGY AND PRODUCT STRATEGY

When people create a new product, they must answer two broad questions: what should we develop and how do we do it? *What* is the product concept that is informed by the firm's vision for its future state and serves to achieve the firm's strategic objectives? *How* is the methodology employed in the product development process? To develop sustainable products, we must amend the traditional approach to establishing *what* and selecting *how*.

The *what* is the utility function that would be optimized in product development and includes the product's functional and economic performance, as well as its contribution to sustainable development. What business are we in and what do we envision our position in the market and society will be in the future? Envisioning sustainability as a moral imperative and an opportunity for a better world deeply informs the *what* of product development. For example, a firm would most likely not pursue the development of products that make coal mining more efficient—because coal power plants are a major contributor to greenhouse gas (GHG) emissions and global warming. Perhaps the firm would redirect its strategic outlook in the energy sector and focus its resources on developing products that can be used to manufacture wind turbines. In the automotive industry, a desire to reduce the firm's environmental footprint could redirect the strategy at General Motors Corporation away from developing Hummer-type products and toward investing in electric cars and high-efficiency cars like the Prius. Ray C. Anderson, the founder and chair of Interface Inc., transformed his company by redefining both the *what* and the *how* of his products. Anderson established a vision of Mission Zero that led the company to develop new technologies, redesign products using renewable materials, and reduce or eliminate waste and harmful emissions from manufacturing processes and operations. The goal of developing sustainable products might guide a firm to explore market opportunities with products that improve efficiency in energy consumption.

Products of violence and war, like guns and other weapons, fail the sustainability test for improving human well-being and should not make it to a firm's strategic portfolio of business opportunities. Similarly, software games that promote violence and domination instead of love and caring for others and nature fail the sustainable product test and should be excluded from the list of opportunities for investment.

The *how* in product development includes the human-centered process of designing a product that is desirable to users, technically feasible, and commercially viable. *How* in sustainable product development is informed by the sustainability frameworks of Chapter 3 and uses design-for-excellence (DfX) and design-for-sustainability (DfS) tools and metrics. (The DfX and DfS methodologies are discussed in detail in Chapter 8.) DfS tools include the life-cycle assessment (LCA) methodology discussed in Chapter 4, which ensures that a design's full life-cycle environmental and health impacts are assessed, and inform decisions that optimize the design. On the other hand, because sustainable products use recycled materials, the manufacturing and sourcing strategies of the firm become an important element of the sustainable product strategy.

Product Strategy

Product strategy is at the intersection of a firm's strategies for business, market, technology, and operations, as shown in Figure 5.1. In other words, the decisions regarding *what* product to develop and *how* to design it must serve the firm's objectives along the four vectors of business, market, technology, and operations. Although not explicitly included in Figure 5.1, human well-being and the sustainability of

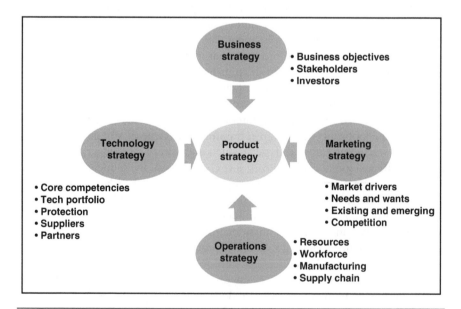

Figure 5.1   A framework for product strategy

earth's sources and sinks must be integral to all aspects of the product strategy—in the business and market opportunities that we pursue, in the technologies we develop, and in our operational practices.

There are four parts to each of the previously mentioned strategies—a vision for the future state, the objectives we aim to fulfill, an assessment of the organization's strengths and weaknesses, and an action plan to achieve the objectives. The vision for the future state must articulate the firm's place in sustainable development—that is, how the firm sees its role in contributing to and enabling sustainable development. These parts in the business, market, technology, and operational strategies are briefly discussed in the following paragraphs.

Business Strategy

The business strategy must define business objectives but also the firm's relationship with its stakeholders in fulfilling these objectives. When developing sustainable products and delivering triple-bottom-line outcomes, the stakeholders extend beyond investors, employees, suppliers, and partners to include the natural environment, the local as well as global society, and future generations. The firm's business strategy must clarify how it aligns the multitude of potentially competing requirements from different stakeholders. The business strategy also must identify the business risks and an associated mitigation plan. The burgeoning risk of adaptation to the consequences of climate change and other unsustainable production and consumption patterns must be included.

An example of business strategy that integrates a vision for sustainability is presented at the end of this chapter. In this particular case study, Millipore Corporation's aspirational sustainability goals and short-term action plans to reduce GHG emissions are discussed. This company declared that *striving to be a sustainable company is partly about responsibility—it is simply the right thing to do.*

Marketing Strategy

A marketing strategy is a plan to realize market opportunities, to meet the competition under advantageous conditions, and to gain maximum customer value and loyalty. A marketing strategy must state the firm's desired position in the value chain (toward customers, competitors, suppliers, distributors, and partners). The strategy should assess the industry's structure, market forces, and trends and devise a plan to achieve the desired position. The existing or new basis of competition in the market shapes marketing requirements and informs the necessary differentiating features and capabilities of a new product. For a new-to-market product or technology, the basis of competition evolves as the product penetrates the market following the technology adoption (or diffusion) curve shown in Figure 5.2.[1] The technology

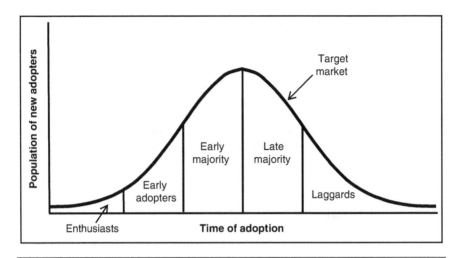

Figure 5.2   Diffusion of innovation and adoption of new technology

adoption curve is a bell-shaped curve that shows the population of new participants in the market as a function of the adoption time.

In a new market or with a new technology, the first customers are innovators and enthusiasts who generally are motivated by the technology and functionality of the product. Later, the basis of competition (in penetrating the market and acquiring early adopters, early majority users, and late majority users) changes to product reliability, ease of use, and eventually price as the product becomes a commodity.

The marketing strategy must identify existing opportunities for sustainable products and plan to create demand for a product that contributes to sustainable development with a low ecological footprint. In other words, the marketing strategy must strive to change the basis of competition to the sustainability of the product—having a long life, being made of recycled material, emitting few harmful by-products over the product's life cycle, and above all improving human well-being. This marketing strategy deviates from traditional strategies significantly. Currently, marketing strategies call for rapid product obsolescence through making technology innovations and promoting consumerism. Sustainability demands a 180-degree change in this approach. Although technological changes are welcome for improving product performance, a marketing strategy must plan a product in which the platform design is extendible over many cycles of technological innovation and allows product upgrades and backward compatibility.

Technology Strategy

Technology strategy provides a blueprint for developing, acquiring, and applying technology to gain competitive advantage and to implement the aggregate business and marketing strategy effectively. Technology can be developed in-house or licensed from a third party. Also, firms can access supplier technologies by outsourcing the design and manufacturing of the product (or its components).

Products result from the application of technology to a market context, and the development of new products has a bidirectional relationship with technological innovation, as illustrated in Figure 5.3.

For example, General Motors Corporation developed the extended-range electric vehicle technology (in the Chevy Volt) to compete with the Toyota Prius and the electric vehicles of other manufacturers. These existing market needs inform new technology and product development strategies. On the other hand, technologies are developed to create new markets or enable new applications in existing markets. Personal computers, Facebook, and genetic inheritance testing applications are in this category. New technologies could create new needs of their own or technology-driven needs. Many of these needs are created by the harmful externalities associated with the production and use of unsustainable products. For example, new drugs must be developed to mitigate the side effects of other drugs like antidepressants—and special drugs are needed to minimize the pain or to heal the damage caused by products of war and violence (like Agent Orange or phosphate

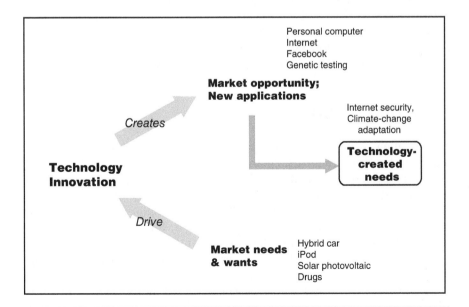

Figure 5.3 Technology innovation and market interaction

bombs). Many of the geoengineering technologies (and products) try to respond to technology-driven needs, too. Dispersing iron particles in oceans has been proposed to reduce ocean acidification caused by GHG emissions. The ubiquitous application of communication and commerce on the Internet has created a need for Internet security technologies.

Any sustainable technology strategy must be developed holistically in the three previously described categories. In existing markets, the strategy must direct technology development to improve the sustainability of existing products. Prius hybrid drive technology is an excellent example of a technology that significantly reduced emissions of GHGs and other pollutants from standard internal combustion engine vehicles. The case of Toyota's Prius development is discussed in Appendix A.

When new market creation is the aim, the technology strategy must be constrained by the sustainability requirements to prevent or minimize harmful externalities. Chemical technology development based on further exploitation of fossil fuels is not sustainable. Alternatively, a chemical company can adopt a technology strategy for developing new green-chemistry products and replacing existing fossil-based chemicals. Genetic-technology road maps must be broadened beyond a mere focus on functionality to include a holistic assessment of the harm that the proposed technologies could inflict on ecological and biological systems.

The cornerstone of a technology strategy—particularly for leading-edge technologies such as biotechnology, where the state of knowledge is primitive—must be the precautionary principle. All new technologies should be considered guilty of unsustainability unless proven innocent through a holistic examination of the externalities created by their production and use, along with the associated harms to human life and ecological systems in a generational timescale. The precautionary principle mandates the establishment of sustainability-assessment criteria for all new technologies before they can be released for commercialization. One of the criteria must be avoidance of technology-created needs by the new technology!

Operations Strategy

The operations strategy establishes plans for manufacturing capacity, equipment, process technology, production control, quality control, new product transition, and facilities. It also includes the supply chain sourcing strategy, human workforce makeup, and performance management system. The outsourcing strategy and design of the product platform must be well integrated to protect the firm's intellectual property and to prevent suppliers from moving up the value chain and becoming a competitor. In other words, those aspects of the design that are outsourced should not reveal any information about the product or its underlying technology that is a source of competitive advantage.

The operations strategy and practice directly impact the life-cycle environmental footprint and social sustainability of a new product. Sustainability requirements must be built into every element of the operation. Sustainability leadership in operations starts with assuming ownership of all three levels of operational activities—Scopes 1, 2, and 3. Scope 1 is a set of activities over which the firm has direct control (including buildings, in-house manufacturing, and a corporate fleet of vehicles). Scope 2 is defined as the energy used by Scope 1 activities (to power the buildings and machinery). Scope 3 is everything else, including activities undertaken by the suppliers.

The sustainable operations strategy envisions zero waste across all three scopes, aims to minimize consumption of resources such as water and energy, and places labor safety (including exposure to hazardous chemicals) on the list of high-priority concerns. (In Chapter 10, an inherent safety by design in manufacturing and operations is discussed in further detail.)

The design of the supply chain structure and the sourcing strategy regarding globalization versus localization are of paramount importance to the sustainability of the product and its production. Many prevailing globalization practices—such as manufacturing in low-labor-cost regions that have lax labor and environmental protection laws—fail the sustainability test. As discussed earlier, supply chains should be redesigned as supply loops, and to the maximum extent possible, local suppliers should be used. The supply-loop design enables a circular economy with local production for local consumption in harmony with the earth's local and seasonal endowments. The production and consumption of food products demonstrate this approach: locally grown and marketed organic food provides fresh and seasonal supplies without managing long-distance logistics and virtually importing or exporting nitrogen, water, and other resources.

Aggregate Strategy Framework

Figure 5.4 depicts a framework that aggregates business strategy with the internal and external factors that determine success in achieving a firm's business objectives. The business strategy is placed at the center and is represented by business objectives, the strategic value proposition, the value model, and the sustainability outlook of the firm. The next layer shows the factors that determine success in execution or the ability of the firm to realize its business objectives. These factors are customer intimacy, product leadership, value-chain leadership, and operational excellence. The firm carries out its operation within the organizational context that is shown as the next layer of the aggregate strategy in the figure. The organizational context is shaped by corporate culture, resource capability, organizational structure, and the firm's business processes.

The environment external to the firm establishes boundary conditions by defining product and market requirements and imposing constraints on business operations. The external players are the customers, investors, partners, and value-chain suppliers. The earth's natural environment and global society shape the overarching external environment whose well-being defines the sustainability requirements. To

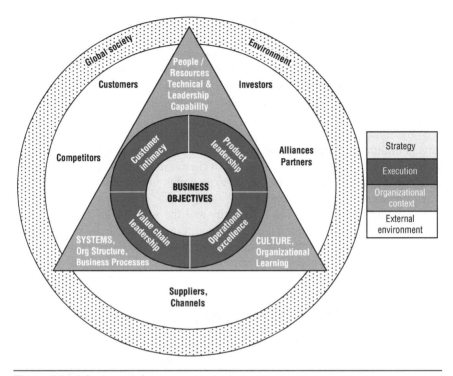

Figure 5.4   A framework for an aggregate strategy

integrate the sustainability requirements in the aggregate strategy, business objectives must include a triple-bottom-line outcome, and the organizational context must have a deep understanding of the sustainability requirements and support the necessary initiatives to meet these requirements. In the upcoming text, you will find an outline for a sustainable business strategy.

An Outline of a Business Strategy

1. **Vision:** The future state of the firm in market position, business, product mix, resource capability, and sustainability
2. **Objectives:** Strategic objectives for leadership in value creation, business results, market share, product and technology, operational excellence, and sustainability
3. **Opportunities and threats in the strategic context:** Market environment and trends, opportunities to capitalize on, threats (competitive landscape, value-chain structure, risks, technological challenges, and resource gaps), sustainability opportunities, and risks

4. **Strategy and action plan:** (1) A list of specific actions to meet the objectives by taking advantage of opportunities, defending against threats, and mitigating risks (or turning them into opportunities); (2) project plans for implementing the actions (what, when, who)

The product strategy is either driven by the market or drives the market. As illustrated in Figure 5.5, market-driven strategies aim to capitalize on existing business opportunities and are informed by customer preferences, market forces, and social factors that are present or are anticipated within the planning horizon. On the other hand, strategies that drive the market, create new opportunities, and strive to change the world are inspired by latent customer needs and social factors and are informed by expected market forces in the future. The strategies that support sustainable development are often of the latter category. Current market conditions, customer preferences, and investor perspectives maintain the status quo economic activities, products, and services that are mostly unsustainable.

Technology-to-Market Value Chain

Often companies engage in applied research and development (R&D) of innovative technologies in new materials, chemicals, software algorithms, drug formulations, designs, or new fabrication processes. Technology-to-market (T2M) analysis explores market opportunities for the technology and helps the firm develop product-realization strategies that are aligned with the firm's business strategy and core competency. A T2M value chain is often complex and involves multiple intermediary products, process equipment, and market makers. The T2M value-chain analysis is useful in business decision making in multiple ways. It can help identify optimal market entry where the firm can add value with comparative

	Driven by the market	Driving the market
Strategy	Capitalize on existing opportunities	Create opportunities – change the world
Impetus	Customer preference; market and social factors	Latent customer needs and societal factors – future market forces

Figure 5.5   Strategy in product development

advantage. It helps assess whether technology licensing is the preferred exit strategy. The T2M value-chain analysis is also important for understanding complementary products at every point along the chain and the need for partnership with suppliers of these products.

Product realization is a pathfinding endeavor that hones the direction of research toward a product concept and product platform design. The developers engage in an iterative process of matching technology to market context by understanding customers, users, and the use environment. Alternate product concepts and designs are validated through rapid cycles of prototyping. In emerging markets and applications where user needs are not established, the product concept is evolved in a bidirectional and iterative process where user preferences are discovered by engaging them in the development of the product concept and in an evaluative feedback process. The pathfinding is concluded with the demonstration of technical feasibility and commercial viability of the technology and product concept. (These steps are described in more detail in Chapter 6, as elements of the overall product development and commercialization process.)

The T2M value-chain concepts are presented with the following case study of solar photovoltaic products.

Case Study: Solar Photovoltaic T2M Value Chain

Figure 5.6 maps out the solar photovoltaic (PV) T2M value chain for the generation of electricity from solar energy. The figure shows both lab-scale and production-scale stages of the chain. The lab-scale stage starts with the invention of the PV cell design, the selection of the materials, and the development of the fabrication process sequence. The fabrication equipment might already be available from

Lab scale				Production scale		
Photovoltaic cell technology • Physics • Small (1 cm²) samples	Manufacturing process and equipment technology • Sputtering, evaporation • Printing	Photovoltaic module • Flexible substrate • Tubular • Flat rigid	Product for the market ⟹	• Consumer electronics • Residential and commercial energy • Utility-scale energy	• Original equipment manufacturers (OEM) • Building owners; construction companies • Utilities	
	Raw materials: existing or new	Complementary products and technologies • Encapsulation • Packaging		Basis of competition • Efficiency, W/m² • Cost, $/W • Levelized cost of energy, $/kWh	Complementary products and technologies • Inverter • Installation	

Figure 5.6   The solar PV T2M value chain for the generation of electricity from solar energy

adjacent markets, but often new equipment must be designed and built. And even if existing equipment is used, it needs to be modified and customized to produce the intended cell design.

The lab-scale PV cell development is focused on achieving high solar conversion efficiency. However, the commercial viability of the PV technology depends not only on its efficiency but also on the fabrication cost. The cost estimate at the lab-scale stage has a large uncertainty band because volume-production data is lacking, and the actual costs are based on the production of a small quantity of the product in a lab environment. Developers extrapolate the lab-scale cost to volume-production cost by applying the rules of economies of scale and the learning-curve effect. When the production volume is high, the fixed cost of production is amortized over a large quantity, which lowers the unit cost. Further cost reductions are achieved with quantity by learning how to improve the process efficiency.

The next phase in the T2M chain is the production-scale fabrication of the cell and PV modules. A module is an assembly of cells that are interconnected in series and parallel circuits to produce a specified output voltage and power level under standard solar radiation (such as 1,000 watts per square meter). Several module design configurations are possible. PV cells might be produced on a flexible substrate or, as is most common, on a flat and rigid substrate like glass. The fabrication equipment that was used in the lab to produce small cells (1 cm^2), must be modified to fabricate large cells (6×6 cm squares) in volume production. New materials are needed for the interconnection and encapsulation of the cells into a working module. Additional equipment for assembling multiple cells into modules must also be designed.

To build a volume-production facility, large amounts of funds must be secured. When the technology is new, as PV was a decade or two ago, investors had to be convinced that high-efficiency cells and modules could be manufactured at low cost and the market opportunity was large enough to realize the desired return on their investment.

The market segments and customers for solar PV cells and modules are shown on the right side of Figure 5.6. There are multiple applications and market segments, such as consumer electronics, small power modules for communication stations, residential and commercial power-generation systems, and utility-scale power plants. The required power in these applications is from a few watts to hundreds of megawatts.

For power-generation applications, such as rooftop applications and utility-scale power plants, in addition to the PV modules, other complementary products and services are required, including inverters to convert the direct-current output of PV modules to alternating-current electricity, aluminum racks to string modules together, power devices to connect the system to the utility grid, and control electronics to operate the system.

In the above discussion, we presented the T2M chain sequentially from R&D to volume production for the end-use markets. The basis of competition in these markets is different and determines the technical feasibility and commercial viability of alternate-cell, module, and PV system technologies and designs. Today, the market price of a PV module for distributed power generation is less than $1 per watt.

The price that the end-user pays is distributed among various providers across the chain according to the perceived value of their offering by their customers. For example, a commercial building owner who desires to install a one megawatt rooftop solar PV system might contract with a solar installer and pay $2.50 per watt for the turnkey system. The system installer buys PV modules from a module producer, buys a power inverter and balance-of-system equipment from other suppliers, and hires installation labor to build the PV system. The module producer in turn acquires the process equipment in his factory from a third party. The $2.50 per watt market value is distributed among all these providers according to the perceived value of their offering. Therefore, the players and providers of various products and services in the value chain must be cognizant of the market structure, the requirements for performance and cost of their product, and their relative power position in the market.

To capitalize on the business opportunity in the solar PV market, different companies may decide to enter at different points in the T2M value chain based on their business strategy, their core competency, and the areas where they can compete. Sunpower Corporation started as a technology company producing high-performance cells and modules and has grown vertically to become a provider of turnkey power systems. Solar City Corporation entered the T2M chain as a distributor of modules and installer of residential rooftop PV systems and has grown to be one of the largest system providers offering innovative financing to alleviate the initial capital cost burden on end-use customers. Some of the innovative PV cell design companies did not enter the market and instead licensed their designs to other companies that mass produce and sell modules. The suppliers of process equipment in the PV T2M chain are generally independent companies whose core competency is process equipment design and manufacturing. Some equipment suppliers serve the R&D market only at private companies and universities for the development of future generations of PV cells and modules.

Success of the T2M Endeavor

Innovation at every step of the value chain, including early-phase research, is inspired by a perceived market application that satisfies an unfulfilled need in an existing market or creates a new market opportunity. The risk of commercial success for early-phase scientific research is usually very high, and only universities, R&D centers at large corporations, and government laboratories engage in such research. Venture capitalists do not invest in fundamental scientific research and prefer to invest in the early product-realization phase of the T2M cycle.

The successful development and commercialization of a new technology—that is, T2M—depends on the four factors depicted in Figure 5.7. These factors are interdependent and form an innovation ecosystem as described in the following section.

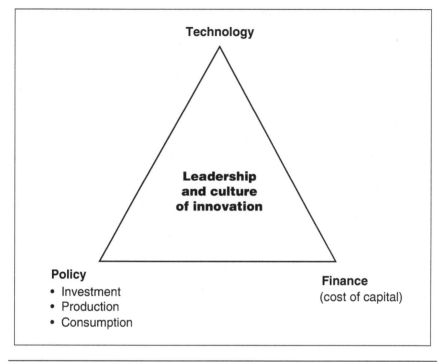

Figure 5.7   A framework for a T2M ecosystem

Technology

Technology development fuels entrepreneurial opportunities, and its success requires a commitment to a strong R&D program, a supportive infrastructure of information technology, and rapid prototyping capability within the firm. Furthermore, to sustain its innovation process, the organization needs a pipeline of engineers and scientists from universities.

Research and teaching universities are indispensable members of the innovation ecosystem. They carry out strong research programs and promote entrepreneurship through multidisciplinary studies and student collaborations. These universities provide experiential and project-based learning opportunities for students and build an ambience that facilitates creativity and interactions among students and researchers. Finally, these universities provide networking opportunities for students through incubators and contacts with industries, investors, and alumni.

Finance

The availability of capital is essential for T2M success. The source and cost of capital vary across the T2M cycle by the risk that alternate investors perceive in the technical feasibility and commercial viability of the technology, as shown in Figure 5.8. The three main phases in the T2M cycle are concept development, commercialization demonstration, and large-scale production and sale of the product. In this figure, the typical sources of capital at each phase and the associated phases of the new product development process are shown below the graph.

In the concept phase, alternate conceptual designs for the application of a T2M context are developed, and their technical and commercial feasibility are established. In this phase, the risk of success is relatively high, and typical sources of capital are *angels*—wealthy individuals, venture capitalists, and governments that provide R&D funding. In the commercialization phase, the technical performance of the design is demonstrated with engineering prototypes, and the manufacturability of the product is demonstrated with pilot-level production. Usually, substantial capital is required in the commercialization phase, and it is not easy to find an investor who would support this phase. This could lead to the so-called valley of death for entrepreneurs who are trying to take their invention to the market. Government

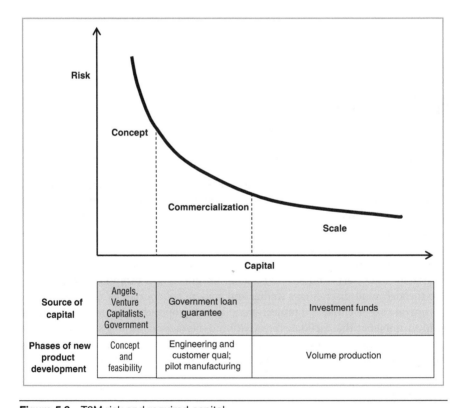

Figure 5.8   T2M risk and required capital

loan guarantees could be an enabling risk-mitigation instrument in the commercialization phase. The scale phase of the T2M cycle is for volume production and sale of the product. The capital required in this phase for building manufacturing facilities and the supporting infrastructure could be very large. At this phase, the risk of failure should be low, and risk-averse investors like investment banks might entertain the opportunity. However, these investors demand demonstrated *bankability* of the technology, which means having sufficient technology performance data based on customer feedback. As is mentioned in the next section, policy instruments can alleviate the capital requirements in this phase.

Policy Instruments

Policy instruments are designed to enable the development and commercialization of target technologies. For example, the government of the U.S. conducts R&D on high-risk technologies at government research labs, and this R&D is later made available to private enterprises. Federal and state governments also provide investment and production tax credits and underwrite loans to encourage private investment in the mass production of new products. The U.S. government has used these instruments to accelerate the commercial viability of wind and solar energy technologies at scale. The German government has used a feed-in tariff mechanism to guarantee an attractive market price for solar and wind energy.

To promote sustainable technologies, governments might levy taxes on the pollution externalities of competing unsustainable technologies and products. For example, a carbon dioxide tax can increase the cost of electricity from coal power plants and hence improve the commercial viability of renewable sources of energy like wind and solar.

The legal infrastructure of a society also plays a critical role in encouraging technology innovation, entrepreneurship, and risk taking. Patent laws, effective enforcement, and regulations that facilitate the formation of corporations create a business environment that is conducive to entrepreneurship and investment in new technologies.

Leadership Prowess and a Culture of Innovation

In the final analysis, the company's leadership and its people invent the technology, convince investors to fund their new products, and promote regulations and policy instruments that enable sustainable technologies and products to succeed. Leadership must build a corporate culture that promotes creativity, experimentation, and risk taking. Some Silicon Valley companies give their employees the freedom to spend 15% of their company time on technology innovation and the development of a product of their choice outside their normal job assignments. Innovative companies institutionalize an innovation process that encourages rapid prototyping, failing fast to succeed sooner, networking, working in multidisciplinary teams, and team building with diversity and the inclusion of women and people of minority backgrounds.

The innovation process within a company, however, could be propelled or constrained by the societal cultural values and practices of the region where the company operates. Silicon Valley's entrepreneurial culture is built on a culture that values individualism, networking, and mobility.

Sustainable Product Strategy

The strategy for technology innovation and pathfinding for commercial success is seriously impacted when the overarching aspirational strategy is sustainable development and social well-being. As Alan Kay, a pioneer in personal computing, graphical user interface, and object-oriented programming, once said, "The best way to predict the future is to invent it." Sustainable product development is a way to invent a just and prosperous future in harmony with nature.

The sustainable product strategy seeks innovation opportunities in the sustainability white space or blue ocean. Solar and wind energy systems, energy efficiency, green chemistry, sustainable agriculture, human-healing-centered health care products, and sustainable transportation are just a few of these opportunities. However, these opportunities face an uphill battle in attracting investment capital and becoming commercially successful under the prevailing consolidated capitalist economy and business decision-making rules. We must fully account for the cost of harmful externalities in the production and use of products over their life cycle and adopt business decision rules that maximize customer well-being rather than shareholder profit.

Tim Kraft and his colleagues model the decision making of a firm that sells a product containing a potentially hazardous substance.[2] Although the substance is not regulated, the firm believes regulation may occur in the future. The model aims to devise the optimal strategy in terms of the timing and intensity of investments for the development and implementation of a replacement substance. The approach in this study demonstrates the prevailing business decision optimization methodology, which aims to minimize costs based on certain external and internal risk factors. The alternative approach, which is required in developing sustainable products, is to adopt a precautionary approach to harm and replace the hazardous substance in the product because it is the right thing to do.

The business strategy for developing the highly fuel-efficient Prius hybrid vehicle at Toyota Motor Corporation is a good example of using innovation in sustainability to drive the (automobile) market. As described in Appendix A, Prius was the product of a visionary imagining of twenty-first-century imperatives—environment strains and scarce resources. This successful product established Toyota as a technology leader and helped the company gain business leadership in the market. In contrast, General Motors Corporation adopted a reactionary strategy for developing the Chevy Volt, an extended-range electric vehicle, a decade after Prius, as described in Appendix B. Although the Volt is highly fuel-efficient and qualifies as a sustainable product, the strategy behind its development was to compete with Prius rather than contribute to sustainable development. The difference in the strategy reveals its impact on decision making at GM throughout the Volt development program. For example, the sustainability attributes of the product were not listed as benefits in the product positioning and marketing, which negatively impacted its market-penetration rate.

Innovation Opportunities in Pursuing Sustainability

The following innovation opportunities are crucial to the creation of commercially successful sustainable products, to inclusive social justice, to an equitable economic system, and to sustainable development:

1. The reengineering of the current system of monopoly capitalism and the creation of models of a sustainable economy that is inclusive of ecological economics and offers a comprehensive business model for triple-bottom-line results.

2. Public policy that regulates an equitable sharing of common goods on global and temporal scales. The current options for the protection of common goods are privatization or coercive governmental regulations. As has been argued elsewhere,[3] privatization of natural capital leads to misplaced priorities in investment decisions. And the formulation and enforcement of effective governmental regulations to protect common goods on a global scale have a low probability of success. The new economy and supporting regulatory regime must look beyond the limitations of these options for solutions that are local, democratic, and inclusive of stakeholders. Elinor Ostrom, the 2009 Nobel Prize-winning economist, has shown in her work that community ownership of resources in rural communities can foster the evolution and adaptation of sustainable resource use.[4] Private ownership or government regulations are not more efficient than community practices. Ostrom posits that shared values for doing what is right and proper against *self-interest with guile* is a social capital that prevents and solves problems of common pool resources.

3. Inventions that enhance human development and are in harmony with nature's bioevolution. These include food production that is organic, seasonal, local, and diverse rather than synthetic and mass-produced; a water supply that is local and sanitary; and energy systems that are fueled by the sun and wind and support sustainable storage products.

4. Green chemistry-based materials and pharmaceutical products.[5] Green chemistry has no human or ecosystem toxicity, is biologically benign and degradable, and is non-bioaccumulative or persistent.
5. Entertainment products such as video games and movies that promote community, peace, love, diversity, harmony with nature, and social justice rather than those that promote aggression, violence, and domination of one group over others or of humans over nature.
6. Technologies that prevent harm versus those that mitigate, fix, or manage harm. For example, we should innovate products and technologies that prevent health or environmental degradation and prioritize those that prevent diseases rather than fix them.
7. Research to uncover root causes of problems rather than *correct* the symptoms. For example, research to discover the causes of cancer and autism should be given a high priority on the roster of research programs sponsored by the government or private corporations. To be effective in this research, we must take a systems approach rather than follow the customary single-disciplined methodologies. For example, technologists, social scientists, policy experts, and economists focus narrowly in their respective fields rather than examining intersectoral root causes and solutions.
8. Refraining from developing technologies and products that are intended for committing violence, war, and destruction. These products fail to satisfy the criteria for being sustainable because of *what* they do, irrespective of *how* they might have been designed or made. For example, a gun is not a sustainable product even if it is manufactured from recycled materials and with renewable energy.
9. Systems simulation and decision-optimization models for sustainable investment and risk management. For example, how should we model well-being and value natural capital without using the current methodologies that assign monetary value to every asset (including social, human, and environmental capitals) and that discount future gains and harm?
10. Integration of LCA tools with traditional design tools, such as computer-aided design software.

Case Example: Corporate Strategy at Millipore Corporation

Sustainability at Millipore Corporation is reported in a Harvard Business School case study[6] that describes how the company integrated sustainability goals and projects with its business strategy. Millipore's filtration products served the biotechnology, pharmaceutical, and beverage manufacturing industries, and in 2009, the company's revenue was $1.6 billion.

In a 2007 memo to company employees (and in its annual report), the company's chief executive officer presented an encompassing sustainability vision for the firm. He stated that sustainability is a moral responsibility and the right thing to do, and that voluntary and collective actions are essential at both individual and company levels to adjust lifestyles and lower our ecological footprint.

Millipore set out two aspirational goals—to become carbon neutral in 15 years and independent of oil in 25 years. The company devised action plans to reduce its contribution to climate change, reduce its dependence on petroleum-based products, and reduce waste from operations and products.

Millipore put in place actions to save energy (by improving the lighting system in buildings and composting waste from its campus cafeteria) and to disclose and reduce the company's GHG emissions. Millipore joined three organizations that support the industry's sustainability efforts—the Carbon Disclosure Project (with other S&P 500 members), the Environmental Protection Agency's *Climate Leaders* (to set reduction targets and report emissions), and the Corporate Council of the Environmental League of Massachusetts (a lobbying group for progressive policy).

Millipore also decided to disclose GHG emissions from all facilities. In its rationale for investing in the GHG-reduction program, it stated that climate-change risk reduction was demanded by institutional investors, regulatory preparedness was needed in anticipation of a tightening of future regulations, transparency was called for in response to non-governmental organizations pressure and consumer interest, opportunities were available for competitive differentiating and branding through the GHG reduction program, and *it was the right thing to do.*

Questions and Exercises

1. In this chapter, 10 innovation opportunities are listed in pursuing sustainability. Identify at least one private or public-sector product and service in each area that can enable the stated goal.
2. What is the best approach in employing the strategic outlook (and tools) described in this chapter when it comes to the selection of new products and projects? Consider formal product portfolio analysis, corporate strategic planning, employee education, and a corporate culture of sustainability.
3. What is the role of employees as citizens in realizing the innovation opportunities in the local and global society?

Endnotes

1. Everett M. Rogers, *Diffusion of Innovations* (Glencoe, IL: Free Press, 1962).
2. Tim Kraft, Feryal Erhun, Robert C. Carlson, and Dariush Rafinejad, "Replacement Decisions for Potentially Hazardous Substances," Production and Operations Management 22(4) (2013): 958–975.

3. Robert C. Carlson and Dariush Rafinejad, "Economic Models for Environmental and Business Sustainability in Product Development and Manufacturing," *International Journal of Environmental, Cultural, Economic and Social Sustainability* 7(4) (2010): 199–210.

4. Elinor Ostrom, *Governing the Commons: The Evolution of Institutions for Collective Action* (Cambridge, UK: Cambridge University Press, 1990).

5. Paul T. Anastas and John C. Warner, "Principles of Green Chemistry," *Green Chemistry: Theory and Practice*, pp. 29–56 (Oxford, UK: Oxford University Press, 2000).

6. Michael W. Toffel and Katharine Lee, "Sustainability at Millipore," Harvard Business School Case 610-012, July 2009, rev. January 2014.

CHAPTER 6

THE PRODUCT CONCEPT AND DEVELOPMENT PROCESS

In this chapter, the process of developing sustainable products is examined. The methodologies presented here are informed by the best practices in the industry, including those researched by the author as well as those found in the published literature. Throughout the discussion, the significance of sustainability and the ways that the traditional best practices must be amended for developing sustainable products are highlighted. First, the general product development methodology is presented, and then certain nuances unique to different types of products—such as software, hardware, or service—are discussed.

Figure 6.1 illustrates the flow of activities in the life cycle of a product. The user need is the prime mover of product creation and informs the product's conceptual design. The technical feasibility and commercial viability of the concept is demonstrated before the so-called product design development phase is begun. In this phase, the product is designed in detail and thoroughly tested to demonstrate that its performance meets the requirements. Product transition in the figure comprises manufacturing qualification (for hardware products) and customer evaluation with beta testing. The product is sold to the customers directly and through the distribution channels (retail stores, sales representatives, and online). Following the sale, many products require customer support that is offered by the supplier or a third party. At the end of the product's useful life, customers dispose of the product (Chapter 9).

The new product development and commercialization process focuses on the early phases of the product life cycle in Figure 6.1—from research into user needs, to the product launch in the market. The process is discussed in detail later in this chapter, after a few key concepts are introduced—beginning with the definition of a product.

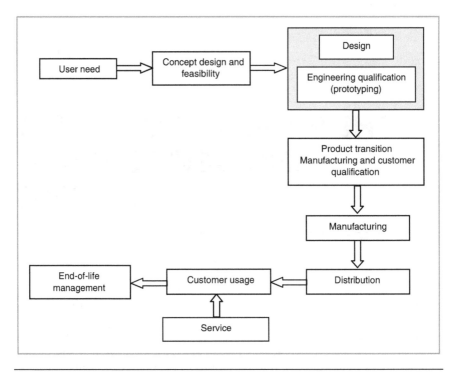

Figure 6.1   The flow of activities in a product life cycle

What Is a Product?

A product is the application of technology to context. It can be a physical object, software, a process (such as a manufacturing recipe), or a service in the value chain. In many cases, some of these characteristics are combined in the product. For example, an e-book reader is both hardware and software, whereas an operating system for a computer or mobile device is software, a photovoltaic solar panel is hardware (or a physical product), and a recipe for baking a cake is a process. Service products, such as diagnostics testing by a lab and software programming services, are also common.

Successful products match technology to the needs and wants of the product stakeholders in the market space and in the application (or use) environment. They create a compelling differentiated value experience for the customer who chooses to buy the product among competing alternatives.

Successful products are products that serve an attractive market, deliver a substantial financial return, and contribute to the customer's well-being. Successful products create customer loyalty and keep them returning to buy future models of the same product or buy other products in the company's portfolio. Successful products have a high profit margin—that is, the cost of making, delivering, and servicing the product is significantly lower than the selling price. The gross margin of the product funds the firm's research and development (R&D) programs and carries the costs of sales, general, and administration. Furthermore, successful products are manufacturable, can be accessed by customers through low-cost sales channels, and are serviceable.

The Whole-Product Concept

A product is a cluster of value attributes that shape the totality of customer experience in the product's life cycle. To the user, the basic or generic function of the product is important, as is how it is sold, delivered, and serviced after sales. Figure 6.2 illustrates the whole-value concept of a product. A customer who visits her eye doctor to improve her vision receives a prescription (a piece of paper or the electronic version of it) for a pair of glasses that the doctor subsequently orders a laboratory to make. The product that the patient cares about is not the prescription, but the eyeglasses, which satisfies her need. However, customer satisfaction in this case is shaped by a cluster of values that she receives or expects to receive, and the eyeglasses are just one of those values. The quality of eyeglasses assessed by the patient's ability to see well is the generic value that the customer expects to receive. However, the patient expects the glasses to be ready on time as promised, and when she returns to the doctor's office to pick up the glasses, she expects them to be delivered in a case with a cleaning cloth. The patient also expects that the new eyeglasses will be fitted to her face. Although the generic product is a pair of eyeglasses, the customer's happiness depends on receiving the expected product—which includes quality, on-time delivery, a carrying case, and adjustment services by the doctor. The totality of the generic and expected values form the product that the customer is buying. However, the doctor's services might go beyond what the patient expects. Think of a patient who must catch a plane in a hurry and does not have time to visit the doctor's office to pick up the new glasses that she must have on her trip. If the doctor delivers the eyeglasses to the patient at the departure gate of the airport (at no additional cost), the customer would be delighted. She is likely to become a loyal customer and return to buy her next pair and perhaps buy a pair of sunglasses, too. The unexpected *delighter* augments the value bundle and becomes a compelling competitive differentiator for the service that the doctor offers.

The whole-product concept illustrated in Figure 6.2 is represented by concentric circles of value (to the user), increasing from the center outward. The generic product delivers the basic function of the product (like the eyeglasses in the above example, which perform the generic function of vision correction). The expected product represents the values that the customer expects to receive above and beyond the generic product value. These expectations are shaped by the products and services that competitors offer. The augmented product offers a value that is beyond expectations and delights the customer. The potential product offers values that are

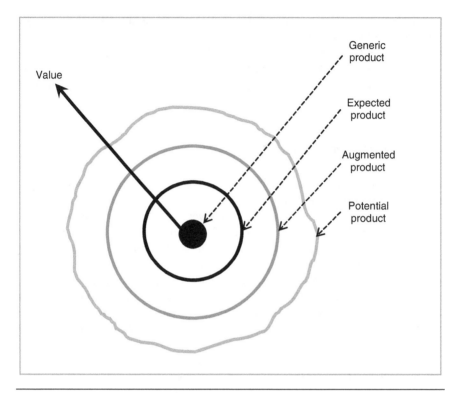

Figure 6.2   The whole-product concept as a bundle of value

possible in the future. For example, extendability of a product to future technology generations is considered a potential value.

According to the whole-product model, firms cannot compete by offering only generic and expected products. Products can be differentiated only with augmented and potential values. However, values in the whole-product cluster shift in time. The values that once were augmented become expected by customers if all or most competitors provide the same values. Firms must be vigilant of this shift, continuously assess their competitive position in the whole-product cluster, and augment their products to remain competitive.

Stakeholders and Product Success

Multiple stakeholders affect or are affected by a product, and their needs and preferences must be satisfied for the product to be successful. First and foremost is the firm. Products are designed and commercialized to satisfy the firm's strategic objectives within its resource constraints and risk tolerance. The next stakeholder is the shareholder of the company who expects to receive an acceptable return on his or her investment in the product. Customers as the next stakeholder demand satisfaction of their needs and wants by using the product. The economic buyer of the product, who might be different than the user, is also a stakeholder. For example, if the product is a children's toy, parents are economic buyers, and the child is the user. Parents might care about the safety, educational value, and price of the product—but the child only cares about its entertainment value and ease of use.

For a tangible product, the manufacturing operation is the next stakeholder. The product must be designed so it can be manufactured with high quality at low cost. The necessary design documentation and assembly instructions must be provided by the designers to the in-house or outsourced manufacturing organizations. The second-tier suppliers who provide the materials and components of a product as an input to manufacturing are the next stakeholders whose performance directly impacts the product success. Another stakeholder is the distributor, as an intermediary between the firm and the customer who plays a pivotal role in the commercial success of the product. In the retail market, for example, distributors like Walmart and Whole Foods Market, which hold dominating power positions in the market, might demand high distributor fees or unique performance and packaging requirements for the product.

The employees of the firm, local and global society, and the natural environment are the next three stakeholders whose needs must be satisfied. The inclusion of these stakeholders in the product development practice is quintessential to the sustainability of the product. Table 6.1 lists the stakeholders that were previously discussed, their primary needs, and the expectations that must be satisfied in new product development.

Table 6.1 Products must satisfy stakeholder needs and expectations

Stakeholder	Needs and expectations
The firm	Profitability, market share, growth
Shareholders	Return on investment
Customers (end users)	Value experience (in the whole-product concept)
Manufacturing operation	Manufacturability, cost to manufacture, documentation
Supply chain partners	Manufacturability, cost to manufacture, documentation, communication, collaboration
Distributors	Easy to store, transport, and display; shelf life; service
Employees	Reward and recognition, safety, health, worthiness of the product
Society	Common welfare, regulatory compliance (environmental, health, and safety)
The natural environment	Sustainable use of the earth's sources and sinks

The firm and its stakeholders are linked in a network that is illustrated in Figure 6.3. The flows of information, products, and services among the stakeholders are also shown with arrows connecting various players. At the center is the firm, along with its employees and its shareholders. The upstream suppliers, partners, and alliances provide the input to the firm for design, manufacturing, and delivery of its products and services. Some of these inputs might be delivered through inbound logistics services of other companies. On the downstream side, the finished goods and services of the firm are delivered to the end users directly or through intermediaries using outbound logistics. As Figure 6.3 demonstrates, the timely flow of information is central to the efficient operation of the entire network, including the flow of materials, products, and services. Information flow communicates the input and output of every stakeholder, including demand forecast, price, performance requirements, and delivery.

The entire network of supply chain players shown in Figure 6.3 is situated within global society and the natural environment. The stakeholder network for a sustainable product must be designed to contribute to the well-being of society and not to

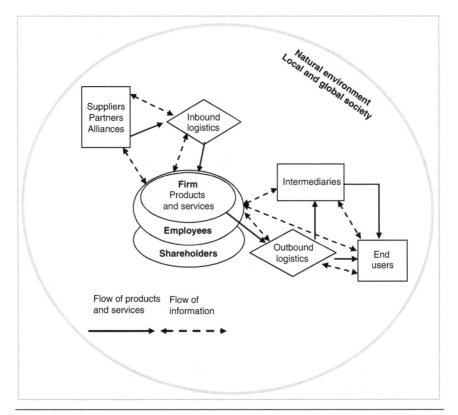

Figure 6.3 The network of product stakeholders

harm the ecological functions of the natural environment. Holistic thinking and strategic planning to serve the interests of all stakeholders in the network are fundamental to the development of a sustainable product.

To ensure inclusion of the right product features and attributes in the design, developers might construct a matrix that relates the design to stakeholder values. The concept for constructing such a matrix is shown in Figure 6.4. This is a three-dimensional matrix listing stakeholders along the horizontal axis and the whole-product values on the vertical axis. The product features are listed along the third axis, perpendicular to the plane. The developer can ask, for example, what features should be designed to meet the expected values of the customers. Conversely, the developer can test the necessity or importance of a design feature by asking which stakeholder this feature would serve and what level of (whole product) value it would provide.

Application Environment

As stated earlier, a product is the application of technology to context. The context is shaped not only by the needs and preferences but also by the application environment where the product is used. Developers must understand users' skills and resources, governmental regulations for safety and environmental protection, and

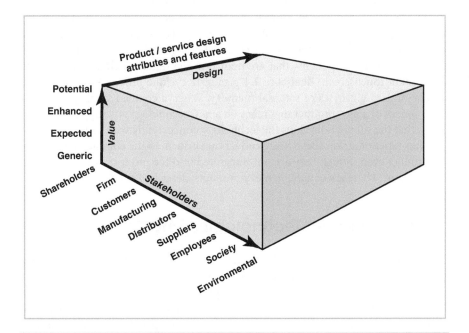

Figure 6.4 The product stakeholder, value, and design matrix

packaging requirements for transporting and distributing the product. For example, designing a rooftop solar power system for a customer in the U.S. would be different than a system that is installed on the rooftop of a house in a remote area of India. The U.S. homeowner is more likely to be skilled in monitoring the performance of the system and to have access to skilled technicians for maintenance. Because the remote Indian homeowner lacks these skills and resources, his or her solar system design and installation must be more reliable and robust, and the suppliers must provide post-installation maintenance service as part of their product offering. Packaging is another important design task that might strongly depend on the application environment. In remote areas of Africa, drugs are often reported to spoil because of difficulties and delays in distribution and warehousing in warm climates. Recognizing these realities, the drug manufacturer must provide thermally insulated packaging for delivery of the drugs to these remote areas versus delivery to hospitals in a metropolitan area in a developed country.

Technology Development

To satisfy unmet needs in the target market, to build competitive advantage, or to create new market opportunities, it is often necessary to develop new technologies. The new technology might be developed in-house and in partnership with other organizations (such as universities), or it might be acquired or licensed from a third party. The suppliers of components and subsystems of the product could be another important source of technology innovation. For example, Apple Corporation's iPhone benefits from the leading-edge technologies of several suppliers. Some of the innovative components that are built into the iPhone include the 4.7-inch LED-backlit touchscreen, dual-core 1.4 gigahertz cyclone processor, 8 megapixel camera, and 16 gigabytes of internal memory. When a company embarks on the development of a new product that relies on a new technology at a supplier, it must ensure that the supplier develops the technology concurrently with its products.

Other types of technologies and products are critical to the commercial success of a product even though they are not integrated into the product as a component or subsystem. These are complementary products, described below.

Complementary Technologies and Products

Complementary technologies and products are those that the user must have to make your product fulfill his or her needs or to perform the intended function. For example, the Windows operating system, a product of Microsoft Corporation, is the complementary product of laptop computers designed and sold by Dell Corporation or other suppliers of personal computers. A can opener is a complementary product of tomato paste sealed in a can. The user cannot access the tomato paste, at least not conveniently, without the can opener.

Product developers must be aware of complementary products and ensure that they are available or concurrently developed with their product. Unavailability of complementary products can be an impediment to the market adoption of new technologies. For example, hydrogen fuel-cell vehicles have been developed and tested by several automobile manufacturers for a long time, but they have not penetrated the market. The missing link is hydrogen fuel as the complementary product, which is not readily available at filling stations on the road.

The Product Development and Commercialization Process

The product development and commercialization process (PDCP) is laid out in Figure 6.5. This general methodology is applicable to the development of any new product, regardless of whether it is a hardware, software, or service. However, this general methodology should be customized to the product type to improve the efficiency of its application. (The nuances of the process for software and service products are discussed later in this chapter.) On the other hand, is the general process in Figure 6.5 suitable for developing sustainable products?

Sustainable product development follows the same generic process, but requires a holistic systems approach throughout. At every step of the process, developers must consider the impact of their strategic decisions and design choices on the economic, social, and environmental performance of the product throughout its life cycle. The PDCP starts with a strategy for sustainable product development and a decision regarding *what* technology and product to develop. The next step is user-need research and product concept development, which must focus on the well-being of the user and ways to improve it. The subsequent PDCP steps for a detailed design of the product must follow the sustainability guidelines described in Chapters 3, 7, and 8 and use the life-cycle assessment tools that were discussed in Chapter 4.

The product development plan and the firm's outsourcing strategy must be integrated to ensure that sustainability goals are pursued across the entire supply loop. Later in this chapter, sustainable practices in outsourcing and supplier management are reviewed. The following sections describe the purpose, scope, and expected output of each phase of the PDCP that are shown in Figure 6.5.

Phase 0: The Product Development Proposal

The purpose of Phase 0 is to identify a market opportunity that can be realized by a new technology and product concept and to identify the desired value attributes of the proposed concept. The new product idea might be derived from R&D at the

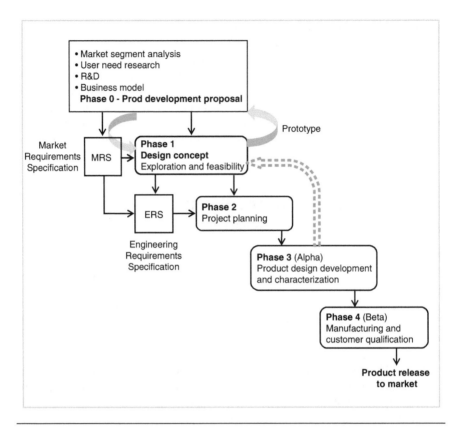

Figure 6.5 The PDCP

firm or at a university. The output of this phase is a proposal to initiate the product development process and to fund the implementation of Phases 1 and 2 that are shown in Figure 6.5. This proposal might be presented to corporate management or, in the case of a start-up company, to external investors, such as venture capitalists. The scope of work in Phase 0 includes a preliminary market segmentation and target user analysis to identify an opportunity in an existing or new market. Furthermore, the realization of the market opportunity must be supported by a preliminary business model for revenue generation—that is, how would we make money? The intellectual property protection, patentability, and risks of the proposed technology also must be included in the proposal at the end of Phase 0.

At the end of Phase 0, there will be many unanswered questions and uncertainties about the technology and realization of market opportunities. However, the outcome of this phase must capture the imagination of investors and corporate executives and create excitement about the proposed opportunity to deliver economic and social value without adversely impacting the natural environment.

Phase 1: Product Concept Exploration and Feasibility

Phase 1 is a pathfinding process, and its purpose is to narrow the market focus, gather detailed user-need data, conceive alternate product design concepts, and select the optimal concept for detailed development and commercialization. The output of this phase is the conceptual design of the optimal product and demonstration of its technical feasibility and commercial viability. In this phase, a preliminary market requirements specification (MRS) should also be prepared. Later in this section, the purpose and content of the MRS document is discussed. (The methodology for user-need research based on a human-centered design approach is described in Chapter 7.)

The scope of Phase 1 includes several cycles of learning in concept development that involves prototyping candidate designs to gather more user information and to solve technical problems. In the upcoming paragraphs, several important tasks in Phase 1 are discussed, including prototyping and assessment of the technical feasibility and commercial viability of alternate product concepts.

Prototyping

Prototyping of alternate product concepts is essential in Phase 1. Prototypes bring ideas to life and help gather high-quality user information. When a prototype is shown to users, they can tell the developer whether or not it meets their expectations and satisfies their needs. This is particularly true for a new-to-the-world product—when the user has not seen anything like it in the past. Prototyping is also important for testing the functional performance of the product and reducing design risks. In Phase 1, prototypes of the entire product, which could be costly and delay the program, are not necessary. Prototyping the new and high-risk components of the product would be adequate. These are called *bench prototypes*. Multiple and rapid prototyping as early as possible in Phase 1 is strongly recommended. For service products, prototypes are process diagrams that lay out the flow of services and funds across the value chain.

Technical Feasibility

To demonstrate the technical feasibility of the proposed design, the development team must assess the design risks, intellectual property landscape, and resource availability. Developers must identify the product-design risks and plan a mitigation strategy. The competitive intellectual property landscape related to the proposed design concept and technology must be carefully assessed. You should determine if the proposed technology or design is patentable and if it is necessary to license patents from a third party. Finally, you must demonstrate that the organization has the necessary resources to carry out the design of the proposed concept according to the specified performance requirements.

Commercial Viability

In Phase 1, the development team must gather sufficient data or make an informed estimate (for new-to-market products) that the target market over the planning horizon is attractive. Attractiveness is subjective and dependent on the firm's business objectives and investors' expectations. Furthermore, the competitive landscape and market assets must be analyzed to understand what the basis of competition is and whether the firm could create adequate competitive insulation to attain the desired market share. Based on this analysis, the team should demonstrate that the proposed product concept has the necessary features and attributes to create a compelling comparative advantage.

The commercial viability of the product also depends on the product's *should-cost* amount in production and the product development timing. The should-cost amount is the estimated cost to produce and deliver the product at expected production volume and operational efficiency. This cost estimate is necessary to determine if a reasonable profit margin is attainable from sales of the product—given the price that customers are willing to pay. On the other hand, for the product to capture the desired market-penetration ramp, the product development timing—that is, the time to carry out the design and other development tasks to market introduction—must fit within the window of market opportunity. As part of the commercial viability demonstration, you must clearly state the value proposition, assess the distribution channels for customer acquisition, and identify the required complementary products.

In summary, in commercial viability assessment, the following questions need to be asked:

- Is there a market for this product category?
- Would customers buy the product from you?
- Would you make a profit by making, delivering, and servicing the product?
- Would you be able to create customer loyalty to sustain and grow the business?

Value Proposition

A value proposition is a description of the core functions and differentiating benefits of a product. In stating the value proposition, several additional pieces of information should be identified to make it useful as the overarching goal of the product development process. The following is a list of information that should be included in the value proposition:

- Targeted users and customers and their characteristics
- Application environment (and its characteristics)
- Proposed value (that fulfills an unmet need of users and other stakeholders)
- Competitive differentiation of the proposed value
- Compelling benefits to the user (the benefits that entice the user to purchase the product)

- Relationship of the value proposition to the value bundle (an integrated collection of values—such as hardware, software, and service—that users need to satisfy their needs)

A convenient and effective way of stating the value proposition is to fill in the blanks (inside the parentheses) in the following sentences: For (target customer) who (statement of the need or opportunity), the (product name) is a (product category) that (key benefit and compelling reason to buy). Unlike (primary competitive alternative), our product (statement of primary differentiation).

Assessment of Alternate Product Concepts or Market Segments

In the pathfinding exploration of technology to market, forks might be encountered on the path; thus, there is a need to identify the optimal direction. We might encounter questions like these: What is the best design among two or three competing concepts? Which is the optimal served-market segment among competing opportunities? The following five-step process can help decision makers answer these questions.

1. **Create a set of selection criteria.** The selection criteria should encompass strategic alignment, extent of the opportunity, and the probability of success of alternate choices. Criteria should be included that indicate alignment with the company's strategy for social responsibility, business, market, and technology. For example, strengthening the existing product portfolio and helping to diversify in adjacent markets might be two corporate strategies that could be included in the criteria set. The extent of the opportunity could account for business potential or contribution to sustainability and social justice. The probability-of-success indicators might be newness of technology, competitive insulation, and resource availability. Additional factors that might be included in the set of selection criteria are ease of market entry, technology fit, time to penetrate the market, and market complexity.

2. **Assign appropriate weight to different criteria.** Not all of the criteria are equally important, and decision makers should assign a corresponding weight to each criterion. For example, a range of 1 to 10 can be assigned, indicating the least to most important criteria. The choice of degree of importance is often subjective and value-based.

3. **Rank candidate alternatives in how effectively they satisfy each criterion.** Use a numeric correlation factor to rank candidate alternatives (such as product concepts or market segments) in satisfying a given criterion. For example, a score of from 1 to 5 could be used, where 1 indicates weak and 5 indicates strong correlation.

4. **Calculate the aggregate score for each candidate.** The aggregate score for a candidate is the sum of the candidate's rank in all criteria multiplied by the corresponding weight.

5. **Choose the opportunity that has the highest score.** Because of the uncertainty and subjectivity of the weights and ranking in this methodology, the team should not take the results literally and instead should use this process primarily to sharpen its understanding of the risks and rewards of candidate concepts and to create shared knowledge among project team members. Furthermore, an important factor that is not included in the above methodology is the team members' passion and enthusiasm for a technology, product concept, or market opportunity. This factor might, in the final analysis, be the determinant of success.

Market Requirements Specification

The MRS describes the features, capabilities, and business requirements for the commercial success of a product in the target market. This document is developed over several phases of the product development process, starting at Phase 0. As the PDCP moves forward through various phases, more definitive knowledge is attained about the market, the needs and preferences of users and other stakeholders, and the competitive landscape. By the end of Phase 2, the MRS should be essentially complete, although it might have to be amended later because of findings made in Phases 3 and 4.

As shown in Figure 6.5, the early phases of the product development process are not linear, and there is a significant amount of iteration between Phases 0 and 1 and, to a lesser degree, between Phases 3 and 1. For example, the evaluative research with early prototypes in Phase 1 might reveal that the initial target market is not ideal, and developers must pivot to a different market application or segment. This finding would require a repeat of the user-need research that was carried out in Phase 0. As another example, the detail design of the product in Phase 3 might reveal a higher manufacturing cost than was previously assumed in Phase 1, when the design was at the conceptual level and the details were not yet well understood. This finding might necessitate a return to Phase 1 and a modification of the conceptual design of the product. Table 6.2 lists the outline of an MRS.

Phase 2: The Project Plan

The purpose of Phase 2 is to prepare a detailed project plan for completing the remaining tasks of the product development process in Phases 3 and 4 and the product release to market, as shown in Figure 6.5. Although the most important strategic decisions in product development are made in Phases 0 and 1, the bulk of the work and the commitment of resources (people and investment) are done in Phases 3 and 4 and the product releases to the market.

The preliminary MRS that was prepared in Phase 1 should be finalized in Phase 2, and an engineering requirements specification (ERS) should be prepared. The purpose and content of the ERS are described later in this chapter.

Table 6.2 An outline of an MRS 127

1. Executive summary	
2. Economic conditions	Macro and industry trends that impact the planned product line
3. Market analysis	Market segmentation and target segment characteristics
	The customer's unfulfilled product and technology needs and application context
	Technology trends (for business-to-business, the customer's technology road map should be included)
	Technology context (including intellectual property and other issues)
	Firm's context: strengths, weaknesses, opportunities, and threats; constraints and preferences
	Competitive analysis
	Business model and opportunity: size of the served available market; growth in 3 to 5 years; market-share target; price target
4. Market-penetration strategy	Competitive advantages and differentiators
	Compelling reasons for the customer to buy the product
	Window-of-opportunity timing
	Initial (first-year) commercialization approach: minimum viable product, beta customers, and early adopters
5. Product performance requirements	Product description: name and primary functions
	Target applications, baseline configuration, and options; hardware and software process performance capabilities; customer interface specification; reliability, productivity, maintainability, environmental-health-safety, and sustainability attributes; target cost and cost of ownership
	Other requirements: future needs and "nice-to-have" features of lower priority
	Product specification
6. Project-execution plan	Key program milestones, critical deliverables and dates
	Beta-testing criteria
	First-year market share and profitability targets
7. Business plan	Business model canvas[a]
	Pricing strategy
	Profit-margin requirements
	3- to 5-year cash flow
8. Product life cycle road map	Evolution of the product line over the planning period
9. Key assumptions	Economy, market, technology, customers, and competitors and their responses
10. Risk analysis	Top three risks
	Sensitivity of business plan and return on investment (ROI) to top three risks

[a]See page 139 for more about the business model canvas.

The project plan in Phase 2 should start with a statement of work (describing the project objectives and scope of work) and should accompany a detailed work breakdown structure (WBS) and schedule. The work breakdown schedule lists all tasks that must be carried out in the project and should be in sufficient detail to include all tasks that are one week or longer in duration. A Gantt chart should be prepared to depict the schedule for completing each WBS task and to show task interdependencies—the Microsoft Project tool is recommended. The Phase 2 plan should include the product platform and system preliminary designs that form the basis for the project plan and should list the recommended prototyping and qualification tests.

The project plan must be aligned with the MRS. For example, the plan must include the tasks that are necessary to design the product features and capabilities that are listed in the MRS. Furthermore, the completion date in the overall schedule—that is, the date to introduce the product to market and to deliver the first unit to a customer—should be the same as specified in the MRS.

The project plan should include estimated resource requirements and associated costs. The plan must describe the sourcing strategy and specify if any of the tasks are outsourced and estimate the cross-functional staff needed to carry out each of the project tasks. The project cost must account for direct labor, overhead, and other direct costs (like materials and equipment). The codevelopment customers and strategic partners must also be highlighted in the plan.

The Phase 2 project plan will be reviewed by corporate executives and external investors (such as venture capitalists) who will approve the proposed budget and authorize the product development to proceed. Therefore, the plan should include the estimated return on product development investment, the top three risks in executing the plan, and a risk-mitigation strategy.

Engineering Requirements Specification

The ERS translates the MRS into an engineering design specification. Whereas the MRS focuses on *what* the market requirements are and *why*, the ERS emphasizes *how* the product is designed to meet the requirements. The ERS defines product hardware, process, software, and service design requirements—including decision criteria (for selecting among alternate design choices) and other design guidelines. For example, if the product is a backpack, the MRS might specify that the product must be light. However, to design the product, engineers need to know what light means—that is, how much should the product weigh? To translate the MRS requirement of being light into an engineering specification might mean stating that the backpack should not weigh more than five pounds. Table 6.3 shows an example of the topics covered in the MRS in contrast with the ERS. The ERS is generated by the R&D and engineering team and is reviewed by the marketing team. Alternatively, the MRS is developed by the marketing team and reviewed by engineering. Marketing and engineering team leaders approve and sign both the MRS and ERS.

Table 6.3 Product MRS and ERS content

Market requirements specification	Engineering requirements specification
• Target market	• Design concept
• User characteristics	• Platform architecture
• Use environment	• Materials of construction
• Functional requirements	• Technology
• Requirements to create satisfactory user experience	• Functional performance criteria
• Attractive form and user-interface requirements	• Design-for-excellence attributes (manufacturability, serviceability, sustainability, repair-recycle-reuse)
• Sustainability	• Should-cost target
• Packaging	• Manufacturing sourcing strategy
• Price and profit-margin targets	
• Distribution and sales strategy	
• End-of-life management strategy	

Why Is Planning the Development Process Important?

As mentioned before, the product development process in Phases 3 and 4 consume most of the development resources, including staffing, cost of outsourced tasks, and prototype and pilot manufacturing tooling expenditures. Therefore, a well-thought-out plan needs to highlight the assumptions and risks of technology, the product design, and the execution plan; provide justifications for the assumptions; and include mitigation strategies for the risks.

Figure 6.6 shows the importance of early-stage planning when management's ability to change is high and the cost of change is low. As the project progresses toward completion, consequential decisions get made, design details solidify, and the cost of making prototypes and manufacturing tooling is committed. In short, as the project progresses through Phases 3 and 4 and market launch, the cost of change increases, and hence management's ability to effect change is diminished.

During the execution of the project, many changes can occur as the result of changing external conditions, such as the actions of competitors or customers. New technologies that were not initially planned might become available to the technical team. The project team might encounter unexpected technical challenges that require a change in technical direction or in the schedule. In each case, the project team must respond to the new reality and decide what to do. To make the project execution efficient, the Phase 2 plan should identify the *decision rules* for change management and call out the decision-making authority in the organization by subject and management level. The Phase 2 plan is also an opportunity to build *flexibility*

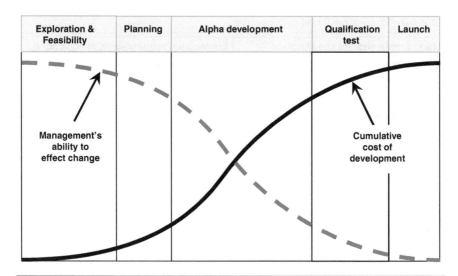

Figure 6.6   Planning enables managers to effect change at low cost

in the product design and development process for an agile response to changes in the external conditions and unanticipated events or roadblocks by the project team.

What Is Flexibility?

Market and technological uncertainties require a rapid response and flexibility in product development. *Uncertainty* refers to the manager's ability to predict future market conditions (user needs or preferences) and changes in the underlying technology. Accuracy of forecasting reduces significantly with time. Flexibility reduces the cost of accommodating the change.

Development flexibility is inversely proportional to the incremental cost of modifying the product design or project plan in response to external and internal changes. Examples of the cost of change include the cost of incorporating a new technology to meet customers' unexpected requirements or the cost of accelerating the schedule to fend off a new competitive threat. The higher the cost of response to a change, the lower is the firm's flexibility. Investing in flexibility pays only when product attributes are highly uncertain.

Flexibility can be enhanced through the choice of technology, product platform architecture, and design of the development process. Versatile technologies allow fast and low-cost changes in product design and enhance flexibility. A flexible platform architecture uses a modular product structure, isolates volatility in design, and reduces coupling between subsystems and modules.

Flexibility also can be enhanced through the development process. Rapid prototyping and market sampling of the product help generate knowledge in lockstep with customer requirements, precluding surprising changes. Furthermore, the team can use the methodology known as *piecewise locking of requirements*, where the requirements that have low uncertainty are locked in first, allowing the design to proceed in those areas while the uncertain requirements are set aside pending further market research or technological investigation until their uncertainty is mitigated. Finally, the project team should sequence the development of subsystems and give priority to the modules that have a weak or well-established interface with the other subsystems of the product. Defining the subsystem (module) interfaces and freezing them are effective product development processes that increase the speed of execution by allowing multiple teams to work on different parts of the product. These interfaces are referred to as an application programming interface for software products and an interface control document for hardware products.

Phase 3: Product Design Development and Characterization

The purpose of Phase 3 (or the alpha phase) is to complete the detailed design of the product based on the conceptual design developed in Phase 1. All hardware and software modules of the product are designed in this phase, with sufficient detail to build and test fully functional prototypes of the product. The engineering tests in this phase must be focused on the performance characterization of the product to ensure that the features and capabilities of the MRS and ERS are fully functional and reliable. The shortcomings and performance gaps revealed by the qualification tests should be corrected by appropriate design changes. The project plan for this phase must specify the number of prototypes that are built and tested in this phase and the success criteria for exiting Phase 3. The success criteria should establish the acceptable levels of functional performance, reliability, unresolved software bugs, and the life-cycle environmental impact of the product. The output of this phase is fully documented software and hardware designs to procure, build, and ship beta units to customers for evaluation in Phase 4.

Phase 4: Manufacturing and Customer Qualification

The objectives of Phase 4 (or the beta phase) are twofold—(1) to evaluate the product performance by customers in their environment and (2) to build several units of the product in pilot manufacturing and assess its manufacturability and production costs. A beta evaluation agreement should be signed with customers to set expectations and define mutually beneficial objectives.

In evaluating the product, customers look at the functionality of the product and its user-friendliness, serviceability, and cost of ownership. Customers usually do not buy the beta units that are sent to them for evaluation, and the cost burden is on the supplier. The number of beta customers strongly depends on the product type. For an application software in consumer markets, beta units might be sent to hundreds of customers. However, in the case of complex process equipment for integrated-circuit manufacturing that costs several hundred thousand dollars to build, two or three beta customers might be all the supplier can afford. To decide on the optimal number of beta customers, considering budget limitations, the product development team should ask these questions:

- What information do we like to receive from beta customers?
- How many beta units are necessary to make sure that the customer data is representative of the market with high confidence?

The exit criteria from this phase should be established at the beginning of the phase. The shortcomings that are revealed concerning customer satisfaction, manufacturability, and cost should be corrected before exiting Phase 4. The output of this phase is a complete hardware and software design, operation manual, manufacturing and sourcing plan, and ROI analysis based on the actual manufacturing cost and projected market-penetration ramp.

Product Release to Market

The objective of this phase—as the concluding step in the product development and commercialization process—is to launch the product in the marketplace and to achieve the desired penetration rate and profitability. In this phase, steps should be taken to update or prepare the following: a product business plan, a product pricing strategy at the launch and subsequent planning periods, a product positioning and marketing communication statement, product naming and trademark registration, a launch roll-out plan.

It is advisable to release the minimum viable product (MVP) at the initial release of a new product. The MVP includes the shortest set of features and functions that are critical to make the product successful in the initial target segment of the market. When the product is complex and has the potential to grow in features and capabilities and to serve multiple market segments, it is best to define the MVP and release it to the market segment that it is most differentiated. Focusing on the MVP also allows the firm to enter the market expeditiously rather than continuing to build features and capabilities and miss the market opportunity. Additional features and capabilities should be developed later and introduced to the market as derivative products subsequent to the MVP introduction.

A project leader should be assigned for this phase, and the team should include representatives from the marketing, sales, customer support, executive management, engineering, and manufacturing organizations.

Product Development Funnel

The tasks of the product development process that are discussed in previous sections are executed like a flow in a funnel, as depicted in Figure 6.7. In the wide opening section of the funnel, information is gathered, and knowledge is generated about

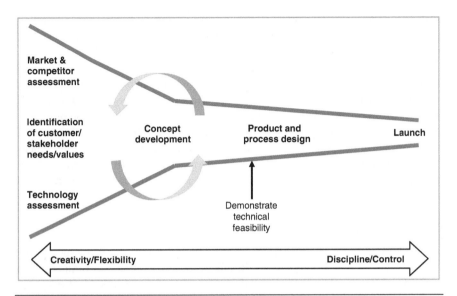

Figure 6.7   The product development funnel

the market and competitors, the needs and values of customers and stakeholders, and existing and emerging technologies. At this opening section of the funnel, new product concept development is an iterative and recursive process that is built on the exogenous knowledge discovered in this early stage and on the creativity of the project team members.

Following the concept development phase (Phase 1 in Figure 6.5), the funnel narrows with sharper focus on the product and process design development. This leads to further narrowing of the funnel to launch the product in the marketplace.

The flow of product development activities down the funnel is characterized by flexibility and creativity at the early stages and by discipline and control during the concluding stages. It is the responsibility of management to keep a delicate balance while guiding the team from one end of the funnel to the other. In the creative phase, process flexibility is high, and new ideas and changes are welcome. In contrast, on the right, at the narrow side of the funnel, when the design is completed and the product is nearing the market launch, discipline and control are exercised, and design changes are discouraged.

Additional challenges in managing the product development process from creativity to discipline arise from external factors such as changes in market conditions and the emergence of new technologies during the march down the funnel (Figure 6.7). How should team members respond to external changes when discipline is called for and they are supposed to focus on the chosen concept and target market? A couple of approaches can mitigate the impact of external changes. One is keeping a short time to market. If the time to market is short, the likelihood of changes occurring during the development cycle would be reduced. Another is building flexibility into the development process (as described earlier in this chapter) so that the project team can effectively manage change.

The phases of the product development process do not have to be sequential, and many tasks in different phases can overlap, as shown in Figure 6.8. This approach, which is referred to as agile development, allows multiple developers to design various parts of a module concurrently, based on an agreed-upon application programming interface and control design interface, and hence accelerate development of the module. Additionally, by piecewise locking of requirements, the development process can proceed rapidly to incorporate the requirements that are certain (and not wait for the uncertain requirements) and to march down the phases of the product development process.

Metrics of a Successful Product Development Process

So far in this chapter, the process of developing and commercializing new products has been discussed. But how are the effectiveness and efficiency of the process assessed and improved for the benefit of future projects? You need to identify appropriate metrics that link the process to the firm's business objectives and monitor the metrics over the development cycle until one or two years after the market introduction of the product.

Table 6.4 lists the metrics of the efficiency and effectiveness of a product development process in five categories. For each category, the corresponding areas of assessment are listed, and for each area potential metrics are identified. The development team should specify the desired value (or goal) for each metric, continuously monitor the actual performance versus goals, identify shortcomings of the process, and take corrective actions to improve it.

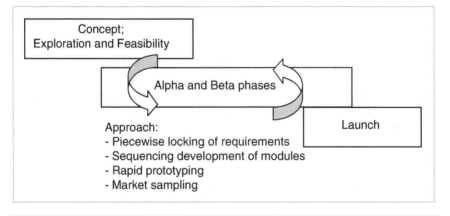

Figure 6.8 Flexible or agile process

Table 6.4 Metrics of the efficiency and effectiveness of the product innovation, development, and commercialization process

Category	Area of assessment	Metrics
Innovation-matching the technology context	Perceiving market and technology opportunities and capitalizing on them	Percentage of the firm's revenue and bookings from the product line one year after market introduction
	Productivity of the innovation process	Number of patent disclosures, filings, and awards
	Product performance: compliance with market requirements with comparative advantage	Competitive standing of the product in key market-value parameters (use a spider or radar chart)
Commercialization and life-cycle leadership	Market-penetration agility	Time to first customer satisfied or time to money
	Market position	Share of market one year after product introduction and penetration at key customers
	Business momentum	Rate of increase in market share
	Competitive advantage	Competitive advantage period: number of years during which a firm can generate economic profits by creating and sustaining competitive advantage
	Value growth	Number of derivative products; operational efficiency improvement and cost reduction
Customer experience	Cost of ownership	Purchase price, installation, operation, and maintenance costs
		Product productivity, reliability, maintainability, and cost of consumables and spares
	Environmental, health, and safety (EHS)	Metrics of EHS best practices, compliance to codes, and standards
	User-friendliness and simplicity	Ease of operation, ease of functionality, intuitiveness, self-diagnostics and troubleshooting, error recovery
	Proactive customer relationship management and support	Customer satisfaction survey

Firm's business objectives	Cost structure	Product production cost (manufacturing fixed and variable costs, including tooling, material, labor, and overhead)
	Value capture: strength relative to other value players (customers, competitors, suppliers)	Trends in average selling price, gross margin, profitability, and ROI
	Environmental and social sustainability	Compliance with worldwide standards and treaty requirements
		Resource efficiency in the supply chain
		Zero waste (emissions) in manufacturing
		Recyclability or reuse at end of life
		Use of renewable and recycled materials and resources in manufacturing
		Environmental life-cycle assessment footprint in scope 1, 2, and 3 categories[a]
Effectiveness and efficiency of the development process and implementation project	Product quality	Compliance with MRS metrics
	Project management	Schedule: actual versus planned
		Project cost (investment): actual versus budget
	Following the PDCP	Quality of documentation for manufacturing, suppliers, and service organizations, according to the users
		Compliance with the product development process
		Corporatewide knowledge retention and reuse

[a] Scopes 1, 2, and 3 refer to (1) activities directly controlled by the firm, (2) energy input to the firm's facilities, and (3) all other product-related activities at suppliers and other entities.

Product Type and Customization of the Product Development Process

Figure 6.9 depicts a framework for the product and project types that a firm might encounter over the life cycle of a product and technology.[1] These types correspond to the state of technologies that enable the functions and features of the product and to the market perception of the value that customers receive from the product.

Radical technologies that deliver a new core value to customers are called breakthroughs and are developed during the R&D in Phase 0 of the product development process (Figure 6.5). The focus of these types of projects is developing the technology and pathfinding the technology to market (T2M). When the technology is developed to a state that is ready for productization, the rest of the activities in Phases 0 and 1 are undertaken.

The new product development process in Phases 0 and 1 often starts with the development of a new platform. These types of projects deploy next-generation technologies to deliver new benefits to the market. Well-conceived platforms allow the product line to have a long life by introducing successive derivative products that are enabled by incremental technologies and deliver improved benefits to the customers. The product-line longevity is extended further with support products. These products use base technologies and correct product shortcomings, like software bugs, that are often sources of customer dissatisfaction.

The generic PDCP shown in Figure 6.5 should be scaled and customized to the type of product and project that developers encounter. For example, most support projects and some derivative products would not need to go through Phases 0 and 1 and can start in Phase 3 of the PDCP. Furthermore, the project team makeup could be limited to one or two engineering disciplines.

The Software Product Development Process

The product development process depicted in Figure 6.5 is comprehensive and applies to all types of products, including software. However, as previously noted, the generic process should be customized to the product type. In this section, the methodologies that are unique to software development are reviewed.

In the traditional software development process or waterfall method, consecutive phases are executed sequentially with stage gates separating the phases. In this methodology, software product requirements are defined first, followed by the software design including structure charts and pseudo code. Next, the software coding, unit test, and integration of multiple units are carried out. The software product is released after the final system integration and test. This methodology usually takes a long time and is not efficient in integrating user needs into the product.

A more efficient or agile software development methodology was needed to respond to the ubiquitous application of software products. The agile methodology breaks the development process into series of build-test-learn cycles to shorten the process of feedback from the user. A multidiscipline team of product manager (owner), developer, quality tester, and integration manager is formed to work closely together while providing continuous visibility to the user. In this methodology, the

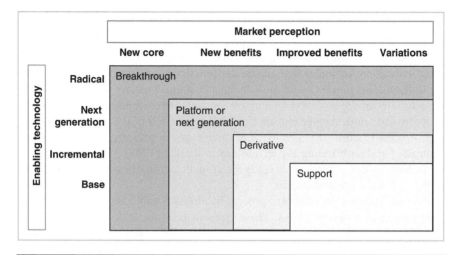

Figure 6.9   A framework for product and project types

software development effort is divided into short *sprints* (approximately two weeks long), and the team is referred to as the *scrum* team. The agile methodology in sprints in shown in Figure 6.10.

In the agile process shown in Figure 6.10, first the product backlog is created, and software tasks are prioritized. Each task might have several subtasks, which are shown in a structured hierarchy (for example, Tasks 1.1, 1.1.1, 1.1.2). The process is managed in three steps—planning, daily communications, and review. During the planning step, the overall backlog is reviewed, and a two-week sprint backlog is created. The team of project (product) manager, developers, and quality tester commits to this schedule. During the two-week period, the team meets daily (usually while standing up) to review the work done, the work planned for the day, and the impediments to meeting the initial schedule. There are several commercial software tools that can be used for managing this process. These tools categorize the software tasks in the sprint cycle as backlog, in progress, and completed. The status information is updated daily and discussed at the daily standups. The last step in the sprint, after the final integration and test, is *review*, in which performance of the software is demonstrated to the product owner for approval. If the product is not approved, changes are identified, and the next cycle starts, and if it is approved, the product is released. The frequency of release and bundling of features and capability are decided in the initial MRS and subsequently modified by product managers, depending on the competitive market conditions.

The scrum method has its own limitations because it might encourage conservatism. The pressure to commit and meet short-cycle goals might discourage developers to take innovative steps for highest performance and quality. An alternative approach is having the schedule for each cycle be determined dynamically

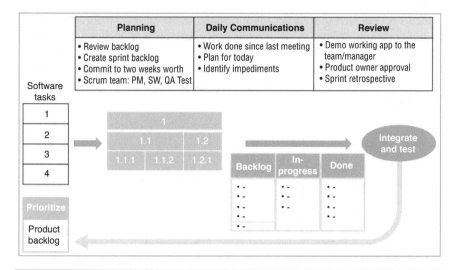

	Planning	Daily Communications	Review
Software tasks	• Review backlog • Create sprint backlog • Commit to two weeks worth • Scrum team: PM, SW, QA Test	• Work done since last meeting • Plan for today • Identify impediments	• Demo working app to the team/manager • Product owner approval • Sprint retrospective

Figure 6.10   Agile software development sprints and scrums

and by the multidisciplinary team of developers, quality tester, product owner, and project manager.

Software development (like the development of hardware, service, or hybrid products) must start with design-thinking that puts the user experience as the principal goal of product development. The design-thinking approach to optimizing the whole product requires knowing the user and the user environment and striving to delight the user. It is also important to motivate team members by the vision for the product and to empower them by full transparency and an open decision-making process. If all team members understand the whole product and the user-experience objectives, they are more likely to be effective in executing the sprint cycles and integrating various tasks.

Business Model Canvas[2]

The business model canvas shown in Figure 6.11 is a useful checklist of the items that must be incorporated in a business plan. The product's value proposition takes center stage and is related to the customers in the served market on one side and resources and activities on the other side of the canvas. The business results are at the bottom, including the cost of carrying out the activities to deliver and support the value proposition and the revenue that is recognized as the result of value capture in the market. The key trends and driving forces shaping the business model are listed on the margins of the canvas.

Figure 6.12 depicts the business opportunities in the value chain for taking T2M. These opportunities (marked with a business plan canvas in Figure 6.11) exist in multiple stages in T2M. For example, there are opportunities to serve the R&D market, to supply manufacturing process equipment, to manufacture the product for the user-facing supplier, and to offer system operation and maintenance services to the end user.

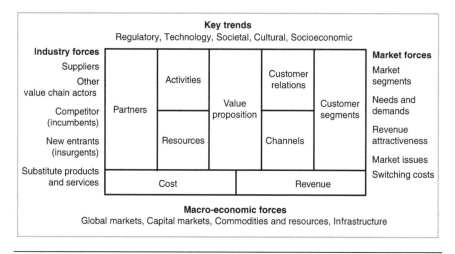

Figure 6.11   The business model canvas and the driving trends and force

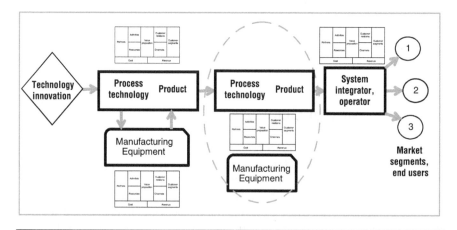

Figure 6.12   Business opportunities across the value chain

Questions and Exercises

1. How can the whole product concept (Figure 6.2) be applied to the offerings of a nonprofit organization? Demonstrate your answer with an example.
2. How would you customize the generic PDCP in Figure 6.5 to different types of products and projects depicted in Figure 6.9?
3. Some software developers argue that the agile development process in Figure 6.10 inhibits creativity in design and encourages mediocracy. Do you agree? Why?

Endnotes

1. Marco Iansiti, *Technology Integration: Making Critical Choices in a Turbulent World* (Boston: Harvard Business School Press, 1997).
2. Alexander Osterwalder and Yves Pigneur, *Business Model Generation: A Handbook for Visionaries, Game Changers, and Challengers* (Hoboken, NJ: Wiley, 2010).

CHAPTER 7

USER-INSPIRED INNOVATION AND DESIGN THINKING: USER-NEED RESEARCH

In this chapter, the innovation ecosystem and the process of creating a commercially viable product concept are explored, with a focus on how to apply design thinking and human-centered design (HCD) methodologies to carry out user-need research and to ideate new product concepts. Also discussed are disruptive technology and lead-user innovation concepts. (The technology-innovation and new-product ideation activities take place during Phases 0 and 1 of the product development process that is shown in Figure 6.5.)

Innovation

Innovation is a disciplined process and is not merely an act of a lone genius. A multidisciplinary team often is needed to carry out the innovation process—to create a new product concept, bring it to life by prototyping, and realize its business potential by commercializing the product. The process is facilitated by supportive management in an organizational context that is conducive to creativity. Such an organization has a structure that enables efficient communication and decision making in teams and has a strong culture of creativity, teamwork, and experimentation. In short, successful innovation is made possible in an ecosystem of disciplined process, efficient organization, supportive management, and creative culture.[1]

To sustain a pipeline of innovative technologies and products, companies must create and maintain the innovation ecosystem within the company. As shown in Figure 7.1, the four essential elements of an innovation ecosystem include a disciplined

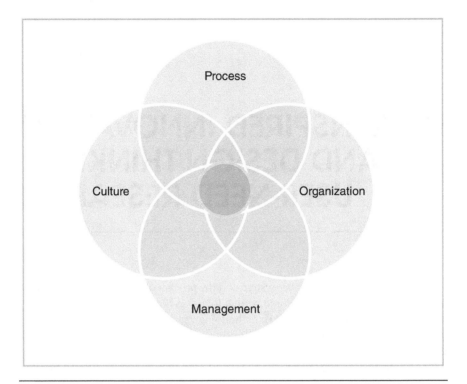

Figure 7.1   The innovation ecosystem

process, an efficient organization, a supportive management, and a company culture that is conducive to creativity and innovation:

- **Process:** The innovation process is a structured methodology that starts with heuristic user-need research to collect market-trend data, discover users' persona, and understand the characteristics of their use environment. A deep understanding of users leads to the ideation of solutions that might satisfy their unmet needs or address their pain points. This user-inspired process is a design-thinking methodology that also is followed in two methodologies discussed later in this chapter—HCD[2] and problem finding, problem solving (PfPs).[3] The innovation process utilizes deep-dive brainstorming and rapid prototyping techniques that are described in more detail in subsequent sections.
- **Organization:** Multidisciplinary teams are more likely to be creative. The product-development process should be carried out by project teams that comprise diverse skills and backgrounds representing multiple functional units of the organization. Efficient communication and an exchange of ideas among the team members and functional units greatly facilitate innovation.

Therefore, the company's organization should be structured in small units with a flat hierarchy.

- **Management:** Project leaders and company management play a crucial role in the innovation process. They must insist on the democratization of ideas so that new ideas are assessed based on their merits, irrespective of who they came from. Furthermore, managers must empower employees to pursue their new ideas and to take the initiative in carrying out their tasks. Empowerment motivates team members and enhances ownership and accountability for the outcome. An innovative workplace has flexible work hours, and rules are simple (including decision-making rules). Although decision-making authority must stay with the project team, managers might find it necessary to intervene occasionally to remove obstacles and refocus the team. Managers should participate more actively in the early phases of the product development process (Phases 0 and 1), when the impact of decisions on business, technology, market, and operational strategies is greatest.

- **Culture:** An innovative company has a playful environment and has a culture of trust in employees. Experimentation and failure in cycles of learning are permitted, and new ideas are respected and freely shared. Establishing a culture of innovation within an organization might be challenging, particularly if the norms and mores of the broader society are not compatible or supportive of democratization of ideas, experimentation, and risk taking. These challenges can be overcome if company leaders walk the talk as role models and demand and reward the desired behaviors.

User-Inspired Innovation

In order to succeed, new product concepts must be inspired by users and be technically and commercially feasible. Three success factors—desirability, technical feasibility, and commercial viability—shape the HCD framework depicted in Figure 7.2:

- **Desirability:** The desirability condition is satisfied when a product fulfills the unmet needs or preferences of users. In an existing market, unmet needs often stem from dissatisfaction with other products in the market. To discover the unmet needs, disciplined user-need research must be carried out (described in the next section). On the other hand, product innovation can create new market opportunities when it delivers unprecedented customer value. For example, a disruptive technology that lowers the cost of ownership of a product makes it accessible to a new set of users who could not previously afford the product.

- **Technical feasibility:** Technical feasibility, as the second pillar of the HCD framework, means that the new technology and product concept can be reduced to practice and be produced at an affordable cost. (The success factors for demonstrating the technical feasibility of a product concept in Phase 1 of the product development and commercialization process are discussed in Chapter 6.)

- **Commercial viability:** Commercial viability, as the third pillar of the HCD framework, means that the proposed product has a compelling comparative advantage over alternate solutions that are available to the target user. The user-need research methodology is helpful in gathering competitive intelligence and uncovering the shortcomings of alternate solutions available to the user. Furthermore, a commercially viable product delivers an attractive rate of return on investment (ROI), which is needed to develop the product. Commercially viable products are also profitable—that is, the price that the user is willing to pay for the product exceeds the total cost of making, delivering, and servicing the product in fulfillment of the user's needs.

To satisfy sustainability requirements in new product development, the meaning of the HCD concepts of desirability, technical feasibility, and commercial viability must be expanded. The desirability of a product is now defined as its ability to

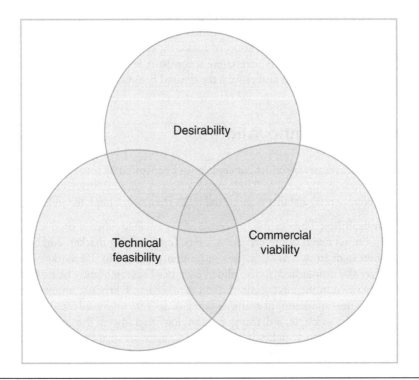

Figure 7.2   An HCD framework

satisfy an unmet need that enhances the user's well-being without harming others or nature in space and time. The technical feasibility of a technology and product must mean both the feasibility of reducing the invention to practice at an affordable cost and also compliance with design-for-sustainability requirements (described in Chapter 8). And finally, commercial viability requires an attractive ROI with a full cost accounting of the externalities in space and time and without discounting the future harm.

Solar Energy Lighting Company (SELCO) in Bangalore, India, exemplifies HCD thinking and innovation for sustainability. The story of how SELCO has provided sustainable energy solutions to the poor is described in a case study published by the Indian Institute of Management Bangalore.[4]

The Sources of User-Inspired Innovation

There are several paths to innovation because the relationship between technology and market application is bidirectional. Existing market opportunities can drive technology and product development, and conversely, the technologies invented by research and development can inspire new application opportunities in existing or new markets. Three important paths to technology and product innovation are customer discovery, lead user need, and disruptive technology.

Customer Discovery

The customer discovery path runs through user-need research and the application of problem-finding and problem-solving methodology. In this approach, the product development team sets out to understand the market, observes users in the use environment, and ideates new product concepts that could solve a pain point and fulfill an unmet need in the market. The innovative ideas might exploit existing knowledge and build on them, or they might be new knowledge created through exploration. The optimal strategy is to have an adaptive knowledge-generation system that maintains a balanced portfolio of exploitation and exploration. New ideas have a higher risk of return compared with existing incremental ideas, and the benefits of new ideas are realized in the future, while those of incremental ideas are short-term gains.

Lead-User Innovation

Suppliers innovate technologies and new products so that they can benefit by making and selling the product. On the other hand, lead users develop products so that they can benefit by using the product.[5] Lead users face a need for products that do not exist, and some will seek to innovate on their own. Sometimes, lead users experience needs months or years ahead of the market. In such cases, the lead user's innovation might be an idea for new product development. The engineers at General Motors Corporation were the lead users of extended-range electric vehicle (E-REV) technology that was commercialized by the company ten years after they experienced the need. The engineers were involved in designing the company's first electric vehicle (called EV-1) in the mid-1990s. However, because the car's battery had a short life, they could not take the prototypes out for long test drives to check reliability. The solution was to attach a diesel generator to the back of EV-1 prototypes to give them an extended-range capability. These engineers were the lead users of the E-REV or Chevy Volt that GM commercialized 10 years after the EV-1 product line was discontinued.

Often, lead users do not productize their invention or pursue commercialization of their product. In such cases, other entrepreneurs or corporations might attempt to license or copy the lead user's innovation, particularly if it is open-sourced. When conducting user-need research, the new product development team should watch for lead-user inventions that they can learn from or acquire. Lead users can be found in the target or in analogous markets. Some may be involved in satisfying just one or a few of the important attributes of the users' problems in the target market.

Disruptive Technology

Clayton M. Christensen, who coined the term *disruptive technology*, observed that many large, successful companies fail to see emerging market opportunities that are enabled by disruptive technologies and filled by obscure innovators.[6] The root cause of this phenomenon is that incumbents listen to their existing customers and sustain their products to satisfy the increasingly smaller segments of their customer base that demand higher performance. The focus on these sustaining products and technologies creates an opportunity for disruption by lower-performing products that are offered at a significantly lower price. The lower prices, simplicity, and ease of use of disruptive technology products often create an entirely new market that was not accessible to the high-performing and expensive products.

When personal computers (PCs) were developed and introduced to the market, they disrupted the mainframe computers, which were far more computationally powerful. Mainframes could be used only by scientists and sophisticated users in large organizations (like government labs and research universities) that could also afford their high prices. PCs, on the other hand, were like toys in comparison, but they were orders of magnitude cheaper, easier to use, and hence accessible to a new class of users—like students who wanted to do simple computations or secretaries who wanted to type and print a letter.

Ultrasound echocardiogram scanners disrupted the monopoly of expensive and powerful image-scanning devices that produced computerized tomography scans and magnetic resonance imaging scans. Surgeons who demanded the highest-quality images did not find ultrasound machines useful and continued using the top-end scanners and continued to demand higher-quality images (such as three-dimensional images) from suppliers like General Electric (GE) Corporation. On the other hand, ultrasound machines that were physically smaller, an order of magnitude cheaper, and simpler to operate penetrated cardiologist offices and appealed to nurses who wanted to perform simple tasks in doctor's offices or in hospitals. The incumbents of image-scanning equipment (like GE) did not pay attention to ultrasound technology and continued listening to their existing customers, who were surgeons at leading hospitals. New entrants, such as Hewlett-Packard, disrupted the image-scanning market with ultrasound technology and served a new segment of users.

Camera films manufactured by market leaders like Kodak were replaced by digital photography that did not need film. Ironically, digital photography was invented at Kodak, which did not recognize its disruptive power. It did not take long before Kodak was made irrelevant by new players like Nikon, which successfully commercialized digital photography.[7]

Over time, the performances of most disruptive technologies improve (often at a higher rate than the sustaining technologies), and their performance gap narrows. The image quality of digital cameras and the powerful versatility of today's PCs far exceed what was imagined even a few years ago.

Disruptive technologies languish in leading firms that offer sustaining technologies not only because they do not meet the needs of existing customers but also because they require different business models, operational infrastructures, and distribution channels than the sustaining products. A disruptive technology is more likely to succeed in an independent company serving a new segment of the market that is not served by the sustaining technology. Therefore, disruptive technology is an opportunity for smaller companies that cannot win against established companies in the sustaining product space.

User-Need Research

User-need research is about customer discovery. Its goal is to understand how and why the user interacts with a product or system. We want to discover user behavior, demographics, and psychographics characteristics and also understand the users' context and the environment in which they use the product. Furthermore, user-need research is about discovering opportunities, user pain points, and unmet needs and wants in the market.

User research draws on multiple disciplines, including sociology, anthropology, cognitive psychology, social psychology, and human factors psychology. Based on cost-benefit optimization, consumers' buying behavior might be rule-based (universalism)[8] or focused on relationships (particularism).[9] Customers might have their own criteria for assessing value and price, or might assess value in reference to associative measures (what others perceive as valuable or are willing to pay for the product). Moral systems of value (like buying only fair-trade coffee) and respect for the norms of the community also shape consumers' behaviors.

In the generative phase of user-need research, we seek the answers to questions like:

- Who are the users?
- What do the users do—and how and where?
- What are the opportunities for a new product or service and why?

In the evaluative phase, our questions are:

- How usable is the product?
- What is the user experience (with the prototype)?
- Did the product design reflect the generative research findings?

In the user-need research process, the user context goes beyond the attributes of the product and focuses on the consumer problem, not the product. Often the entrepreneurs who conduct user-need research focus on the product that they have in mind, and try to find the data that validates their ideas. Such an approach prevents the entrepreneur from collecting insightful data and discovering novel product ideas. The opportunity for innovation—including sustainability—lies in a deep understanding of the user's persona and use environment.

There is a distinction between user-need research and marketing research, and both types of research are needed to gather a complete set of data for product concept development, business model development, and ROI justification. Table 7.1 compares the information gathered through the two types of research.

The Process of User-Need Research and Concept Development

In this section, the details of the new-product user-need research process and design process are described. (The HCD and PfPs documents cited before should be consulted for additional information.) The process is depicted in Figure 7.3 and comprises three sets of activities—generative research, ideation or concept design, and evaluation testing of prototypes.

Table 7.1 Data collected in user-need research versus marketing research

User-need research	Marketing research
Informs the design	Informs the business strategy
Focuses on product experience	Focuses on product features and pricing
Emphasizes qualitative nondiscrete data (but includes some quantitative data) to reveal preferences	Emphasizes quantitative discrete data (for trends, stated-preference surveys, and analysis)
Uses unstructured interviews and usability tests, and emphasizes ethnography	Uses structured interviews, surveys, and focus groups
Uses holistic personas	Uses discrete demographics and segments

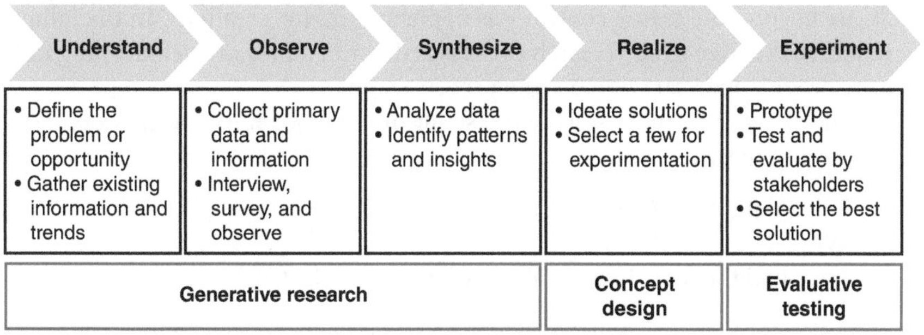

Understand	Observe	Synthesize	Realize	Experiment
• Define the problem or opportunity • Gather existing information and trends	• Collect primary data and information • Interview, survey, and observe	• Analyze data • Identify patterns and insights	• Ideate solutions • Select a few for experimentation	• Prototype • Test and evaluate by stakeholders • Select the best solution
Generative research			Concept design	Evaluative testing

Figure 7.3   User-need research and concept development

The process starts with the *understand* step, where we define the problem, state the opportunity, and gather existing information and trends in the market (through secondary data sources). The *observe* step in user-need research is carried out to create a deep understanding of the users and their environment. In this step, we identify key stakeholders and their needs. In the *synthesis* step, the secondary and primary data collected in the first two steps are analyzed to identify patterns and insights about market opportunities, customer pain points, and customers' unmet needs. The *realize* step is for ideation of solutions and alternate product concepts that can fulfill the unmet needs in the market. The ideation is carried out through a brainstorming process with the active participation of team members with diverse experience. A few product concepts are selected for evaluation in the next step. In the *experiment* step, prototypes of the chosen few concepts are made, and their merits in fulfilling the product development objectives are assessed, including the underlying assumptions, technical quality, and desirability of the solution according to the stakeholders. The optimal design concept is then selected, and its performance in meeting the market requirements specification (MRS) is verified.

The user-inspired design or design-thinking process outlined in Figure 7.3 is nonlinear, recursive, and iterative. Perceptions of the market opportunity and product concept might change as we march through the process. The team might have to pivot and repeat some prior steps to gather more information or clarify initial assumptions. The process requires a high level of operational flexibility and creative thinking, particularly during the initial steps. As the team nears the end of the process, it has to practice a higher level of discipline and control to converge and select the optimal solution concept to exit Phase 2 of the product development process.

The user-need research and concept development process is most effective in a creative work environment and with strong collaboration and teamwork. The team should be multidisciplinary and represent a diversity of skills and experiences, including marketing, sales, engineering, customer support, and manufacturing. The team must remove internal obstacles to innovation by not taking no for an answer and by viewing constraints—particularly those imposed by exogenous factors, which are beyond the team's control—as opportunities for creativity. In the following sections, the user-need research process is described in more detail, and guidelines are provided for carrying out the process steps.

User-need research must start with establishing the *primary research objectives* and answering these questions:

- What data should we collect?
- Why?
- If we had the data, how would it inform our objective?

The next step is to *identify target users* for the research, including demographics and psychographics. It is helpful to include the extreme users in the research because they do things in a unique way, push the boundaries, and often are ahead of the market. Sometimes it might not be possible to reach a user (such as the CEO of a company) for a personal interview or online survey. In such cases, the researcher should look for a proxy user who exhibits similar behavior. The next step in the research process is to *recruit* the target users, particularly the candidates for personal interviews. The number of users in the primary research should be large enough to be representative of the market segment. In the following sections, the methodologies for data collection and data synthesis are examined.

Data Collection

There are a number of methodologies that the research team can deploy to gather user-need data and to create an empathy map of what users think, feel, see, hear, say, and do. A few of these methodologies and their benefits and shortcomings are listed here:

- **Shadowing:** Shadowing is a passive observation of users in their context. The users are not disturbed, and their actions are not biased by the researcher.
- **Contextual inquiry:** Contextual inquiry includes observations and interviews with users in their natural environment. This method is excellent for capturing a broad sense of the user and identifying his or her latent needs and preferences.
- **Unstructured interviews with open-ended questions:** Using unstructured interviews with open-ended questions also captures a broad sense of the user, but is more efficient than shadowing and contextual research. However, contextual information is not collected.
- **Structured interviews focused on getting discrete answers from the user:** Using structured interviews focused on getting discrete answers from the user is useful in gathering information that can be compared directly across users. However, it is not useful for discovering latent and unexpected needs.
- **Surveys with questionnaires:** A large number of subjects can be reached with surveys using questionnaires, but this method is not very helpful for discovering the latent needs and persona of the users.

- **Focus groups:** Focus groups are similar to structured interviews, but they are conducted in a group setting. They can quickly and inexpensively gather information from a representative sample of users, but they require expert facilitation to gather valid data.

Interview Guidelines

An interview is an opportunity to understand a person's thoughts and motives, as well as his or her choices and behavior. This understanding helps to uncover unmet needs and create solution concepts that fulfill those needs. Interviewers should ask open-ended questions and encourage stories rather than yes or no answers. Ask "Why?" and let the conversation develop. Do not ask biased questions that encourage the participant to respond in a certain way or be led to agree or disagree. Do not ask a compound question that embeds more than one question. Pay attention to body language and emotions. Before proceeding to the next question, pause and allow the interviewee to reflect on what has been said and to reveal additional information. For further details on conducting primary research, the reader should consult the Purdue University and Stanford University d-School websites.[10]

It is best to have two researchers at the interview—one to ask questions and the other to take notes. Recording the interview is recommended. Right after the interview, the research partners should compare notes and capture what their impressions are and what they have learned.

Synthesis

Synthesis is an emersion process and one of the most challenging steps in user-need research. It is about coalescing all the data that was gathered in the primary and secondary research, establishing patterns, and succinctly articulating the user's persona and unmet needs. The process should start with qualitative emersion in the data, in a group setting where every team member (who participated in the research) tells a story to report his or her findings and observations. Team members should capture their insights in writing and post them on a board accessible by all team members (sticky notes work well). The next step is to analyze and group the insights and data into common categories. All team members participate in this activity in silence by moving the sticky notes close to other notes that have similar or related information. This can also be done in group discussions with a facilitator guiding the effort.

The outcome of data synthesis should be a description of the user profile or persona and a prioritized set of needs and preferences. Personas are archetypes of the users, based on the primary and secondary research, and help team members focus during the product-ideation process. If appropriate, the team should follow up the previous qualitative analysis with a quantitative analysis of the data from the primary and secondary research to support or refute the insights gained from the emersion process.

Brainstorming for Product Ideation and Conceptual Design

Following the synthesis of the research data, the team engages in brainstorming discussions to create solutions that fulfill the user's needs and preferences. The brainstorming session should be guided by a facilitator following the seven rules depicted in Figure 7.4. Rule 1 is the most important because judgment is the antithesis of innovation and creativity. The primary inhibitor is self-judgment, which prevents team members from thinking freely and pondering new ideas without the fear of rejection by others. The facilitator should encourage the expression of new and wild ideas (Rule 2) and discourage the other team members from judging the ideas as good, bad, impractical, or difficult to implement. The team should have no fear of failure. Rule 3, building on the ideas of others, necessitates intent listening and empathy for different points of views. Because brainstorming starts with a divergence of ideas, it is easy for the team to defocus and engage in unrelated topics and issues. The facilitator must keep the team focused (Rule 4) and ensure that only one

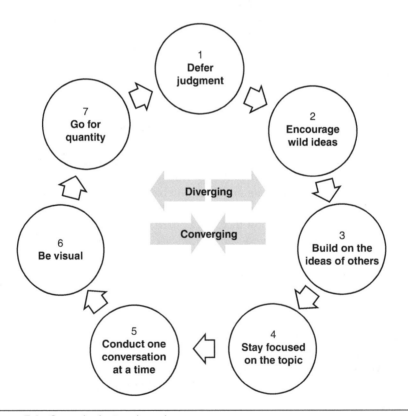

Figure 7.4   Seven brainstorming rules

conversation is going on at a time (Rule 5). Being visual (Rule 6) means writing down or sketching ideas and posting them for everyone to see. Capturing the ideas in writing helps in the post-brainstorming analysis and convergence phase of the process. Rule 7 encourages the generation of as many ideas as possible without inhibition of time or other constraints.

The first time that this brainstorming process is used is during the initial divergence for idea generation. In the second part of the brainstorming process, convergence, the facilitator follows the same approach used in data synthesis to categorize the brainstorming ideas. The product ideas across different categories are then merged by picking the best idea for creating a whole product conceptual design. One or more competing product concepts might emerge from the brainstorming session. To identify the optimal product concept, the competing ideas are assessed based on desirability, technical feasibility, and the commercial viability criteria in the subsequent evaluative phase of the process in Figure 7.3. The evaluative phase starts with experimentation and prototyping, as described in the following section.

Prototyping and Experimentation

Prototypes bring ideas to life and help team members evaluate the desirability of a concept by showing the prototype to users and seeking their feedback. Furthermore, the performance of the concept design against specifications can be assessed by the functional test of the prototypes. Rapid prototyping and multiple cycles of learning are essential to successful product development. The team does not have to wait until the detailed design of the entire product is completed before starting the prototyping and test cycle. The team should prototype and test the high-risk and uncertain components and modules of the product as early and as often as possible. The initial prototypes do not have to be functional and can be mock-ups of the product design in a realistic scale, shape, and form to enable evaluative testing and user feedback.

Experimentation accelerates learning of what does or does not work and how a product concept can be improved to achieve the desired performance. Running an experiment or test is easy, but running a disciplined experiment in multiple cycles of learning is difficult. The six steps of experimentation are listed here:

1. Start with a hypothesis and a plan. The plan must clearly state the purpose of the experiment (that is, what the team intends to learn or demonstrate).
2. State the success criteria and the supporting logic and assumptions. The criteria might be based on target performance specifications (in the MRS or the engineering requirements specification), or on predictions.
3. Run the experiment, measure results, and document observations.
4. Compare the test results with the predictions and success criteria.

5. Identify gaps and lessons learned.
6. Modify the design, and go back to the first step to repeat the process until the prediction methodology is reliable and success criteria are met.

Prioritizing User Needs

The synthesis of the data collected by user-need research often results in a long list of user needs and preferences. The list gets even longer when it includes the product design requirements demanded by other stakeholders, like manufacturing operations, distributors, and post-sale service providers. These needs and requirements must be prioritized because they are not of equal value to customers and stakeholders. Furthermore, if all the requirements are incorporated in the product design, time-to-market and product profitability goals might be compromised; the product development effort will take longer, and the production costs of the product are likely to increase.

In the following sections, the Kano model is reviewed, conjoint analysis methodology for prioritizing product attributes is looked at, and the product value matrix (PVM) for cataloguing stakeholder needs and requirements is examined.

The Kano Model

Named after Noriaki Kano, the Kano model[11] is used to illustrate the *degree of importance* of product features and attributes to customers in satisfying their needs and expectations. According to this model, product attributes can be grouped into four categories (shown in Figure 7.5)—must have, delighter, linear satisfier, and indifferent:

- *Must-have* capabilities or attributes of a product are essential to customer-need satisfaction (such as the generic value in the whole-product concept shown in Figure 6.2). For example, the must-have attribute of a camera is an ability to take high-quality images. If a must-have capability in a product meets a customer's expectations, the customer will be neither satisfied nor dissatisfied. On the other hand, if the must-have attribute falls short of a customer's expectation, his or her satisfaction declines sharply.
- *Delighters* are not expected by customers and can create a compelling competitive advantage. Wi-Fi capability in a camera to upload images to the user's cloud storage might be a delighter feature.
- *Linear satisfiers* are the values that increase customer satisfaction in proportion to the extent that they are offered. For a camera, price and weight are linear satisfiers. Customer satisfaction would increase if the camera was cheaper or lighter. However, there might be an upper or a lower threshold for a linear satisfier. If the camera was *too light* or *too cheap*, it might be perceived to be of low quality.

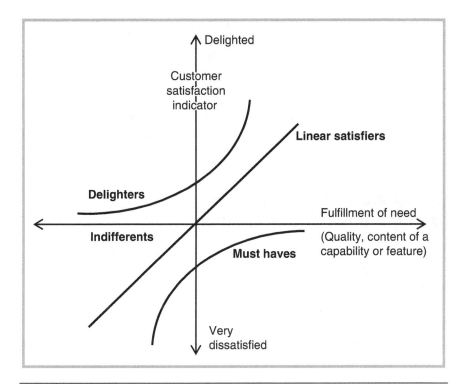

Figure 7.5   The Kano model

- *Indifferents* are not important to the customer; their presence or absence does not impact the user's satisfaction. The manufacturing source of a product might be an indifferent attribute for some customers.

Conjoint Analysis

Conjoint analysis is a statistical multi-attribute preference method for assessing the relative importance of product attributes in satisfying the user's needs. This method is used by market research professionals to rank various product attributes based on customer survey data. Various combinations of the product attributes and associated price options are presented to a representative sample of customers to rank them. The response determines the importance of a design attribute to the customer and her or his willingness to pay for it.

The Product Value Matrix

The PVM is a framework for listing the user and other product stakeholders and their requirements. This tool helps the product development team design a total solution that satisfies the needs of the end user and other stakeholders in the value chain, including distributors, manufacturers, suppliers, and post-sale service providers. For example, packaging material, design modularity, and ease of access to service and repair might not be important design attributes to the end user, but they are important to other stakeholders. Table 7.2 illustrates the conceptual framework for a PVM. Note that the framework includes society as a stakeholder whose well-being must be considered in product development. The needs of society include a lack of pollution and other harmful externalities during product use and sustainable management of the product at the end of its life.

The Competitive Landscape and the Basis of Competition

The commercial success of a new product requires a deep understanding of the competitive landscape and the basis of competition in the target market. As the developer of a new product, you need to answer these questions:

- What is unique about our product?
- What is its competitive advantage?
- What is the switching cost to the customer who chooses our product over alternate choices?
- Who are the influencers in the customer's purchase decision?
- What would be the competitors' response after we introduce our product?
- Would the competitors be able to copy our invention—basically, is our invention protected by patent or other means?

The basis of competition is where you need to differentiate and deliver a compelling competitive advantage—it might be technology, price, or brand. As a new product penetrates the market and moves along the adoption curve depicted in Figure 5.2, the basis of completion changes according to the user group. For example, newness of technology and functionality would be the basis of competition for the enthusiasts; enhanced values that enable users to improve their performance form the basis of competition in the early adopter segment; and reliability, quality, and eventually price are the basis of competition for the early and late majority adopters.

The competition for a new product can come from several sources—existing suppliers, new entrants, and other means that are available to customers to satisfy their needs. Existing competitors do not stand still. They continuously improve their products to remain relevant in the market. In other words, the market is a moving target, and, using a hunting metaphor, you need to shoot ahead of the target. In other words, your product must create a compelling competitive advantage over the future products of competitors and not over what they currently have in the market.

Table 7.2   A product value matrix (PVM) framework

Factors	Stakeholders in the target market				
	Buyer or user	*Manufacturer*	*Distributor*	*Post-sale support provider*	*Society*
Purpose: Needs and expected values					
Physical: Functional attributes					
Cognitive: User interface and knowledge					
Emotional: Aesthetics, etc.					
Sustainability					

If your product or technology is new to the market, you might have to change customers' behaviors to encourage them to switch to your product—and changing customer behavior might be the most difficult barrier to market penetration.

A useful tool for analyzing a product's competitive standing in the market is a market print (also known as a spider or radar chart), as shown in Figure 7.6. The product attributes are called out on the spokes, and their performance is scaled at the concentric circles. In using this tool, only the attributes (that is, product features and capabilities) that are important in the customer's purchase decision should be listed. Figure 7.6 shows an example of the market print for a solar photovoltaic module. The product attributes are module efficiency, price, ease of installation, energy yield, sustainability, and performance degradation over time. As illustrated in this example, it is important to be quantitative and scale the increasing level of value in the outward direction. In Figure 7.6, the concentric circles represent the market trend over time.

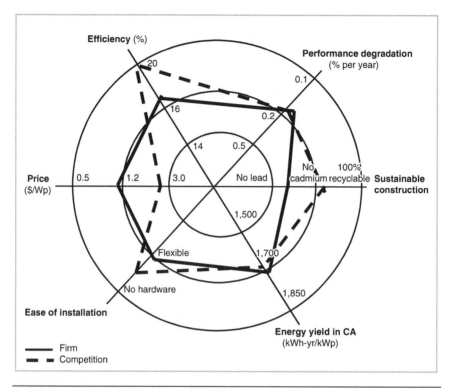

Figure 7.6 The market print for a solar photovoltaic module

For example, the outer circle represents the anticipated market requirements in 2018, and the other two circles reflect the 2017 and 2016 requirements, respectively. The market positions of the supplier and its competitor are highlighted with the solid and dotted lines connecting the points on different spokes.

Questions and Exercises

1. Some entrepreneurs or non-governmental organizations who develop products to solve the unmet needs in developing countries forego the user-need research methodology described in this chapter and rely solely on secondary data sources on the Internet. What are the advantages and disadvantages of this approach? What would be the risks in understanding the users and their use-environment?

2. How effective is the innovation ecosystem of your company (or a company of your choice)? Use the model in Figure 7.1.

3. The HCD methodology starts with the desirability of a new product. How would you satisfy the desirability requirements for a new-to-market product that potential users have not seen or experienced before?

Endnotes

1. The case study discussed in this chapter demonstrates the innovation culture and process at IDEO Corporation, an international product design firm. It is adapted from Stefan H. Thomke and Ashok Nimgade, "IDEO Product Development," Harvard Business School Case 600-143, June 2000, rev. April 2007.
2. IDEO.org, "Design Kit: The Human-Centered Design Toolkit," 2nd ed., 2015: http://www .ideo.com/work/human-centered-design-toolkit.
3. Sara Beckman, "Problem Finding, Problem Solving," internal report, Haas School of Business, Berkeley, CA, 2010.
4. Sourav Mukherji and P. D. Jose, "SELCO: Harnessing Sunlight to Create Livelihood," Indian Institute of Management Bangalore Case No. IMB 321, 2010.
5. Eric von Hippel, *The Sources of Innovation* (New York: Oxford University Press, 1998).
6. Clayton M. Christensen, *The Innovators Dilemma: The Revolutionary Book That Will Change the Way You Do Business* (Boston: Harvard Business School Press, 1997).
7. See the full story at James Estrin, "Kodak's First Digital Moment," Lens: Photography, Video and Visual Journalism, blog, New York Times, August 12, 2015, http://lens.blogs.nytimes .com/2015/08/12/kodaks-first-digital-moment/?nytmobile=0&_r=0.
8. Universalism is the belief that practices can be applied everywhere with few modifications. Practitioners tend to focus on formal rules.
9. Particularism is the belief that circumstances need to shape how practices are applied. Practitioners tend to emphasize relationships.
10. "Creating Good Interview and Survey Questions," Purdue Online Writing Lab, Purdue University, http://owl.english.purdue.edu/owl/resource/559/06/; Hasso Plattner School of Design, Stanford University, https://dschool.stanford.edu/
11. Kano, Noriaki, Nobuhiku Seraku, Fumio Takahashi, and Shinichi Tsuji (April 1984). "Attractive quality and must-be quality," Journal of the Japanese Society for Quality Control (in Japanese). 14(2): 39–48. ISSN 0386-8230.

CHAPTER 8

DESIGN FOR EXCELLENCE AND SUSTAINABILITY

The traditional best practices in design for excellence (DfX) include guidelines for superior product performance, low cost, simplicity, and excellence in other aspects of the design that create a satisfactory user experience. Unfortunately, many products do not follow design-for-sustainability (DfS) guidelines, which also are important in the market today.

The product design must incorporate the requirements listed in the market requirements specification (MRS) and engineering requirements specification (ERS). However, creating an excellent design entails a deep understanding of the product's utility, customer experience, and purpose. Designers often focus on the object to be designed and its functionality, not on why the user wants the product. Behind every product's utility is a purpose—or several layers of purpose. An effective way of gaining a deep understanding of the product purpose is to use the five-why method by asking "Why?" repeatedly for every product requirement. Often, by asking the question up to five times, the root cause of a situation, either a need or a problem, is uncovered. For example, if you were designing a navigation map for a mobile device, you might ask the following questions: "Why would a user want the map?" To locate an address. "Why?" To drive to the address. "Why?" To go to a restaurant. A good navigation application software would have a restaurant locator capability. Furthermore, because the ultimate purpose of a product must be user happiness and well-being, it is essential for designers to adhere to the DfS guidelines.

Design for Excellence

The guidelines in the DfX methodology encompass six elements—product performance, cost, user friendliness, manufacturability, serviceability and maintainability, and simplicity and efficiency—as described in the following sections.

Performance

The product design must satisfy both the MRS and the ERS to deliver differentiated functional performance. Product performance must be predictable, repeatable, robust, and extendable. Predictability is about fulfilling customer expectations without surprise. Customers want to know what they might experience by using a product. Repeatability and reliability mean producing the same results under the same conditions (or use environment). Robustness is a measure of variability in product performance as a result of variability in the external conditions. Robust products are insensitive to such variability. For example, a robust mobile phone functions normally in both hot and cold weather and after an accidental drop on the ground. Extendable products have a platform and a design architecture that allow developers to design derivative products with additional features and capabilities that extend the product's life. An extendable design of a portable phone enables the developers to incorporate a front-facing camera (in addition to the original back camera) or voice-recognition capability without a major redesign of the hardware and operating system.

Cost

Design the product for low-cost manufacturing and use. This capability benefits both suppliers and customers. Low manufacturing costs improve the profit margin in selling the product but also gives salespeople greater flexibility in price negotiations. The product development team should set cost targets in the MRS and the ERS, including cost of manufacturing, delivery, warranty, and service. Low-cost designs have fewer parts and use standard (rather than custom-made) parts. Design simplicity is another significant contributor to achieving the low-cost objective. A low cost of consumables (COC) benefits customers directly and also enhances the competitive differentiation of the product. For example, the COC of an automobile can be reduced by designing an efficient engine that consumes less fuel and has tires that have a long life. The maintenance cost and hence the cost of ownership can be further reduced by a design that allows ease of access for repair, uses standard parts, and has fewer parts. Reliable designs also lower the warranty cost and cost of repair.

User Friendliness

User friendliness means that a product has been designed from the user's point of view. User friendliness must be built into the design of the product for ease and intuitiveness of installation, configuration, feature access, and error recovery. Designers who do not have a deep understanding of the users and their use environment will not appreciate the true meaning of user friendliness. These designers subconsciously project themselves onto the user, forgetting that as designers, they are experts in their field, are experienced with the product, and have many support tools at their disposal. In other words, a product that is user friendly to an expert designer might not be so to a novice user. For example, the usability of many *help* functions on computer programs are dubious. Difficulties arise when the user does not ask the *right* question and when the developer has not anticipated a particular problem. Either case must be addressed by design. Simplicity in design, such as having fewer steps to perform a function and intuitive operations, significantly improves its user friendliness.

Manufacturability

A product needs to be designed so that it can be manufactured at a low cost, without making mistakes in assembly (right the first time), and with high quality (without defects). The principle of poka-yoke (*mistake-proofing* in the Toyota production system) is an important requirement of design for manufacturability (DFM). It calls for a design that can be assembled or used only the correct way. DFM requires a careful design—of the product architecture, modularity, components, and materials of construction—that considers the impact on the supply chain strategy and sustainability of the product. Proven parts and adequate design documentation are also important in DFM. Manufacturability requirements should be developed at the onset by a team of design and manufacturing engineers in conjunction with the ERS.

Serviceability and Maintainability

Ideally, a product will never fail and will not need maintenance in its useful life. However, even great products have consumable parts and must be serviced occasionally. The brake pads of automobiles wear out and need to be changed after a certain number of travel miles, and a computer occasionally freezes. Ease of troubleshooting, diagnostics, and error recovery makes the user experience with product failure less painful. A car that alerts the driver about worn brake pads improves product safety, and a design that allows the technician to access the brake pads easily and change them quickly lowers maintenance costs. A computer that can recover from a freeze easily and without loss of data would be much appreciated by users and would help make them loyal customers.

Serviceability and maintainability require an intelligent design that monitors and, when appropriate, graphically displays system performance parameters. An intelligent design enables optimal system operation, timely maintenance calls, and an archive of valuable information that can be used to improve future designs.

The maintainability of a product extends its useful life and improves its sustainability, too. If you cannot repair a product that has failed, you have to discard it (most likely to a landfill) and replace it with another unit. Design for maintainability also can delay product obsolescence caused by advances in technology. The user can upgrade the product with the latest technology and save it from going to a landfill. Design for serviceability and maintainability should allow intuitive troubleshooting and repair by a less-skilled user. A good metric of design for serviceability is mean time to repair.

Simplicity and Efficiency

Simple products and components use fewer parts, are easier and cheaper to build, and have fewer failures. Simple systems are modular and have clear interfaces and minimal interdependencies between the modules.

An efficient product design demands minimal consumption of resources in its construction and operation. An efficient car is light and has high miles-per-gallon performance. A 100% efficient paint booth in automobile manufacturing uses only the amount of paint that ends up coating the car. Energy efficiency is another important consideration that often is lacking in the manufacturing and the ERSs of many products—partly because energy is quite cheap in the United States. Many electronic devices (like computers and televisions) are not energy efficient and consume energy even when turned off. In an effort to minimize resource consumption, we should be mindful of the life-cycle environmental impact of our choices. For example, we might substitute one material for another to reduce weight, but end up increasing the life-cycle carbon emissions of the product.

Efficient designs create minimal waste across the product life cycle and have the lowest life-cycle resource consumption and environmental impact—using the life-cycle assessment (LCA) methodology. An efficient product design might not have the lowest initial cost. But it is worthwhile to trade off higher initial costs for a lower cost of ownership and minimal environmental impact.

Another efficiency consideration is the efficiency of carrying out the product development and commercialization process. An efficient process relies on the methodology discussed in this book to maintain a balance between flexibility for creativity and discipline for productivity. Designers should first develop a deep understanding of the users and their use environment and ask many "Whys?" before designing the hardware or coding the software. An efficient product development process relies on upfront flexibility and iterative cycles of learning. Efficient project implementation precludes rework. Rework means correcting mistakes that could have been prevented. Rapid prototyping and experimentation are for knowledge creation and learning in the early design phases and are not the same as rework.

Design for Sustainability

To develop a sustainable product (as defined in Chapter 2), the development team should follow the DfS guidelines provided in this section. In DfS, the goal is to go beyond the traditional goal of designing for market share and profitability and instead to design a product that has a positive social impact and minimal environmental impact. In other words, a sustainable design meets the needs of customers and shareholders, but also is mindful of the life-cycle consequences of the product here and elsewhere, now and in the future.

To assess the environmental impact of alternate design concepts, designers need to follow the frameworks of industrial ecology (discussed in Chapter 3) and the LCA methodology (Chapter 4). An efficient product design enables a circular supply-loop process (instead of the traditional supply chain process) and produces no waste. In Chapter 9, we discuss the end-of-life (EOL) management issues in more detail and review an initiative at Cisco Corporation that diverted waste from the landfill and improved operational profitability.

Attributes of a Sustainable Design

A sustainable design:

- Efficiently incorporates environmentally preferred materials and finishes
- Requires a minimal consumption of resources in all stages of the product life cycle, including energy, water, and other resources in manufacturing; consumables in use; and natural footprint (such as land for disposal) at the end of life
- Minimizes the material content in products
- Uses green chemistry-based materials and avoids materials that upset the ecosystem in production and use
- Uses recycled material and refurbished assemblies and components
- Minimizes the use of dissimilar materials
- Allows its components to be reused and its materials of construction to be separated and recycled at the end of a product's life (recycling technology is rapidly advancing, and design engineers must be aware of best practices and the possibilities of recycling)
- Causes minimal solid, liquid, and gaseous discharge into the atmosphere, water streams, and land in manufacturing and in use
- Has a long life, is repairable, and is efficient in use (requiring the least amount of energy and other consumables without harmful emissions)
- Can be upgraded to extend the product's life
- Has high reliability and maintainability with low cost of repair
- Is in harmony with people and nature at the point of use
- Is optimized across time and space by using LCA to assess the product's environmental impact and to prioritize design decisions
- Both sustainability and commercial viability criteria are used in design decisions to ensure that the product enhances customer's well-being

Example: Even Small Things Make a Difference

The invention in 1976 of the stay-on pop-up tab opener on aluminum soda and beer cans meant that the formerly discardable tabs stayed with the can, therefore passing back through the recycling process rather than being thrown away and

Figure 8.1   An aluminum can's stay-on pop-up tab

ending up in a landfill (Figure 8.1). The recycling of those tiny tabs saves 16,000 tons of aluminum and around 200 million kilowatts of electricity per year in the U.S. It also prevents 136,000 tons of carbon dioxide emissions.

In the remainder of this chapter, we discuss the integrative nature and interdependence of product design with the manufacturing process and supply-loop strategy.

Manufacturing and Sustainability

A product's life-cycle impact on the environment and society is caused not only by how it is used but also by how it is made. The latter includes the manufacturing operations at the firm and its suppliers. Figure 8.2 depicts a manufacturing supply loop and highlights how at the end of its life, the product can be collected and diverted away from disposal to a landfill and back into the manufacturing cycle. The product or its components at EOL are refurbished and reused, or its material is recycled to substitute the virgin material that would otherwise be extracted from the earth. Such a closed-loop manufacturing cycle reduces demand for virgin materials (the earth's resources) and for waste reprocessing (the sink functions of nature).

The sustainability requirements for closed-loop manufacturing must be considered in the planning and design of the manufacturing system, in the determination of order quantity and forecasting, in the supply chain strategy and management, and in the management of manufacturing operations at a firm.[1] Below, the salient factors are examined in more detail.

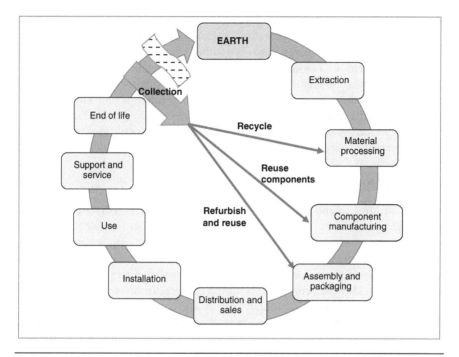

Figure 8.2   A manufacturing supply loop with reuse and recycle at EOL

Production Capacity

Production capacity is based on the forecasted demand for the product in the planning horizon, which in turn is impacted by the expected product life. Sustainable products have a long life and can be repaired and refurbished to extend their useful life. Sustainable designs reduce the required manufacturing capacity in comparison with the capacity for traditional products, which often are designed for obsolescence and a short life to increase their demand.

Facilities

Facilities location and size, consumption of electricity and water, and waste generation are all impacted by the design of the product and its manufacturing process. Sustainable operations require an efficient building design to minimize energy consumption and a safe and comfortable workspace for workers. The manufacturing facilities should use renewable energy from onsite solar thermal and photovoltaic generation. There should be provisions for on-site water recycling, and facilities should adopt a zero gaseous, liquid, and solid waste-generation strategy. Closed-loop manufacturing and process design helps reduce waste. If necessary, a landfill or waste processing units (such as incinerators) should be located near the production facilities to avoid transportation of waste away from the source. Building a strategy for by-product synergy (BPS) is another effective approach to sustainable waste management. BPS (which is discussed in more detail in Chapter 9) aims to use the waste from one manufacturing process as an input material (or feed stock) for another manufacturing process. The BPS approach can be adopted inside a company or across the manufacturing processes of different companies. Furthermore, the facilities location should be as close to the market as possible to minimize the costs and emissions of carbon dioxide and other pollutants from transportation.

Supply Chain and Outsourcing

Supply chain strategy and management have profound effects on the life-cycle environmental and social impacts of a product. To develop a sustainable strategy, the purpose of outsourcing should be rationalized, and the criteria for supplier selection should be clarified based on sustainability principles. For example, the desire to access a critical component or technology that the supplier possesses might be a justifiable strategy. However, components should not be outsourced for cost efficiency to low-cost manufacturers that are not socially and environmentally responsible—suppliers that do not pay living wages to their workers, that have unsafe work environments, and that emit pollutants to the air, water, and land. In other words, sustainability needs to be imposed as a decision-making criterion in any supply chain strategy. Manufacturers must assume responsibility for the entire supply chain (beyond the confines of their own facilities) to ensure that suppliers adhere to sustainability principles in their product design and manufacturing processes.

The geographic location of the supplier is important too. Long supply chains increase transportation costs and pollution. On the other hand, local suppliers help create local jobs and retain value where it is created. The terms and conditions of the contract signed with a supplier also should be based on social sustainability considerations.

When a corporation's power relationship with a smaller supplier is asymmetrical, the corporation must establish a win-win relationship with the supplier rather than apply the principle of *the strongest takes all*. Many large corporations negotiate extremely low and unfair prices, particularly with the suppliers of raw materials in developing countries, forcing the supplier to adopt unsustainable practices and create extreme hardships for workers.

The next requirement for sustainability in the supply chain is proactive management of the suppliers. We need to establish key performance indicators (KPIs) for each supplier at the onset and regularly monitor their performance against established targets. The KPIs should measure the supplier performance for cost efficiency, high quality, on-time delivery, and sustainability. The KPIs of a sustainable operation include carbon emissions; waste generation and disposal (with no waste as the goal); consumption of energy, water, and other resources; workers' environmental, health, and safety conditions; and workers' wages based on acceptable living standards.

The assumption of ownership for a sustainable practice at the supplier's facilities encourages information and knowledge sharing and promotes a cooperative relationship with them. For example, firms should proactively develop joint efforts with their suppliers to reuse and recycle components and to use renewable materials. This might involve training or joint research to develop recycling and reuse technologies and design practices.

For in-house manufacturing, firms often purchase process equipment from suppliers that design the equipment based on specifications established by the firm. These suppliers also should be asked to design their equipment according to the DfS guidelines.

Quality and Sustainability

Quality is broadly accepted as a critical operational principle for meeting customer expectations and producing defect-free products. Quality products make customers satisfied and loyal, and lowers the post-sale warranty and service costs. Cost of quality is a concept that has been used to justify the economic value created by building quality in the design, manufacturing, and delivery of products and services. We can extend the same concept to sustainability. The cost-of-sustainability (COS) concept (discussed in detail in Chapter 3) is an indicator of the net value (rather than additional cost) that is created by practicing sustainability in product design and manufacturing operations. The cost of sustainability is a holistic and systems concept in which the environmental and social costs and benefits are added to the traditional business costs and benefits.

Production Control

The principles of reuse and recycling must be applied to achieve the sustainability goals in inventory control, materials planning, and scheduling in production. Reuse and recycling reduce the demand for virgin materials and new components and reduce the finished-goods inventory. The reuse and recycling practices, although desirable, face significant challenges. First, the product must be collected at the end of its life and diverted from the landfill. The EOL collection is particularly difficult for consumer products because the quantities are large and dispersed. Setting up collection points is costly, and consumers do not have the necessary incentives to return the product. The second impediment is an absence of recycling technologies that can be used to replace virgin materials at a competitive price. The majority of existing recycling technologies down-cycle materials. For example, used car tires are not recycled to make new tires. Instead, they are ground and used as construction material.

For business-to-business products, the EOL collection challenge is lessened because the number of users is (relatively) small and are organized entities with whom you can set up and manage EOL collection. Cisco Systems Corporation was successful in diverting EOL products away from the landfill for reuse at its customer service centers and engineering labs. (The Cisco case study is discussed in Chapter 9.)

If the product cannot be reused, you should explore the reuse and recycling opportunities outside the firm, a practice called by-product synergy (discussed in detail in Chapter 9).

Waste Management

Often facilities use specialized equipment to manage hazardous emissions and comply with emission standards and regulations. For example, scrubbers are used to reduce hazardous emissions to the atmosphere. It should be noted that scrubbers and other waste-processing equipment do not reduce waste but only convert waste from one form to another. The best strategy is not to produce waste in the first place by using efficient process design, using closed-loop manufacturing cycles, and adopting the BPS strategy.

Design-for-Sustainability Resources

The following is a list of useful resources related to DfS practices:

- West Coast Climate and Materials Management Forum, https://westcoastclimateforum.com
- United Nations Environment Program (UNEP) and Delft University of Technology (TU Delft), *Design for Sustainability: A Practical Approach for Developing Economies* (Paris: UNEP, n.d.). This excellent introductory manual is available for free in PDF form at http://www.d4s-de.org/manual/d4stotal manual.pdf.
- UNEP—Resource efficiency: http://web.unep.org/resourceefficiency/.
- Dan Lockton, D. Harrison, and N. A. Stanton, *Design with Intent: One Hundred One Patterns for Influencing Behavior through Design* (Windsor: Equifine, 2010). This free toolkit offers many design strategies for designing to influence (sustainable) user behavior and is available at http://www .danlockton.com/dwi/Main_Page.
- Autodesk has some good videos on thinking about life cycles and whole systems:
  □ Whole systems design:
    http://www.youtube.com/watch?v=L06ZgG0FV4c
  □ Lightweighting:
    http://www.youtube.com/watch?v=rEaOa25ik0U&feature=relmfu,
    http://www.youtube.com/watch?v=hoHCjWqQQ9Y&feature=relmfu,
    and http://www.youtube.com/watch?v=e-aVkOSd0IE&feature=relmfu

- ◻ Design for disassembly and recycling:
  http://www.youtube.com/watch?v=tQY1VdpHF4c&feature=relmfu

Questions and Exercises

1. How should a firm justify adherence to DfS requirements by incorporating the *attributes of a sustainable design* that are listed in this chapter. State the justifications for every line item on the list.
2. Can you cite an example of a product for which the COS is negative, i.e., is it profitable to design for sustainability?

Endnotes

1. Robert C. Carlson and Dariush Rafinejad, "The Transition to Sustainable Product Development and Manufacturing," in Karl G. Kempf, Pinar Keskinocak, and Reha Uzsoy, (Eds.), *Planning Production and Inventories in the Extended Enterprise: A State-of-the-Art Handbook*, vol. 1, pp. 45–82 (New York: Springer, 2011), sec. 4.2.6.

CHAPTER 9

DESIGN FOR END-OF-LIFE MANAGEMENT: A ZERO-WASTE STRATEGY

In this chapter, we focus on the waste generated during the manufacturing and use of a product and discuss how to adopt and implement a zero-waste strategy. The zero-waste objective is essential to sustainable product development, even though it might seem unrealistic in view of current industrial practices. Realization of this objective requires leadership by private industry and the creation of a supportive regulatory regime by the public sector. Product suppliers must assume responsibility for the entire supply chain over the product life cycle, consider waste as a resource to be mined, and holistically design the product and manufacturing processes for zero waste. Government policy and regulations must be enacted to accelerate the development of recycling technologies, create financial incentives for zero-waste practices, and facilitate recycle, reuse, and by-product synergy (BPS).

Waste from Use

Today, limited portions of waste from residential, commercial, and industrial applications are recycled or reprocessed, as shown in Figure 9.1. The waste diversion from landfill to recycling, material recovery, and processing (for biogas and energy generation) are usually initiated by organizations other than the suppliers of consumer products. For example, users—on their own initiative or in compliance with local ordinances—sort their waste into bins for recycling, composting, and landfill, and the bins are subsequently collected and hauled to transfer stations or to recycling and reprocessing centers by independent operators. Municipalities facilitate and regulate the collection, hauling, recycling, reprocessing, and landfill operations. The recycling and reprocessing operations are established as a business by entrepreneurs who see a profit opportunity in mining the waste and marketing the recycled

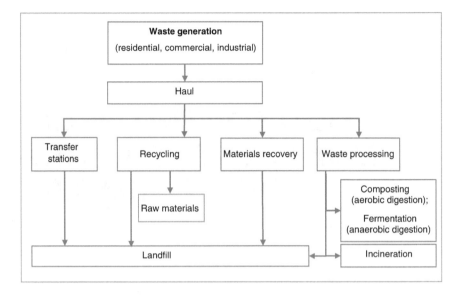

Figure 9.1 A current waste-generation and management system (not including agri-culture waste)

and reprocessed materials. The waste-processing companies also develop the necessary recycling and reprocessing technologies.

The percentage of waste diverted from landfills varies significantly by location in the U.S., but most waste ends up in a landfill. This is true even for products like aluminum, where recycling benefits are evident. The primary production of aluminum from virgin bauxite ore requires 194.7 megajoules per kilogram (MJ/kg), and the energy intensity of recycled aluminum is only 10.3 MJ/kg—a 19-fold improvement in energy efficiency. Nevertheless, according to the International Aluminum Institute, globally, only 30% of aluminum was recycled in 2010. In the U.S., the situation was much better, and 65% of aluminum cans were recycled in 2011.

Today, public policy is not designed to eliminate waste and create a circular economy. Most of the existing regulations in the U.S. are established for short-term environmental protection and for the health and safety of the population. For example, hazardous materials must be diluted below a specified concentration or threshold limit value before they can be discharged to the atmosphere or water streams. Furthermore, codes and standards are in place for the design of landfill sites.

Life-Cycle Strategies for Waste Management

The zero-waste objective is a requirement of sustainable product development and commercialization and requires a holistic three-step life-cycle strategy where waste is prevented by design, eliminated in production, and mined as a valuable resource at the end of the product life. The following discussion describes these three strategies.

First, we must increase resource productivity (that is, use less to achieve the same function) in both product performance and manufacturing. For example, by designing a high fuel-efficiency car, we lower consumption of nonrenewable fossil fuels and reduce life-cycle emissions of carbon. Fuel efficiency by design can be achieved by lowering the vehicle's weight and designing an efficient propulsion system. The lighter vehicle uses fewer materials and hence reduces pollution and waste in the material extraction and manufacturing phases of production. Furthermore, product designers should choose sustainable materials that are extracted from renewable resources and generate low waste in the manufacturing cycle.

Second, all phases of production (extraction, material processing, component manufacturing, and final assembly) must adopt a zero-waste operational strategy. Using renewable energy, recycling water and packaging materials, and adopting BPS are a few necessary steps in the zero-waste operational strategy (BPS is described later in this chapter).

Third, at the end of its life, the product must be collected from the consumers and treated as a raw material resource. Mining the waste eliminates the need for virgin materials from the earth. Reusability, recyclability, and material-recovery capability must be designed into the product at the onset.

Figure 9.2 shows a flow chart for sustainable management of a product at the end of its life. This process flow is based on the assumption of life-cycle responsibility by the product supplier and is a strategy to create a closed-loop life cycle to maximize diversion from landfills. In this process, the objective is to reuse and recycle the

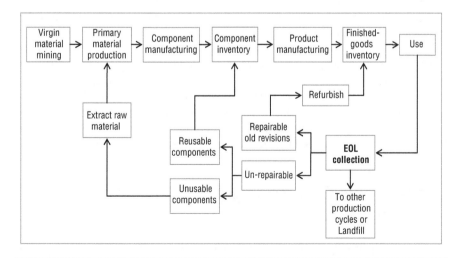

Figure 9.2 Sustainable integration of products at end of life (EOL) into the manufacturing cycle

product as much as possible in the standard production cycle of the product. To the extent that this is not possible, the *waste* should be marketed to other companies for use as input to their manufacturing cycles in a BPS program.

The end-of-life (EOL) waste management model shown in Figure 9.2 and the creation of a supply loop are constrained by an insufficient collection of products at the EOL, the technical and economic feasibility of reprocessing technologies, and a limited market demand for reprocessed material.[1] The removal of these constraints requires product design according to design-for-sustainability principles, investment in recycling and reprocessing technologies, effective EOL collection, supportive governmental regulations, and consumer education and behavioral modification.

To encourage EOL collection, some suppliers offer redeemable value for the used product as a credit against the purchase of a new replacement item. Consumers in California pay a recycling state tax when they buy a new electronic product. The tax is used to recycle the product at the end of its life when it is returned to a recycling center at no cost to the consumer. California municipalities are required to divert 75% of their waste from landfills by 2020, and there is additional pending legislation that would ban organics from landfills. The California senate tasked the California Public Utilities Commission with developing incentives for anaerobic digestion plants through feed-in tariffs or guaranteed wholesale electricity rates.

The recycling technologies for recovering raw materials from waste at a competitive price are not sufficiently developed, and research and development (R&D) in this area is limited. The contributing factors are the low cost of virgin materials and unfavorable governmental regulations that discourage transportation and use of waste.[2] The virgin materials are too cheap because their price does not reflect the social and environmental costs of harmful externalities created in the extraction and production of the material. For example, the adaptation and remedial costs of exposure risks to pollution, climate change, and diminishing ecological functions are not reflected in the market price of virgin materials. Progressive public policy can help internalize the social and environmental cost of virgin material extraction and processing.

The market demand for products that are built from recycled materials is limited because of existing governmental regulations and users' negative perceptions of those products. For example, current U.S. government regulations hinder the transportation of waste and require product declarations if reused and recycled content is used. New supporting regulations that promote a circular economy are needed. And suppliers can change consumer perceptions and purchase behaviors by marketing the health and environmental benefits of reuse and recycling practices.

Case Study: Reverse Logistics at Cisco Systems, Inc.

This case study of reverse logistics at Cisco Systems, Inc., demonstrates leadership in product EOL management. (For the full story, see the original case study, Parts A and B.)[3] In this study, Cisco used product returns to drive sustainability and shareholder value. From a cost sink to a profit-oriented business model, the reverse logistics initiative unleashed entrepreneurial drive, empowered people to discover new ways to deal with old problems, and informed and enhanced every strategic and tactical decision the team made. The result was that an $8 million yearly cost turned into a $100 million profit generator in three years. The idea was as simple as it was powerful.

In 2005, return materials management was an $8 million per year cost center. About $500 million or 6 million pounds of gear, which could cover 12 football fields knee-deep, were scrapped to landfills annually. The product reuse was less than 5%, and there was limited visibility on the disposal.

Christine Fisher, director of Worldwide Reverse Logistics at Cisco, saw an opportunity here and wanted to reverse course. However, the conventional wisdom made many (false) claims to challenge change and rationalize the status quo—for example, that returns are largely defective goods, that the returns process is a hairball and too hard to optimize, that costs can be kept down by treating all returns the same, and that the existing reverse supply chain is probably good enough.

Motivated by a corporate commitment to go *green*, the team posited that Cisco must adopt a reduce, reuse, recycle, and rethink strategy in managing scrap material: reduce products sent to scrap; reuse products to extend their useful life; recycle what is left over, responsibly and visibly; and finally, rethink the way business is done.

Instead of driving a product to its lowest use (scrap), the team aimed to preserve as much of its functional value as possible. Team members surveyed the internal and external markets and identified four opportunities for reusing the product returns. The internal market opportunities were spares/repairs and engineering uses, and the external opportunities were secondary markets and philanthropy. The largest internal customer was the service and support organization, which had a significant need and had to order products from manufacturing, which treated them at a lower priority than Cisco customers. Also, the return products had the advantage of being older revisions that the service organization often needed to service the installed base.

To make the reverse logistics initiative work efficiently, the team treated it as a business with profit and loss responsibility and aimed to reduce operating costs and maximize contributions through reuse. The project was an outstanding success. By 2008, the $8 million cost center was transformed into a $100 million profit center. Internal customers were delighted, and landfill quantities were reduced by 90%.

By-Product Synergy

According to the U.S. Environmental Protection Agency, BPS is: "The synergy among diverse industries, agriculture, and communities resulting in profitable conversion of by-products and wastes to resources promoting sustainability." Inspired by nature's ecology, BPS aims to create an industrial ecology (also referred to as industrial symbiosis) in which the waste of one industry becomes a resource for another. Widespread adoption of industrial symbiosis leads to the creation of a circular economy.

BPS can be applied across the processes within one manufacturing operation and across the boundaries of industrial sectors. BPS leads to measurable and verifiable environmental benefits in pollution prevention, waste reduction, energy efficiency, and raw material use.

The Wacker case study[4] reports on the BPS practice within the chemicals manufacturing plant of Wacker Chemie AG in Germany. By-product recycling and intelligent production loops enabled Wacker to decouple emissions from production volume in a number of processes and achieve the company's environmental goals. For example, a newly integrated chlorine and ethylene production system created opportunities for cross-linking various process areas for BPS. In addition to recycling and reusing hydrogen chloride by-products, the newly integrated system enabled the use of waste heat within the facility that produced it and in the neighboring facilities, saving primary energy.

Industrial symbiosis through BPS engages traditionally separate industries in a collective approach involving the physical exchange of materials, energy, water, and by-products.[5] The keys to the success of industrial symbiosis are collaboration and the synergistic possibilities offered by geographic proximity.

One of the first and arguably the best-known operational industrial symbiosis operations is located in Kalundborg, Denmark (described in Chapter 3). Figure 9.3 depicts the industrial layout of the Kalundborg system. Kalundborg municipality has a population of 49,000 and is home to the world's largest enzyme and insulin factory, northern Europe's largest industrial wastewater plant, and northern Europe's second-largest oil refinery. The network cooperation among key stakeholders helps turn waste products (or by-products) into something commercially useful. The industrial symbiosis started in the 1960s as the result of a water shortage for the water-demanding industrial operations in the area.

Another industrial symbiosis has been reported in Guigang, China, where Guitang Group sugar refining BPS has fueled new enterprises, decreased environmental impacts, and increased employment.[6]

A number of other BPS examples are cited in the Applied Sustainability, LCC case study by Susan Mackenzie and Terry Anderson.[7] The case examines the technical, operational, and commercial challenges and opportunities of BPS.

Figure 9.4 displays the actors in a BPS network and the characteristics of their interactions. The BPS structure is similar to the traditional supply chain, in which the supplier and customer sign a contract that specifies the terms and conditions of the agreement, including intellectual property protection provisions, technical specifications for the incoming materials, rate of delivery, supply capacity, and pricing. The supplier might have to customize the waste to meet the technical specifications of the user (customer). The physical proximity between the supplier's and the user's facilities plays an important role for certain types of products (such as steam) and impacts the cost of transportation, insurance, and permitting. Most BPS initiatives across independent manufacturers use a facilitated process, as shown in Figure 9.4, and are more difficult to sustain.

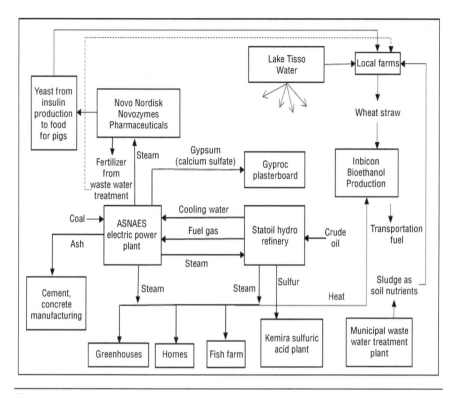

Figure 9.3   Industrial symbiosis in Denmark

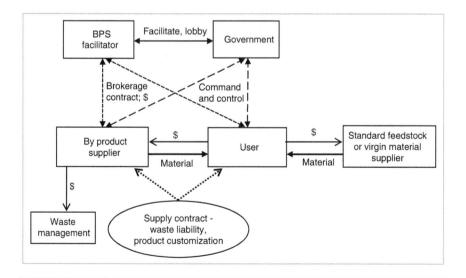

Figure 9.4   A BPS network: actors and interactions

Questions and Exercises

1. BPS is an important strategy for creating a circular economy and eliminating waste. What are the constraints that have inhibited BPS from becoming a mainstream practice?
2. Can you recommend strategies for overcoming the BPS constraints?
3. How could an industrially advanced society promote R&D when it comes to mining-the-waste? Consider both public and private options.

Endnotes

1. R. Geyer and T. Jackson, *Supply Loops and Their Constraints: The Industrial Ecology of Recycling and Reuse*, California Management Review 46(2) (2004): 55–73.
2. The Resource Conservation and Recovery Act (RCRA) was enacted in 1976 and is the principal federal law in the United States governing the disposal of solid waste and hazardous waste. The RCRA amended the Solid Waste Disposal Act of 1965.
3. S. Chandrasekaran, Dariush Rafinejad, and D. Collins, "Turning End-of-Life Product Reprocessing into a Profit Center at Cisco Systems, Inc." (Pts. A and B), Number MS&E-002-2009, Department of Management Science and Engineering, Stanford School of Engineering, 2009.
4. K. Blum, R. Carlson, F. Erhun, and Dariush Rafinejad, "Sustainable Production in the Chemical Industry: Wacker Sets a Good Example at Its Burghausen Site," Number MS&E-001-2008, Stanford School of Engineering, 2008.
5. Marian Chertow, "'Uncovering' Industrial Symbiosis," Journal of Industrial Ecology 11(1) (2007): 11–30.
6. Qinghua Zhu and Raymond P. Cote, "Integrating Green Supply Chain Management into an Embryonic Eco-Industrial Development: A Case Study of the Guitang Group," Journal of Cleaner Production 12(8–10) (2004): 1025–1035; Qinghua Zhu, Ernest A. Lowe, Yuan-an Wei, and Donald Barnes, "Industrial Symbiosis in China: A Case Study of the Guitang Group," Journal of Industrial Ecology 11(1) (2007): 31–42.
7. Susan Mackenzie and Terry Anderson, "Applied sustainability LLC: Making a business case for by-product synergy." Case Number E-118, Stanford Graduate School of Business, 2002.

CHAPTER 10

PUBLIC POLICY AND BUILDING INHERENT SAFETY BY DESIGN

Environmental, health, and safety (EHS) regulations and standards impose constraints throughout a product's life cycle from design to end-of-life (EOL) disposal. For example, regulations might require product safety in handling and use and labor safety in the manufacturing workplace. The distribution, storage, transportation, and EOL waste disposal of products also could be regulated for public safety and environmental protection.

Government intervention for the protection of the common good goes beyond EHS standards and could be designed to impact the evolution of new technologies and products and to support targeted industries. The U.S. government has supported early-phase research and the development of many technologies at a precompetitive stage to enhance the efficiency of market adoption. The human genome project is a good example; it mapped the DNA sequence of the entire genetic system of a human being and enabled significant progress in the biotechnology industry.

Governments could act to reduce risks to industry and suppliers. For example, the U.S. and other governments underwrite safety insurance for nuclear power generation to promote the design and construction of nuclear power plants. Governments also intervene to stabilize the supply and demand of critical commodities like agricultural products, financial services, and energy. The bailout of financial corporations in the subprime mortgage crash of 2008 was critical to saving the U.S. and global economies.

Governments also intervene to support strategic industries. When the manufacturers of semiconductor devices in the U.S. fell behind their superior Japanese competitors in the early 1980s, the U.S. government helped establish and partially fund an industry consortium (Sematech) to develop competitive manufacturing equipment and processes. In the economic crash of 2008, the financial bailout of automobile manufacturers like General Motors Corporation saved the U.S. auto industry from bankruptcy. Technology improvements, market adoption, and manufacturing cost reductions in the solar energy industry have been enabled by strong governmental actions across the globe. The market penetration of solar energy was accelerated in Germany by a feed-in tariff pricing scheme and in the U.S. through investment and production tax credits. The Chinese government helped lower the production costs of solar modules by investing in high-volume production capacity.

And finally, government intervention can level the playing field for emerging renewable energy and other sustainable products and technologies. For example, imposing a carbon tax on products that emit greenhouse gases (GHGs) like oil and coal helps improve the price parity of renewable and clean sources of energy like solar and wind.

The above government interventions can be classified into two categories—penalty instruments with command and control and market and incentive instruments. The command-and-control instruments aim to limit adverse impacts on the environment and human health. The incentive instruments are proactive and drive target strategies.

Over the past several decades, major global corporations and manufacturers of products have gone through multiple evolutionary phases in their outlook toward environmental sustainability. These companies have generally evolved through several stages—including: no concern, pollution control, pollution prevention, and resource efficiency maximization—in lockstep with applicable governmental regulations. However, governmental regulations are uneven across geographic locations (local, national, and global), and various stages of product life cycle (make, use, and disposal) occur at different locations with different EHS regulations. Globalization of production has created an opportunity for companies to manufacture their products in regions where environmental and labor regulations are lax.

The next section provides a brief overview of the historical context that has driven business decisions to comply with EHS regulations and environmental sustainability.

The Evolution of Regulations Driving Design for EHS Protections

Safety- and health-related guidelines in product design and manufacturing were imposed through codes and standards devised by organizations such as the American Society of Mechanical Engineers, American Society for Testing and Materials, National Electric Code, and National Fire Protection Association throughout the twentieth century. Many of these guidelines were developed by professional engineering organizations and adopted by local and state governments as prerequisites for issuing manufacturing or construction permits.

Modern environmental awareness grew in the second half of the twentieth century as a result of several alarming radioactive accidents, oil spills, mercury poisonings, and other mishaps. The U.S. Environmental Protection Agency (EPA) was established in December 1970 and was charged with protecting human health and safeguarding the natural environment. Another U.S. federal agency, the Occupational Safety and Health Administration, was also created in December 1970. Subsequently, the U.S. passed new laws, such as the Clean Air Act (1970), the National Environmental Policy Act (1970), the Clean Water Act (1972), and the Endangered Species Act (1973). These laws provided the foundations for current environmental standards. In 1972, the United Nations Conference on the Human Environment was held in Stockholm, for the first time uniting representatives of the world's governments in negotiations on the state of the global environment. This conference led directly to the creation of the United Nations Environment Program (UNEP).

The common use of the terms *sustainability* and *sustainable development* in the context of the environment began with the publication of the Brundtland Report, which characterized sustainable development as: "development that meets the needs of the present without compromising the ability of future generations to meet their own needs."[1] UNEP has organized several international conferences that have increased awareness and broadened the discourse on sustainability issues. These issues have included the systematic scrutiny of patterns of production of toxic components (such as lead in gasoline or poisonous waste), alternative sources of energy to replace the use of fossil fuels, new reliance on public transportation systems in order to reduce vehicle emissions, and the growing scarcity of water.

An important achievement was the United Nations Framework Convention on Climate Change, which led to the establishment of the Kyoto Protocol in December 1997. Countries that ratified this protocol committed to reduce their emissions of carbon dioxide and five other GHGs by an average of 5% below their 1990 levels or to engage in emissions trading if they wished to maintain or increase emissions of these gases. The Kyoto Protocol, which expired in 2012, was not ratified by the U.S.—the leading emitter of GHGs, in spite of its adoption by almost all other industrial countries of the world. However, the Kyoto requirements were widely recognized to be inadequate in the light of alarming data on climate change that were collected after the treaty was signed. There is a need for much more restrictive measures on GHG emissions (as much as a 50% to 80% reduction by 2050) if environmental and ensuing economic calamities are to be averted.[2]

Multiple UN-sponsored international conferences were held after the Kyoto conference to devise a GHG emission-reduction plan that is agreeable to major polluters and that meets the climate change challenge. The pivotal meeting was the Paris Conference of Parties (or COP 21) in 2015.[3] The agreement that emerged from this conference was based on an *intended nationally determined contributions* approach in which each country agreed to commit to a reduction target of their choosing.

Another important international treaty regulation that significantly impacted product and process development in the 1990s was the Montreal Protocol on substances that deplete the ozone layer. This treaty forced industries across the globe to phase out the production of chlorofluorocarbon (CFC) chemicals (which were invented in 1929) because they are responsible for the depletion of atmospheric ozone, which provides a critical health service to humans and animals by absorbing the harmful wavelengths of ultraviolet sunlight. The depletion of atmospheric ozone was a clear demonstration of how excessive human-made industrial effluents (over a very short period from 1929 to 1987) could exceed the earth's limited capacity as a sink to absorb and process the waste. The widespread adoption and successful implementation of the CFC ban have been hailed as an example of exceptional international cooperation in preventing a global tragedy of the commons. This case also demonstrated that global society can be prepared to make sacrifices in order to live within ecological limits.[4]

In the last decade, the European Union (EU) has led the industrialized world in enacting laws that regulate the use of hazardous substances in product manufacturing and that hold the original equipment manufacturers responsible for recycling the packing material and products at end of life through a take-back program. The following EU directives have impacted many electronic and electrical products: the Restriction of Hazardous Substances Directive,[5] the Waste Electrical and Electronic Equipment (WEEE) Directive,[6] and the Energy-Using Products Directive.[7] The most notable of recent EU directives is the Registration, Evaluation and Authorization of Chemicals (REACH) Directive (enacted in 2006).[8] According to REACH, the burden of proof is on industry to ensure that the chemicals they market do not adversely affect human health or the environment: "authorities should focus on ensuring that industry meets its obligations and takes action to reduce the harmful effects of substances of high public concern or where there is a need for community action."[9]

This is in contrast with the Toxic Substances Control Act (TSCA) of 1976 that is the primary chemical policy in the U.S. The TSCA places the burden of proof on the EPA. The TSCA gave the EPA the ability to track the 75,000 industrial chemicals currently produced or imported into the U.S. To take regulatory action, the EPA must provide *substantial evidence* that there is an unreasonable risk to human health or the environment, that the benefits of a regulation outweigh the cost to industry or lost social value of a product, and that the EPA has chosen the least burdensome solution. Under this evidentiary burden, the EPA has been able to regulate only five existing chemicals (or chemical classes) since 1976.

The TSCA supplements other federal statutes, including the Toxic Release Inventory under the Emergency Planning and Community Right-to-Know Act, which was passed in 1986 in response to concerns regarding the safety hazards posed by the storage and handling of toxic chemicals. These concerns were prompted by the 1984 disaster in Bhopal, India, where the release of toxic chemicals killed more than 3,500 people and injured more than 500,000.[10]

The EU directives have a broad implication for product design by global manufacturers that market beyond the EU territory. Because most manufacturers have a strong preference for common product designs across different market segments, the EU initiative is likely to become the de facto global standard for transnational corporations.

Throughout the short history of environmental protection, there has been strong opposition to government regulations by many corporations (particularly large U.S. corporations) and by political leaders who have been concerned about the negative impacts of environmental regulations on economic growth. Corporations have consistently engaged in intense lobbying efforts to dissuade lawmakers from enacting environmental laws rather than demonstrating imaginative leadership in sustainable product design and manufacturing.

The case of atmospheric ozone depletion and subsequent international cooperation that substantially abated the problem is a success story. It demonstrated that environmentally friendly industrial action need not necessarily harm the economy. Nevertheless, when the problem was first brought to the attention of the public and environmentalists called for urgent action, the reaction from industry and government officials was a predictable denial and economic risk-benefit analysis.[11]

Over the last two decades of rapid globalization of markets and supply chains, sensitivity to environmental and sustainability issues has risen significantly. However, the impact of sustainability issues on corporate strategy has been limited to four areas—risk management, regulatory compliance, customer concerns, and emerging market opportunities.

Globalization has intensified competition and has brought an unprecedented pressure on corporations to increase operational efficiency and reduce costs. This has had an unintended benefit for the environment through reductions in waste. Marketers have taken advantage of this opportunity and have favorably positioned their companies as environmentally friendly while reducing costs. More recently, increased consumer awareness about global warming and other environmental degradations has created additional incentives for corporations to adopt energy-efficiency measures in their operational practices.[12]

The adverse impacts of traditional manufacturing and agricultural practices on the environment and human health have also created opportunities for disruptive technologies such as organic farming and genetically modified crops. The demand for organic food has grown at an unprecedented rate in spite of higher prices and a shorter shelf life, and has enticed mainstream farmers and distributors to enter the market. Riding on the coattails of sustainability, Monsanto Corporation has tried to redefine the agriculture industry by inventing genetically modified crops.

Monsanto's CEO, Robert B. Shapiro, positioned his company's strategy for genetically modified crops as growth through global sustainability:

> The Company has progressed from pollution prevention and clean-up to spotting opportunities for revenue growth in environmentally sustainable new products and technologies. Sustainable development is a discontinuity: the world is a closed system and we are beginning to hit the limits. The traditional model of growth in agricultural output has been to increase

acreage and increase productivity through fertilizers, pesticides, and irrigation. This is not sustainable. New technology is the only answer: biotechnology and DNA-encoded information technology. . . . Sustainability means less stuff and more knowledge and service (delivering functions to the users rather than goods).[13]

The new biotechnology that uses genetically modified organisms (GMOs) is criticized for introducing safety concerns, for endangering biodiversity and indigenous farming (particularly in underdeveloped regions of the world), and for creating even further centralization of global industrial activities. A 2001 EU Directive requires authorization for placing GMOs on the market, in accordance with the precautionary principle.[14]

Other industry leaders have expressed the need for change and have tried to align their product strategies accordingly. Toyota Motor Corporation developed the highly successful Prius hybrid car in a strategic response to an anticipated increase in consumer sensitivity to environmental and resource scarcity issues.[15] Toyota's proactive development of the Prius, which exceeded regulatory emission standards, created comparative advantages for the company by changing the rules of the game and creating competitive barriers.

Charles O. Holliday Jr., Stephan Schmidheiny, and Philip Watts[16] provide an excellent account of the practices of several large transnational corporations and discuss an evolving paradigm in sustainable development. Schmidheiny, a Swiss industrialist, pioneered the formation of a business council of executives in the early 1990s, which led to the formation of the World Business Council for Sustainable Development (WBCSD) in 1995. According to Schmidheiny, "the WBCSD continues to seek ways by which companies can achieve economic vitality while helping the planet toward environmental and social vigor."[17] The WBCSD website routinely documents successful cases that highlight the integration of environmental and social concerns into business operations.

The trend in adopting sustainability as a strategic business imperative is not encouraging. "No firm is yet sustainable," observes Catherine A. Ramus in her research.[18] According to her study, a gap between environmental policies and practices exists in many firms, even in those that are environmentally proactive. In a survey by McKinsey in February 2008, only 30% of the 1,983 global companies in the survey considered climate change in their business strategy.[19] The percentage was even lower (21%) among the 470 U.S. companies in the survey. In a 2011 survey of 4,700 executives, managers, and thought leaders from around the world and from a wide range of industries, only 14% listed the threats and opportunities of sustainability as being among the primary business challenges facing their organization.[20] In a 2014 report for the United Nations Global Compact, 84% of the 1,000 global CEOs surveyed agreed that business "should lead efforts to define and deliver new goals on global priority issues," but only a third said that "business is doing enough to address global sustainability challenges."[21] In this report, only one in 12 companies linked executive remuneration to sustainability performance, and one in seven rewarded suppliers for good sustainability performance.

The motivation in business for tending to environmental sustainability has been weak because the traditional strategies for competitive advantage and sustained value creation have served corporations well. Risk management, branding, and improvements in operational efficiency—rather than triple-bottom-line sustainable development—have been the basis for corporate environmentalism.

Decision Making for Compliance with EHS Regulations

Several factors make the decision making for compliance with EHS regulations challenging. Market incentives for adopting sustainability as a strategic imperative in business are weak, governmental EHS regulations are uneven across geographic locations, and various stages of the product's life cycle (making, use, and disposal) often take place at different locations. For example, if an automobile is fabricated in Mexico and sold to California drivers, the automobile company must abide by Mexico's EHS requirements for manufacturing and by California's EHS requirements for driving. The manufacturing requirements impact the facilities design and set standards for the occupational safety and health of the factory workers. The driving EHS regulations (including passenger safety and tailpipe emission standards) impact the automobile's design.

Firms have four decision options in complying with the EHS and sustainability requirements in developing and commercializing a new product:

- **Minimal compliance:** Comply with local regulations where the product's life-cycle activity takes place.
- **Corporate commonality:** Adopt a firm-wide common strategy of compliance. This option is relevant to large companies that have multiple operations across the world. For example, a garment manufacturing company with factories in Bangladesh and the United States might set corporate-level occupational safety and health standards and demand compliance by both divisions, even if they exceed the governmental regulations in certain locations.
- **Risk minimization:** Voluntarily adopt requirements that are more stringent than existing regulations in anticipation of a tightening of regulations in the near future. This option is applicable when the time to develop a new product and technology is long, competitors are likely to adopt more stringent requirements and gain comparative advantage, and the firm plans to extend its served market to the regions with more stringent requirements. For example, Apple Corporation designed a hazardous brominated flame retardant out of the iPhone product when it faced pressure from nongovernment

organizations and competitors and when the EU banned the chemical following the precautionary principle.

- **Sustainability leadership:** Exceed regulatory requirements in design and operational practices worldwide, and do what is *right*. Follow the design-for-sustainability rules described in Chapter 8, and support regulatory policies that require inherent safety by design. Although this option might not be the lowest-cost alternative, it improves the firm's brand and competitive differentiation.

Questions and Exercises

1. Governments use command-and-control as well as market incentive instruments to enforce/promote EHS provisions. Which approach is more susceptible to creating an unintended adverse consequence? Give an example.
2. How can you design an effective EHS policy that achieves the desired outcome without unintended adverse consequences?
3. What can corporations do to enhance the consumer support for EHS policies?

Endnotes

1. Gro Harlem Brundtland and M. Khalid, *Report of the World Commission on Environment and Development: Our Common Future* (New York: United Nations, 1987), 43.
2. Nicholas Stern, *Stern Review: The Economics of Climate Change* (London: Chancellor of the Exchequer, 2006).
3. United Nations Framework Convention on Climate Change, "Adoption of the Paris Convention," December 12, 2015, http://unfccc.int/resource/docs/2015/cop21/eng/l09.pdf.
4. Donella H. Meadows, Jorgen Randers, and Dennis Meadows, *Limits to Growth: The Thirty-Year Update* (White River Junction, VT: Chelsea Green Publishing, 2004).
5. "Directive 95/EC of the European Parliament and of the Council of 27 January 2003 on the Restriction of the Use of Certain Hazardous Substances in Electrical and Electronic Equipment (RoHS)," *Official Journal of the European Union L* 37 (2002): 13.
6. "Directive 96/EC of the European Parliament and of the Council of 27 January 2003 on Waste Electrical and Electronic Equipment (WEEE)," *Official Journal of the European Union L* 37 (2002): 24–38.
7. "Directive 2005/32/EC of the European Parliament and of the Council of 6 July 2005 Establishing a Framework for the Setting of Eco-design Requirements for Energy Using Products and Amending the Council Directive 92/42/EEC and Directives 96/57/EC and 2000/55," EC of the European Parliament and of the Council, 2005.
8. "Regulation No. 1907/2006 of the European Parliament and of the Council of 18 December 2006 Concerning the Registration, Evaluation, Authorization and Restriction of Chemicals (REACH), Establishing a European Chemicals Agency, Amending Directive 45," 1999.
9. Ibid.

10. Roli Varma and Daya R. Varma, "The Bhopal Disaster of 1984," *Bulletin of Science, Technology and Society* 25(1) (2005): 37–45.

11. Meadows, Donella, Jorgen Randers, and Dennis Meadows. *Limits to Growth: The 30-year Update.* Chelsea Green Publishing, 2004.

12. Lyn Denend and Erica L. Plambeck, "Wal-Mart's Sustainability Strategy," Stanford Graduate School of Business, Stanford University, 2007.

13. Joan Magretta, "Growth through Global Sustainability: An Interview with Monsanto's CEO, Robert B. Shapiro," *Harvard Business Review*, January–February 1997, 79–88.

14. Silvia Francescon, "The New Directive 2001/18/EC on the Deliberate Release of Genetically Modified Organisms into the Environment: Changes and Perspectives," *Review of European, Comparative and International Environmental Law* 10(3) (2001): 309–320.

15. Robert C. Carlson and Dariush Rafinejad, "Business and Environmental Sustainability at Toyota Motor Corporation: Development of the Prius Hybrid Vehicle," MS&E Case Study, Management Science and Engineering, Stanford School of Engineering, 2007.

16. Charles O. Holliday Jr., Stephan Schmidheiny, and Philip Watts, *Walking the Talk: The Business Case for Sustainable Development* (San Francisco: Berrett-Koehler, 2002).

17. Ibid.

18. Catherine A. Ramus, "Organizational Support for Employees: Encouraging Creative Ideas for Environmental Sustainability," *California Management Review* 43(3) (2001): 85–105.

19. P. Enkvist, Tomas Nauclér, and Jeremy M. Oppenheim, "Business Strategies for Climate Change," *McKinsey Quarterly* 2 (2008): 24.

20. Nina Kruschwitz and Knut Haanaes, "First Look: Highlights from the Third Annual Sustainability Global Executive Survey," *Sloan Management Review* 53(1) (September 21, 2011).

21. Sheila Bonini and Steven Swartz, "Bringing Discipline to Your Sustainability Initiatives," McKinsey and Company, August 2014, http://www.mckinsey.com/insights/sustainability/bringing_discipline_to_your_sustainability_initiatives?cid=other-eml-alt-mip-mck-oth-1408.

CHAPTER 11

SUSTAINABILITY STANDARDS AND PRODUCT RATINGS

An increasing awareness of the need for sustainability in product design and operational practices has given rise to the creation of myriad standards and rating systems. These standards include methodologies for the consistent assessment of sustainability efforts and metrics for the characterization of the environmental and social impacts of products and enterprise operations. Some of these metrics are targeted to specific product types and industries, such as electronics products or textiles, while others measure the environmental and social footprint of an organization. In this chapter, a handful of these standards and metrics are reviewed. Although this coverage is not comprehensive, it provides a broad overview of the intent and approach of the standards. This is a dynamic and rapidly changing field. As understanding of the subject matter deepens and sustainability practices become widespread in industry, old standards are modified and new ones are created.

Eco-Efficiency and Eco-Effectiveness

The eco-efficiency of a product is defined as the ratio of its economic creation to its ecological destruction.[1] Economic creation equals the price minus the costs of manufacturing the product and abating its environmental impact. Ecological destruction is the normalized environmental impact of the product based on its life-cycle assessment (LCA). Eco-efficiency improvements can be achieved by redesigning or reengineering the product. Redesigning improves the efficiency of existing products, and reengineering creates a new efficient design. For example, to improve the fuel efficiency of a car, its internal combustion engine can be redesigned or can be reengineered as a hybrid drive system with regenerative capability that recovers lost energy in deceleration. Companies use the framework shown in Figure 11.1 to assess the eco-efficiency of a new product in comparison with a baseline product.

Toshiba Corporation characterizes environmentally conscious products by Factor T, which is a metric of improvement in the eco-efficiency of products[2] and is

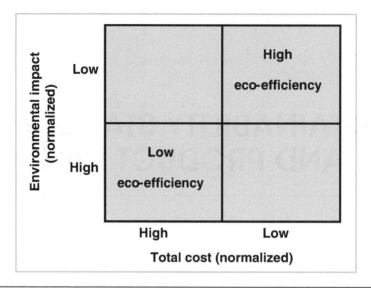

Figure 11.1   A framework for product portfolio analysis with eco-efficiency

calculated by dividing the eco-efficiency of a product subject to assessment by the eco-efficiency of the benchmark product. The higher the eco-efficiency of a product, the larger its Factor T becomes. The benchmark product is usually a previous model of the product, subject to assessment.

Eco-effectiveness means achieving the desired function of a product with the least ecological impact. To achieve eco-effectiveness, the problem often has to be redefined, and a different product concept or business model needs to be invented. For example, instead of redesigning a car to improve fuel efficiency, efficient transportation could be offered by train or rapid bus service.

The International Organization for Standardization Environmental Standards System

The International Organization for Standardization (ISO) develops and publishes international standards and provides practical tools for tackling many of today's global challenges. ISO standards are listed on the organization's website[3] and cover myriad topics, such as quality management, environmental management, and social responsibility.

The ISO 14000 family of standards provides practical tools for many different kinds of companies and organizations that are looking to manage their environmental responsibilities.[4] Table 11.1 lists the existing and upcoming environmental standards in the 14000 family.[5]

Table 11.1   The ISO 14000 series of environmental standards, 2015

Series	Standards area: description or guidelines
14001	Environmental management system
14004	Complements 14001 with additional guidance and useful explanations
14010	General environmental auditing principles
14031	Environmental performance evaluation
14020	Environmental labels and declarations general principles
14040	Guidelines on the principles and conduct of life-cycle assessment
14041	Life-cycle assessment impact assessment
14064	Greenhouse gas accounting and verification
14065	Requirements to accredit organizations that undertake ISO 14064
14063	Environmental communications to external stakeholders
ISO Guide 64	Environmental aspects in product standards (for standard developers and product designers and manufacturers)
14045	Eco-efficiency assessment
14051	Material flow cost accounting
14067	Requirements for quantification and communication of the carbon footprint of products
14069	Calculate the carbon footprint of products, services, and the supply chain
14005	Phased implementation of an environmental management system
14006	Ecodesign
14033	Compiling and communicating quantitative environmental information
14066	Competency requirements for greenhouse gas validators and verifiers

Ecolabels

The ISO 14020 family covers three types of ecolabels: Type I is a multi-attribute label developed by a third party, Type II is a single-attribute label developed by the producer, and Type III is an ecolabel whose award is based on a full LCA. Type III environmental declarations present quantified environmental information on the life cycle of a product to enable comparisons between products that are fulfilling the same function.

Figure 11.2 shows a few ecolabels that have been developed by the U.S. Environmental Protection Agency (EPA), the European Union (EU), the United Nations (UN), and other organizations. These labels are described below with a link to their Internet sources:

Figure 11.2   Selected ecolabels

- **EPA:** The EPA's Energy Star logo is a Type II ecolabel and indicates energy efficiency in products, buildings, and plants. www.energystar.gov
- **EU:** To qualify for the EU's Ecolabel, products have to comply with a rigorous set of criteria. These environmental criteria are set by a panel of experts from a number of stakeholders (including consumer organizations and industry) and take the whole product life cycle into account—extraction of raw materials, production, packaging, transport, use, and recycling. http://ec.europa.eu/environment/ecolabel
- **UN:** The UN's SA 8000 focuses on social accountability based on labor practices in manufacturing and the supply chain. The SA 8000 standard is an auditable social certification standard for decent workplaces across all industrial sectors. It is based on the UN Declaration of Human Rights and conventions of the International Labor Organization, the UN, and national law—and spans industry and corporate codes to create a common language to measure social performance. http://www.sa-intl.org/
- **U.S. Green Building Council (USGBC):** The USGBC's Leadership in Energy and Environmental Design is a Type I ecolabel and signifies the eco-effectiveness of buildings. http://www.usgbc.org/leed
- **Green Seal:** The Green Seal organization's label signifies sustainability standards for products, services, and companies that are based on life-cycle research. http://www.greenseal.org
- **Forest Stewardship Council (FSC):** The FSC provides a sustainable ecolabel for forest products. https://us.fsc.org/en-us

Environmental Product Declarations

Environmental product declarations (EPDs) are ecolabels that disclose the environmental performance of products based on an environmental LCA.[6] An EPD is the Type III ecolabel described in ISO 14025. An EPD resembles a nutrition label and discloses the amount of each environmental impact implied by the product based on the LCA of the product. EU countries are beginning to require EPDs on products sold in the region. An EPD is a verified and registered document that communicates transparent and comparable information about the life-cycle environmental impact of a product. The International EPD® System is a global program for environmental declarations based on ISO 14025 and EN 15804.

The Value Chain Index

The value chain index (VCI) "provides a way to make apples-to-apples comparisons of products on the basis of the impacts that accrue to them at each phase of their journey from raw material to consumed, discarded good."[7] The VCI draws on multiple data categories, such as land use, water, energy, carbon, toxics, and social welfare.

Patagonia's founder, Yvon Chouinard,[8] proposed the following approach for improving the VCI in an industry:

1. An industry coalition defines the VCI for a particular industry.
2. Design for sustainability is implemented across the supply chain to improve the VCI.
3. Investors include the VCI in their assessments.
4. Legislators enact regulations supporting sustainability.

The Ecological Footprint

An ecological footprint is the land and water area that a human population requires to produce the resources it consumes and to absorb its wastes. The concept of the ecological footprint is discussed in more detail in Chapter 1.

The Chemical Footprint Project

The Chemical Footprint Project (CFP) is a new initiative founded by the environmental nonprofit Clean Production Action,[9] the Lowell Center for Sustainable Production at the University of Massachusetts at Lowell, and the sustainability consultancy Pure Strategies. CFP's mission is to transform global chemical use by measuring and disclosing data on business progress in moving to using safer chemicals. The CFP aims to establish a common metric for assessing progress to safer chemicals, bring transparency to chemicals management practices, and benchmark company performance. Similar to carbon footprinting, the CFP applies clear and consistent metrics to help purchasers select suppliers based on how they manage their chemical footprint. These metrics also help investors integrate chemical risk into their sustainability and investments analyses.

Several chemical producers and users are proactive in reducing or banning chemicals of concern (which are known to cause health and environmental harm) such as formaldehyde, triclosan, toluene, diethyl phthalate, dibutyl phthalate, nonylphenol ethoxylates, butylparaben, and propylparaben.

Formaldehyde is a carcinogen found in resins for wood products, building materials, paints, and some consumer products (like cosmetics). Triclosan is a chemical used in antibacterial soaps, toothpaste, and some cosmetics. Triclosan is not known to be hazardous to humans, but some animal studies have shown that it alters hormone regulation, according to the U.S. Food and Drug Administration. Toluene is a colorless liquid that is used in paint thinners, nail polish, and fragrances. Diethyl phthalate makes plastics more flexible and is also used in cosmetics, insecticides, and aspirin. Nonylphenol exthoxylates, which are surfactants, are used in industrial applications and consumer products such as laundry detergent. Butylparabens are used as a preservative in cosmetics. Dibutyl phthalate is a solvent, and propylparaben is another preservative.[10]

The Electronic Product Environmental Assessment Tool

The Electronic Product Environmental Assessment Tool (EPEAT)[11] was created by the electronics industry in 2006 to provide a consumer-facing rating based on more than 50 environmental criteria, including use of heavy metals and toxic flame retardants. EPEAT criteria include reduction or elimination of environmentally sensitive materials, material selection, design for end of life, product longevity or life extension, energy conservation, end-of-life management, corporate performance, and packaging.

The GoodGuide Rating

GoodGuide is a comprehensive resource for information about the health, environmental, and social performance of consumer products and companies.[12] It was founded in 2007 by Dara O'Rourke, a professor of environmental and labor policy at the University of California at Berkeley. Consumers can search or browse over 210,000 foods, toys, personal care, and household products to find better products that are healthy, green, and socially responsible. Consumers can search for a product on the GoodGuide website or use a smartphone application to scan a product's bar code and see a rating. GoodGuide ratings range from 0 to 10: the higher the score, the better the product.

Corporate Rankings

The following sections list a few ranking systems that assess sustainability practices of corporations, including the Newsweek Green Ranking, Global Reporting Initiative (GRI), and Sustainability Maturity Index (SMI).

The *Newsweek* Green Ranking

The *Newsweek* Green Rankings[13] are assessments of corporate environmental performance. The project features eight indicators that are used to assess and measure the environmental performance of the world's largest publicly traded companies. The indicators assess productivity in energy, greenhouse gases, water, and waste; green revenue score; sustainability pay link; sustainability board committee; and audited environmental metrics.[14]

The Global Reporting Initiative

The GRI is a nonprofit international independent organization that helps businesses, governments, and other organizations understand and communicate the impact of business on critical sustainability issues such as climate change, human rights, and corruption.[15] The GRI's vision is to *create a future where sustainability is integral to every organization's decision-making process.*

The GRI provides all companies and organizations with a comprehensive sustainability reporting framework that is widely used around the world. The categories and aspects of the GRI reporting are as follows:

- **Economic**: Economic performance, market presence, indirect economic impacts, procurement practices
- **Environmental**: Materials, energy, water, biodiversity, emissions, effluents and waste, products and services, compliance, transport, overall, supplier environmental assessment, environmental grievance mechanisms
- **Labor practices and decent work**: Employment, labor and management relations, occupational health and safety, training and education, diversity and equal opportunity, equal remuneration for women and men, supplier assessment for labor practices, labor practices grievance mechanisms
- **Human rights**: Investment, nondiscrimination, freedom of association and collective bargaining, child labor, forced or compulsory labor, security practices, indigenous rights, assessment, supplier human rights assessment, human rights grievance mechanisms
- **Society**: Local communities, anticorruption, public policy, anticompetitive behavior, compliance, supplier assessment for impacts on society, grievance mechanisms for impacts on society
- **Product responsibility**: Customer health and safety, product and service labeling, marketing communications, customer privacy, compliance

The Sustainability Maturity Index

The SMI assesses the level of maturity and leadership of an organization in integrating sustainability principles into its business strategy and operational practices. The details of this rating system are described in Chapter 2.

Questions and Exercises

1. Which of the sustainability standards and product rating methodologies described in this chapter are applicable to a software company and its software products? Give an example.
2. How would you utilize the eco-efficiency metric in continuous improvement projects of a product to reduce its environmental impact over its life cycle?
3. Can you identify three products and/or companies that are effective in using ecolabels for competitive advantage?

Endnotes

1. Peter Saling et al., "Eco-efficiency Analysis by BASF: The Method," *International Journal of Life Cycle Assessment* 7(4) (2002): 203–218.
2. Environmental impacts are calculated using the Life Cycle Impact Assessment (LCIA) Method based on Endpoint Modeling (LIME), developed by Japan's National Institute of Advanced Industrial Science and Technology (AIST) through a life-cycle assessment project run by that country's Ministry of Economy, Trade, and Industry (METI) and New Energy and Industrial Technology Development Organization (NEDO).
3. International Organization for Standardization (ISO), http://www.iso.org.
4. International Organization for Standardization (ISO), http://www.iso.org/iso/home/standards/management-standards/iso14000.htm.
5. International Organization for Standardization (ISO), "ISO 14000 Standards: Environmental Management," http://www.iso.org/iso/home/standards/management-standards/iso14000.htm.
6. Rita C. Schenck, "A Roadmap to Environmental Product Declarations in the United States," American Center for Life Cycle Assessment (ACLCA) and Institute for Environmental Research and Education (IERE), 2010, http://iere.org.
7. Yvon Chouinard and Vincent Stanley, *The Responsible Company: What We've Learned from Patagonia's First Forty Years* (Ventura, CA: Patagonia Books, 2012).
8. Ibid.
9. Clean Production Action, www.cleanproduction.org.
10. Lauren Coleman-Lochner and Andrew Martin, "Wal-Mart Asks Its Suppliers to Stop Using Eight Chemicals," Bloomberg, July 20, 2016, http://www.bloomberg.com/news/articles/2016-07-20/wal-mart-asks-suppliers-to-remove-eight-chemicals-from-products.
11. Green Electronics Council, EPEAT, http://www.epeat.net/about-epeat.
12. GoodGuide, GoodGuide Ratings, http://www.goodguide.com.
13. "Green 2015," Newsweek, http://www.newsweek.com/green-2015.

14. The Newsweek Green Rankings are as follows: (1) combined energy productivity (15%); (2) combined greenhouse gas productivity (15%); (3) combined water productivity (15%); (4) combined waste productivity (15%); (5) green revenue score (20%); (6) sustainability pay link (10%); (7) sustainability board committee (5%); and (8) audited environmental metrics (5%).

15. Global Reporting Initiative, https://www.globalreporting.org/Pages/default.aspx, https://www.globalreporting.org/standards/g4/Pages/default.aspx.

CHAPTER 12

DECISION ANALYSIS AND MODELING IN PRODUCT DEVELOPMENT: SYSTEM DYNAMICS MODELING

Sustainable product development involves myriad strategic and tactical decisions related to technology, design, marketing, operations, investment, and other areas. Good (or right) decisions are not the impromptu creations of inspired minds but the result of careful decision analysis, involving both deliberation (which is informed by data, experience, and reason) and intuition (which connects us to our creative essence). Decisions are of three types—right, wrong, and bad—according to their outcome and the process followed in making the decision. Right decisions follow an appropriate process (involving deliberation and intuition) and result in appropriate actions that produce the desired outcome. Wrong decisions follow an appropriate process, but because of uncertainties in predicting the future, do not produce the desired outcome. Finally, bad decisions do not follow an appropriate process and result in an undesirable outcome. Although wrong decisions are unsuccessful, they increase knowledge and help the decision analysis in future iterations of the process.

Decision making requires information about the current state, relevant issues, decision parameters, and knowledge of the system characteristics. It also requires establishing the objective of the decision analysis and the criteria for setting priorities and making choices. And finally, a model needs to be developed for predicting the future state by pursuing alternate decision paths. Because we often are faced with uncertainty in decision analysis, we must make assumptions in the model and assign probabilities to the likelihood of alternate exogenous events. The sustainability requirements in product development introduce an additional degree of complexity in decision analysis because of the time-integrated impacts and nonlinearities in system behavior.

In this chapter, we review a few practical decision-making processes and modeling techniques, including system dynamics that help decision makers uncover leverage points in a system and focus resources accordingly.

The Decision-Making Process

At the onset of a decision-making process, the decision maker must clearly define the problem and decision-making objectives and frame the decision that needs to be made. Often, the optimal decision must satisfy multiple objectives that could be competing—that is, one objective might be met but at the expense of not meeting another.

For example, the goal is to design a product that satisfies three objectives—low manufacturing cost, low environmental impact (according to a life-cycle assessment [LCA]), and short time to market. Each objective has a target value that we desire to achieve. The decision is to choose between two design alternatives proposed by the engineers: one option meets the time-to-market target but falls short of the manufacturing cost and environmental impact targets, and the other option misses the time-to-market and manufacturing cost targets but exceeds the environmental impact target. Which design alternative is the optimal choice? The decision makers' values are pivotal in answering this question because they establish the degree of importance and hence the ranking of the three objectives. Also, the decision makers need to quantify how close each design comes in meeting the targets. A decision model must be created to account for these considerations. In this example, the model might be a simple scoring algorithm where the design option with the highest aggregate score would be the optimal choice. The score in satisfying an objective would be proportional to how close the design comes to meeting the target. The aggregate score of a design, or its figure of merit, would be the sum of the weighted scores where the ranking of objectives would determine their weight.

In the decision-making process, the decision maker who has both the authority and accountability for the decision must be identified at the onset. Many people might contribute to the decision analysis (such as through data collection and model development) and participate in deliberations. However, the decision maker is the person who clarifies the values, establishes the degree of importance of alternate decision criteria, and approves the final decision. Collective decision making by majority vote or consensus are acceptable alternatives but not preferred in product development.

The subsequent steps in the decision-making process are as follows:

1. Identify the critical issues related to the decision.
2. Collect data regarding the critical issues, and develop a decision model.
3. Synthesize the data to arrive at solution options.
4. Apply the model to select the optimal choice, and make a decision.
5. Make a sensitivity analysis of uncertainties and assumptions.
6. Implement the decision.

The critical issues are the parameters that are built in the decision-analysis model to assess alternate paths and choose the optimal decision. The team should thoroughly research the critical issues and collect secondary and primary data. It is important to consult with all stakeholders who will be affected by the decision. Data analysis and synthesis should lead to the identification of a few (not more than three or four) decision alternatives to solve the problem.

The decision model is the tool for assessing decision alternatives and selecting the optimal alternative based on the decision criteria that were established at the beginning of the process. Because the input data might be inadequate and have a high degree of uncertainty, decision makers should perform sensitivity analysis of uncertain variables and assumptions in the model. They also could perform a sensitivity analysis of the priorities and weight factors assigned to different objectives.

The last step in this process is to implement the decision and verify that the problem has been solved or that the desired outcome has been achieved.

Example: Select the Optimum Product Concept in Phase 1 of the Product Development Process

Let's consider a case where a choice must be made among three alternate product concepts that have emerged as a result of user-need research in product development. The concepts have commercial opportunities in different market segments, face different competitors, and require different business models. The critical issues or decision parameters relative to each product concept are sustainability, served-market size (that is, business opportunity), ease of market entry (based on the required investment capital or brand value), difficulty in developing the necessary technology, time to penetrate the market, competitors' strength, intellectual property (IP) protection (whether the concept or technology can be patented or not), and the firm's capabilities and resources for developing and marketing the product. The decision-analysis model is a scorecard where each candidate is assigned a score based on its strength or weakness relative to each decision parameter. Because the decision parameters are not of equal importance, the model is built with a provision for assigning a weight factor to each parameter. For example, market attractiveness might be more important than technological difficulty (because you can mitigate it by hiring a skilled technologist). The model calculates the aggregate score for each product concept as the sum of the weighted scores with respect to each decision parameter. The optimal concept is the one with the highest aggregate score. The model is shown in Table 12.1.

Note that in this simple model, many subjective choices (such as the weights that were assigned to different decision parameters) were made. The strength and weakness scores of a product concept regarding a decision parameter also were subjective and based on the implied probability of achieving the relevant outcome. A more sophisticated model can be developed. For example, the sustainability score of a design concept might be calculated based on a detailed LCA and the LCA impact's

Table 12.1 A concept-selection scorecard

	Sustainability	Market size	Technological difficulty	Ease of market entry	Time to market	Competitors' strength	IP protection	Firm capabilities	Aggregate weighted score
Weight factor (0 to 1)	1.0	1.0	0.5	0.8	0.7	0.5	0.5	1	
Concept 1	3	5	1	4	3	4	5	5	23.36
Concept 2	5	2	4	2	3	4	3	5	21.20
Concept 3	5	4	2	4	5	3	4	3	23.20

Note: 1 = very weak; 5 = very strong.

proximity to a specified environmental impact goal. Time to market might be estimated with a detailed project plan for the development of alternate concepts to market launch.

Even with the simple model in this example, an important value of the decision analysis is to sharpen the decision-making team's understanding of the risks and rewards of the candidate concepts and to create shared knowledge among the team members. After the analysis, intuition and the team's passion for different product concepts should also be considered before the final decision is made.

Pitfalls in Decision Making

Cognitive bias, risk averseness, personal agendas, and undue haste in making a decision may derail a creative decision-analysis process. These faults or traps impact the framing of a problem, the values that help set decision criteria, the data-collection approach, model development, and other aspects of the decision-analysis process. The *hidden traps*[1] in decision making that must be watched for and circumvented in the decision-making process are listed here:

- **Anchoring:** Using initial impressions, estimates, or data to make subsequent thoughts or judgments
- **Perpetuating the status quo:** Choosing the option that creates the least change and risk
- **Justifying sunk costs:** Using previous expenditures to prolong actions based on past (bad) decisions
- **Being biased toward a preconceived outcome:** Seeking out confirming evidence and the information that supports the team's inclinations
- **Being biased when framing:** Stating the problem in a way that establishes anchoring or status quo biases
- **Being overconfident:** Feeling that information is not necessary
- **Exercising overcautious prudence:** Seeking too much information and getting paralyzed by analysis
- **Recalling incorrectly:** Being biased by past events and memories that may not be well calibrated

Risk Assessment in Decision Making

In developing a new-to-the-world sustainable product, we often make many decisions as we choose among alternate market opportunities, technology paths, design approaches, and commercialization strategies. The trade-off studies for selecting the optimal decision are commonly challenged by inadequate information and a lack of appropriate analytical models. For example, market conditions might be turbulent and highly uncertain, we may not have the experimental data or theoretical modeling capability to assess the performance of a design with a high degree of confidence, and there might be uncertainties in evaluating the life-cycle impact of the product on the environment, human health, and society. In spite of these uncertainties, we have to make decisions (even if they are risky) and move forward—by choosing a market strategy, adopting a technology, and selecting a design concept—or risk missing the market opportunity altogether.

Risk is the probability of suffering loss or harm from an event or hazard. Risk taking means making decisions and acting without the necessary knowledge and therefore facing the possibility of loss. Calculated risk taking, on the other hand, means making decisions that are informed by a pros-and-cons analysis of the expected outcome of ensuing action. Innovative organizations promote calculated risk taking and experimentation to learn quickly and improve the accuracy of making predictions.

The decisions in product development aim to optimize one or more utility functions, such as return on investment, time to market, market share, brand equity, liability abatement, and product sustainability. The decision-making process must include risk assessment, including the probability of the occurrence of a harmful impact and the consequence of the impact on utility functions. Risk assessment might be influenced by subjective factors: is the risk feared, is it new and unfamiliar, is the victim known and identifiable, is it equitable? A higher degree of severity is assigned to risks that are feared (like cancer) or unfamiliar. Also, in assessing the consequence of risk, we underestimate the significance of loss if the victims are unknown or represented by a statistical figure.

Three types of risks must be assessed and mitigated in the sustainable product development process:

- **Social, health, and environmental risks:** The risks caused by the product include the probability of the occurrence of a harmful event, magnitude of the impact, and exposure and vulnerability of the subjects
- **Product strategy risks:** These risks include business, marketing, technology, and operational risks
- **Project management risks:** These are the risks in achieving the desired objectives and on-time completion of the product development project[2]

In the remainder of this chapter, selected modeling techniques are discussed that can be used in analyzing decisions and understanding the behavior of systems in sustainable product development and operations.

Modeling

A model is a symbolic representation of a system in the real world. A system is a group of functionally interrelated elements that form a complex whole. The system might be a product comprising several components, a manufacturing assembly process, a supply chain, or a business process. Systems thinking considers the interactions of system elements in analyzing complex problems and making decisions. A model can analyze and explain, optimize a system, predict an outcome, or help us draw conclusions and make decisions.

An example is shown in Figure 12.1, which illustrates a conceptual model adopted by the California Environmental Protection Agency to identify the indicators of climate change and to establish a response strategy for mitigating their impact.[3] In this model, (1) the drivers of climate change establish (2) the climate state manifested by the changes in the climate, which, in turn, results in (3) the impacts on both physical and biological systems, and (4) the response to these effects include greenhouse gas (GHG) emission reductions and adaptation strategies. The response actions impact the pressure (that is, the drivers of the climate change) in a feedback loop shown in Figure 12.1.

Figure 12.2 illustrates the relationship of the real world to the virtual world of a model adopted from John Sterman.[4] In the real world, we make decisions to effect change and achieve a desired outcome. However, our interactions with the real world occur in a closed loop as shown in Figure 12.2. Our decision-making process follows the strategies, structures, and decision rules that we establish based on our mental model of how the real world works. After the decision is implemented, we verify if the desired change has been attained by examining the information feedback from the real world. This information might create new learning and change our mental model of the world, which in turn would persuade us to change our strategy (or even the structure and decision rules). The decision is then amended to change the real world in the next iterative cycle. The cycle of learning and amending the decision continues until the desired outcome is achieved. It should be noted that our mental model of the real world and the information feedback interact in yet another loop within the larger interactive loop. This interactive loop is also shown in Figure 12.2. When we receive information feedback, our mental model of the world might change, which might in turn result in a different interpretation of the feedback information.

In a complex system, the above decision-making process and interactive learning cycle are quite challenging. Consider solving an environmental and social

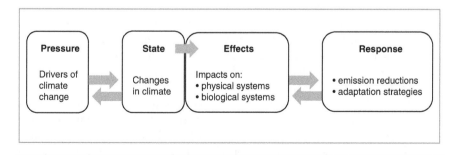

Figure 12.1   A conceptual model for climate-change indicators

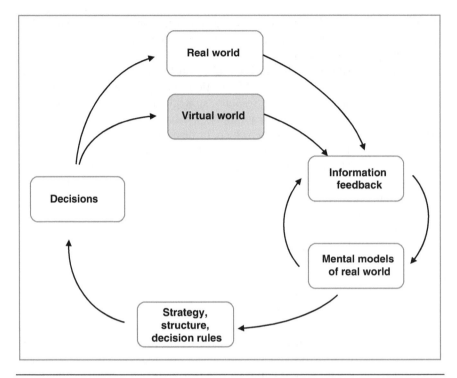

Figure 12.2   Using decision making with modeling in the real world

sustainability problem. There is often a long delay between the time when the decision is made and the time when information feedback about the impact of the decision is received. It also would be difficult and expensive to conduct a controlled experiment to compare the future states of the environment or society with and without our decision. In addition, the interpretation of feedback from the real world and the application of scientific reasoning to shape our mental model are prone to many biases and judgmental errors.

To overcome these shortcomings and limitations, we create a virtual world by means of a model that can be physical or a computer simulation of the real world. With the model as the virtual world, the cycles of learning can be carried out the same way as in the real world. However, after the decision has been optimized with the model, it has to be implemented in the real world, and it must be verified that the desired outcome has been achieved.

Using a model accelerates the process and increases the probability of arriving at a right decision. As John Sterman points out, modeling (or the virtual world) is not panacea and does not overcome the flaws in our mental models. However, creating the model and verifying that it is a reasonable representation of the real world provides opportunities for challenging built-in mental biases and providing a common

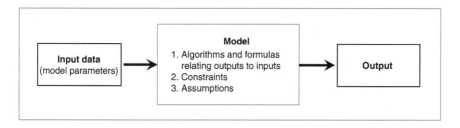

Figure 12.3   A model with its input and output relationships

understanding of the key issues and relationships among the decision makers and other stakeholders. The process of creating and verifying the model also helps improve the scientific reasoning skills of decision makers.

A model comprises algorithms or mathematical formulas that relate output variables to input or model variables. It must have a clear purpose, and it must be able to solve a particular problem. Figure 12.3 shows a schematic of a model.

There are two types of variables (or parameters) in a model—exogenous and endogenous. Exogenous variables are input parameters or independent variables. Endogenous variables are output parameters or dependent variables—things that the model seeks to explain. Assumptions and constraints also are associated with a model. Assumptions include the definition of variables and their interrelations, and constraints bound the problem and the domain of the model.

Models can be static or dynamic, mathematical or physical, and stochastic or deterministic. Different models (such as optimization, simulation, or econometrics models) are suited for different purposes, as explained below.

Optimization Models

Optimization models seek the best way to accomplish a goal. They are normative and prescribe what to do. In optimization models, an objective function is chosen to be optimized—either maximized or minimized. Then the decision variables or the choices to be made are selected. These are determined by the model to optimize the objective function. Constraints in the optimization models are specified to restrict the choices of decision variables.

Many operations problems can be solved by optimization modeling techniques, such as linear programming (LP) and dynamic programming. However, there are limitations to what the optimization models can do. For example, the relationships in the system that are being modeled are assumed to be linear for mathematical convenience, but in complex systems the linearity assumption is often unrealistic. Furthermore, the complex objective functions that we often encounter in solving sustainability problems are difficult to specify in simple mathematical terms. In the following sections, a few examples of the optimization modeling technique in decision making are discussed.

Problem 1: Optimizing Production to Minimize Cost (Analytical Solution)

The issue in this problem is to determine the optimal frequency of production runs in a manufacturing operation, in order to achieve the lowest marginal cost of production. The objective function is the operations cost per unit of time. The exogenous variables are the holding cost of a finished goods inventory, the cost of raw material storage, the setup cost of a production run, and the shortage cost (or cost of losing a customer if inventory runs low). There is only one endogenous variable (the variable that the factory can control), and that is the time between production runs. The constraint and assumption in the model are that all orders must be filled and the size of a customer order is random. Figure 12.4 depicts the variation of production inventory as a function of time. Inventories for raw materials and finished goods are plotted over an order fulfillment period, T. Raw materials are depleted at a faster rate than needed for order fulfillment. Hence, the inventory of finished goods rises over the production run of t days, as shown in Figure 12.4.

In this example, we need to determine the time between production runs that minimizes the production cost per day. We formulate an equation for the total production cost per day as a function of both exogenous and endogenous variables and differentiate it with respect to T to obtain its minima, where:

$$\text{Cost per day } c = \frac{s}{T} + \frac{\left[e(r-f)+df\right](fT)}{2r}$$

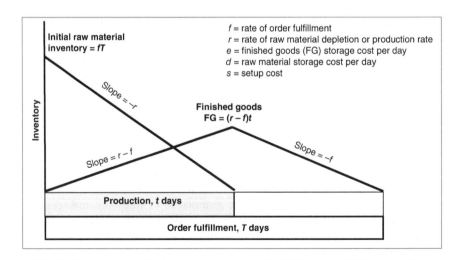

f = rate of order fulfillment
r = rate of raw material depletion or production rate
e = finished goods (FG) storage cost per day
d = raw material storage cost per day
s = setup cost

Initial raw material inventory = fT

Slope = –r

Slope = r – f

Finished goods
FG = (r – f)t

Slope = –f

Inventory

Production, t days

Order fulfillment, T days

Figure 12.4   A production optimization problem

$$C \text{ is minimum when } \frac{\partial C}{\partial T} = 0.$$

Therefore, the optimal values of T and t will be:

$$T = \sqrt{\frac{2rs}{f\left[e(r-f)+df\right]}} \qquad t = \sqrt{\frac{2fs}{r\left[e(r-f)+df\right]}}.$$

This problem is relatively straightforward because an equation can be derived for the total cost per day and the equation had an analytical solution. Other optimization problems, particularly those with multiple constrains, might not have simple analytical solutions and might require the use of other methodologies—such as linear programming, dynamic programming, or computer models—to find the optimum solution.

Problem 2: Using an Energy Mix to Minimize Costs and Carbon Emissions (Linear Programming)

The Community Choice Aggregation (CCA) law in California allows communities to establish their own energy supply organizations independent of the electric utilities that traditionally have had a monopoly on the supply of electricity to the end users. The CCAs are free to purchase electricity from independent producers, which allows them to maximize renewable energy in their portfolio and minimize their contributions to GHG (carbon) emissions and global warming.

The situation in this section is the case of a CCA that plans to purchase electricity from two sources—solar photovoltaic farms and natural gas power plants. The annual energy demand is 100 gigawatt hours (GWh). Solar energy costs more but has lower life-cycle carbon emissions than electricity obtained from the natural gas plant. The CCA likes to determine the lowest-cost mix of solar and gas to satisfy the demand without exceeding the annual target for emissions of 6,000 tons of carbon equivalent. The problem can be formulated as follows, where:

Solar annual purchase (in GWh) = X
Gas annual purchase (in GWh) = Y
Cost of electricity to CCA from solar = 10 cents/kWh
Cost of electricity to CCA from gas = 4 cents/kWh
Life-cycle carbon emissions from solar = 6 tons/GWh
Life-cycle carbon emissions from gas = 600 tons/GWh
Total annual cost of electricity supply in thousands of dollars: $C = 100X + 40Y$

We need to determine the values of X and Y that minimize C while satisfying the following constraints:

Demand fulfillment: $X + Y \geq 100$ GWh
Carbon emissions target: $6X + 600Y \leq 6{,}000$

The above LP problem can be solved graphically or by using a Microsoft Excel Solver routine. The optimal solution is $X = 90.9$ GWh and $Y = 9.1$ GWh. The optimal cost (lowest-cost) solution is \$9,454,500 per year.

Problem 3: Using Decision Optimization in an Uncertain Environment (Dynamic Programming)

Tim Kraft and his colleagues[5] have developed an optimization model for a firm that is faced with a decision about if and when to replace a potentially hazardous material within a product. The substance is not banned by regulations, but there is a chance that regulations might be enacted in the planning period. There is also pressure from some consumers and nongovernmental organizations to find a safe substitute for the material. Furthermore, there is a chance that competitors might remove the substance from their products before the firm does and gain a comparative advantage.

Under these uncertain regulatory and market conditions, the model addresses two decisions—if and when to develop a substitute material and if and when to implement the change in the product. The objective function is the total expected cost—as the sum of the cost of development of the substitute material, cost of implementation in the product, and cost of market share loss if regulations go into effect or competitors develop a substitute before the firm has implemented a solution. (Kraft and his colleagues provide details about how the problem is laid out in phases and how the dynamic programming technique is used to solve it.)

Simulation Models

Simulation models are descriptive and create a virtual world of the real system to help us study its behavior and learn the effects of alternate decision options. Laboratory models (full-scale or subscale) do the same for experimentalists. Simulation models, such as system dynamics, can include nonlinearity, feedback, dynamic behavior, and delays. A simulation model comprises the elements (or actors) and structure of the system and the rules that describe how the system elements work and interact with each other.

The model should be validated by using it to predict the behavior of a system whose performance is known (analytically or experimentally), particularly at the extremes and boundary conditions.

Simulation models have several limitations, especially when they aim to model social and environmental systems. For example, it can be difficult to describe decision rules and quantify soft variables. Also, the choice of model boundary or the system's control volume impacts the determination of both exogenous and endogenous variables and the simulation outcome.

In the following sections, an example of a simulation model is reviewed, and the system dynamics modeling technique (which is particularly relevant to many sustainability problems) is discussed.

Modeling Sustainability in Product Development and Commercialization

In developing a new product, multiple decisions are made to choose the optimal product concept, design, and investment strategy. These decisions are optimized based on both financial and market impacts. In decisions pertaining to the development of sustainable products, we must consider additional factors known as externalities, including the life-cycle impact of the product on the earth's sources, sinks, and ecological systems—and on future generations. The cost of externalities—that is, the cost of harm inflicted on people and the environment—must be internalized as an additional cost of developing, producing, and commercializing the product. For example, costs are incurred when the choices of future generations are limited by depleting nonrenewable resources and by consuming renewable resources at a rate faster than they can replenish. Similarly, the firm should internalize the costs of environmental and social harms caused by the product in manufacturing, use, and end of life.

Compliance with regulations should be treated differently, too. Traditionally, suppliers limit their product strategy to compliance with local regulations. And because many local regulations around the world are below the best-in-class standards, the environmental and social performance of products remains suboptimal in much of the world. Sustainable products must comply with the best-in-class standards irrespective of local requirements.

The aforementioned approach in sustainable product development has been incorporated into a simulation model by Robert C. Carlson and the author.[6] The model's block diagram is shown in Figure 12.5.[7] It depicts the system variables and their interrelationships. In addition to accounting for the cost of externalities, the model includes the following provisions: noncompliance to regulations results in the total loss of market in applicable segments, voluntary compliance above local regulations captures a price premium and market-share advantage, and design for sustainability increases research and development costs. The model's framework can be used to answer the following questions:

- To what extent should the product be designed for recyclability and reuse?
- What is the optimal mix of renewable and nonrenewable resources in design, manufacturing, and consumables?
- How should future environmental regulatory mandates be treated?
- Is it better to wait until the regulations demanding recycled and renewable resources are in effect?
- Should the firm adopt a voluntary and uniform sustainability strategy across all served-market segments?
- Should the firm forego serving a market segment that imposes stringent requirements?

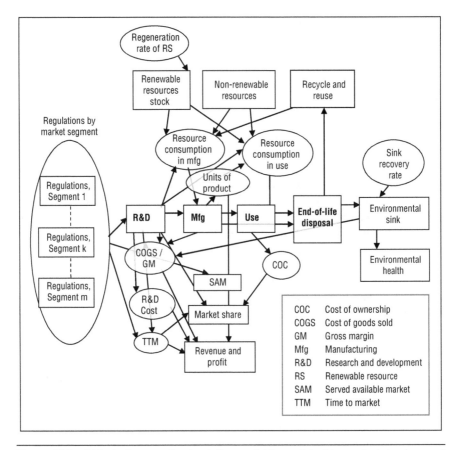

Figure 12.5   A block diagram of a simulation model for sustainable product development

System Dynamics Modeling

System dynamics is a technique for modeling the behavior of complex and nonlinear systems over time with feedback loops and delayed reactions. This technique is suited for analyzing many sustainability-related problems and decisions in business. The system dynamics modeling technique was first developed and used by Jay Wright Forrester.[8] Modeling an urban setting, Forrester demonstrated how the misuse of land resources could lead to the overall economic downturn of an area.[9] John D. Sterman's book[10] is an excellent reference on the subject.

In system dynamics modeling, variables are grouped into three categories—state variables (or stocks representing accumulations in the system), rate variables (or flows that adjust state variables), and auxiliary constants and accounting variables. For example, a system of bunnies, rabbits, and wolves is shown in Figure 12.6. In this causal diagram, there are three stock variables (population of bunnies, rabbits,

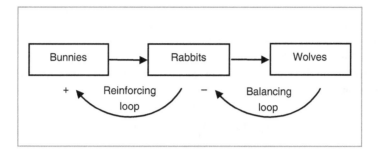

Figure 12.6 A causal diagram of a system of bunnies, rabbits, and wolves

and wolves) and two feedback loops (a reinforcing loop and a balancing loop). An increase in the population of rabbits (a stock variable) causes an increase in the population of bunnies (another stock variable), as depicted by an arrow with a plus sign. And an increase in the population of bunnies increases the number of rabbits. This is called a reinforcing loop, which leads to exponential growth or decay. On the other hand, an increase in the number of wolves (a third stock variable) causes a decline in the stock of rabbits. This is called a balancing loop and is shown by an arrow with a minus sign. Balancing loops lead to dampened fluctuations. Note that stock variables are shown by a box and feedbacks are shown by arrows with a positive or negative sign. Positive or negative feedbacks mean that the variables at the two ends of the arrows move in the same or opposite direction, respectively.

A system dynamics structure of the rabbits and wolves model is shown in Figure 12.7. The flow or rate variables are shown by the symbol of a valve. Causal influences between various variables including the auxiliary variables are shown by arrows with a sign (+ or –).

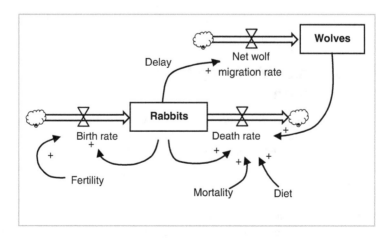

Figure 12.7 A system dynamics structure of a rabbit and wolf habitat

The next step in developing the model in this example is to formulate the relationship between the variables. Let the stocks of rabbits (R) and wolves (W) as functions of time (t) be $R(t)$ and $W(t)$, and let the birth rates (BR) and death rates (DR) of rabbits be $BR(t)$ and $DR(t)$, respectively. BR and DR depend on the fertility and mortality of rabbits and on the wolves' diet. Therefore, we can write the following equations:

$$R(t) = R(0) + \int_0^t \left[BR(t) - DR(t) \right] dt$$

$$BR(t) = R(t) \times fertility$$

$$DR(t) = R(t) \times mortality + W(t) \times diet$$

$$W(t) = W(0) + \int_0^t WMG(t) dt$$

$$WMG(t) = a \times R(t - delay)$$

where $WMG(t)$ is the net migration rate of wolves to the area near the habitat of rabbits, a is a constant, and there is a delay in this causal influence. Note also that $\dfrac{dR(t)}{dt} = BR(t) - DR(t)$, where $BR(t)$ and $DR(t)$ are functions of $R(t)$.

According to the described relationships, the model is a system of differential equations that are solved by a computer program starting at time $t = 0$ and integrating the equations over time. A solution for the stocks of rabbits and wolves is graphically displayed in Figure 12.8. Note that the population of rabbits increases early on when the population of wolves is low but declines as more wolves migrate into the common habitat. Eventually, the stock of wolves peaks with the declining rabbits. The system reaches an equilibrium over a long period of time.

System Dynamics Modeling for a Sustainable Sourcing Decision

Daniel Bryce Greenia has developed a system dynamics model[11] to study the impact of environmental regulations on global versus local product sourcing decisions. Firms in industrialized countries adopt the global (or remote) manufacturing option in developing countries for financial gain because in those regions labor costs are low and environmental regulations are either lax or not enforced. In contrast, local manufacturing is expensive because labor costs are high and there are stringent environmental regulations to minimize the environmental and human health impacts of manufacturing. Greenia's model *accounts for the environmental and*

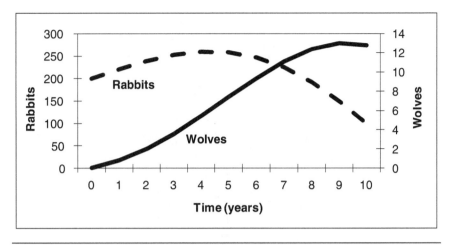

Figure 12.8   A solution to the rabbit and wolf system dynamics model

social costs that are generally ignored when firms decide to source locally or remotely.
The environmental and social costs of pollution in local and remote manufacturing
are accounted differently. The local government imposes a pollution tax or requires
an industry to invest in pollution prevention. The remote government spurs development to increase employment. However, worker productivity in remote manufacturing declines over time as workers are exposed to pollution and manufacturing
cost increases.

The system dynamics model structure discussed in Greenia's paper is shown
in Figure 12.9.[12] This structure is then turned into a system dynamics model with
stock and flow variables, causal influences, and loops. The goal is specified as the
desired ratio of remote to local production as a function of the remote to local cost
ratio. The simulation is carried out over several years of sourcing decisions, which
are revised once a year. From his system dynamics modeling, Greenia makes several
conclusions about the effectiveness of alternate government policies and finds that
*investments in preventive capital and pollution abatement, while initially costly, can
simultaneously stimulate economic development, increase human health, and save on
labor costs over a strategic time horizon.* In other words, local manufacturing in regulated countries should be looked at as a business opportunity, not a liability.

Modeling the State of the World and Limits to Growth

Donella H. Meadows, Jorgen Randers, and Dennis Meadows[13] use system dynamics modeling to *understand the broad sweep of the future—the possible modes, or
behavior patterns, through which human economy will interact with the carrying
capacity of the planet over the coming century.* This model, which is referred to as
World3, relates the demand for the earth's carrying capacity (for sources and sinks)

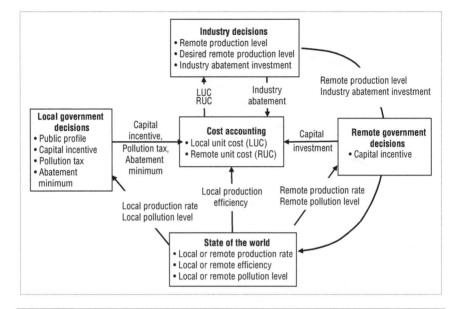

Figure 12.9   The structure of a sourcing decision model

to human population growth and industrial and agricultural production and presents possible scenarios through the twenty-first century if human development is left unchecked. In World3, stock variables include population, industrial capital (factories and machines), cultivated land, nonrenewable resources, service capital (such as health and education services), and pollution. Multiple causal relationships connect the stock variables with flow variables such as birth and death rates, investment in industrial capital per year, and industrial output. Appropriate delays are built into the causal relationships.

As a measure of human welfare, World3 uses a variable called the human welfare index (HWI), which approximates the United Nations' human development index (HDI). The HDI is proportional to life expectancy at birth, the adult literacy rate, and the standard of living as measured by gross domestic product per capita in purchasing power parity dollars.

The reference scenario in World3 is a world society that proceeds in the traditional manner without any major deviation from twentieth-century policies. For this scenario, World3 predicts that the human ecological footprint and human wealth index rise in the first two or three decades of the twenty-first century and decline (collapse) thereafter. By 2100, the HWI would be lower than it was in 1900. In contrast, in the sustainable scenario—where population and industrial output per person are constrained, and pollution, resources, and agriculture technologies from the 2002 levels are deployed—the HWI rises in the first quarter of the twenty-first century and then stabilizes. In this scenario, after an early rise, the human ecological footprint declines to late-twentieth-century levels by the year 2100.

System Dynamics and Leverage Points in Business Operations

R. Scott Marshall and Darrell Brown[14] report on the system dynamics models of business operations they developed for Norm Thompson Outfitters (NTO). These models helped the company to strengthen its sustainability initiatives. NTO, a catalog retail company, had introduced several sustainability initiatives—including using recycled paper in catalogs and merchandizing sustainable products. Marshall and Brown developed two system models for the company—the recycled paper supply and demand system and the sustainable merchandizing system. These models identified the leverage points in the systems and drove corrective actions in the company. According to Marshall and Brown, leverage points are actions that can significantly impact the desired system behavior. The leverage points in the recycled paper supply and demand system were perceived quality of recycled content and price differential between recycled and virgin paper content. The leverage points in the sustainable merchandizing system were the buyers' willingness to use sustainability criteria and the buyers' ability to choose high-margin sustainability products. These leverage points directed the strategy and resources at NTO on the actions that had the highest return on achieving the company's sustainability objectives.

For example, NTO decided to collect customer feedback on recycled paper, communicate the information widely in the industry, and encourage its peers to use recycled paper in their catalogs. Furthermore, the company started to work with suppliers to enhance investments in recycling and to lower the cost of recycled paper.

Responding to the leverage points in the sustainable merchandizing system, NTO's management decided to base its buyers' annual raise on both improvements in their sustainability scores (10%) and traditional performance metrics (90%). Training sessions also were held for the buyers, who were included in developing the sustainability tool kits (for identifying sustainable merchandise).

Questions and Exercises

1. How would you assess the validity of predictions from a model?
2. How would you identify the environmental, health, and cost leverage points in the design of a new product?
3. Can you develop a plan to apply the simulation model of Figure 12.5 to a pair of shoes? How do you determine the model parameters?

Endnotes

1. John S. Hammond, Ralph L. Keeney, and Howard Raiffa, "The Hidden Traps in Decision Making," Harvard Business Review 76(5) (September–October 1998): 47.
2. Project risks can be mitigated by building flexibility in the design and development process to allow rapid adjustment in product development decisions through continuous and real-time knowledge, learning, and feedback. This subject is discussed in more detail in Chapter 8.
3. California Environmental Protection Agency (CalEPA) and Office of Environmental Health Hazard Assessment (OEHHA), "Indicators of Climate Change in California," August 2013, p. 2.
4. John D. Sterman, *Business Dynamics: Systems Thinking and Modeling for a Complex World* (New York: McGraw-Hill Education, 2000).
5. Tim Kraft, Feryal Erhun, Robert C. Carlson, and Dariush Rafinejad, "Replacement Decisions for Potentially Hazardous Substances," *Production and Operations Management* 22(4) (2013): 958–975.
6. Robert C. Carlson and Dariush Rafinejad, "Modeling Sustainability in Product Development and Commercialization," Bulletin of Science, Technology & Society 28(6) (2008): 478–485.
7. Ibid.
8. Jay Wright Forrester, *Industrial Dynamics* (New York: Wiley, 1961).
9. Jay Wright Forrester, *Urban Dynamics* (Cambridge, MA: MIT Press, 1969).
10. John D. Sterman, Business Dynamics. There also are several excellent commercial software products for creating system dynamics models, including Vensim (http://vensim.com/vensim -brochure) and ISEE Systems (http:/www.iseesystems.com).
11. Daniel Bryce Greenia, "Essays in Sustainable Operations and Intellectual Property Management," Ph.D. dissertation, Department of Management Science and Engineering, Stanford University, 2012.
12. Adapted from Greenia, "Essays in Sustainable Operations and Intellectual Property Management."
13. Donella H. Meadows, Jorgen Randers, and Dennis Meadows, *Limits to Growth: The Thirty-Year Update* (White River Junction, VT: Chelsea Green Publishing, 2004), p. 137.
14. R. Scott Marshall and Darrell Brown, "The Strategy of Sustainability: A Systems Perspective on Environmental Initiatives," California Management Review 46(1) (2003): 101–126.

RETURN ON INVESTMENT: INTELLECTUAL PROPERTY PROTECTION

Multiple factors contribute to the financial success of a product. These factors, as shown in Chapter 5 (Figure 5.7), include technology, public policy, cost of capital, and organizational leadership and a culture of innovation. Public policy plays a pivotal role in propelling enabling technologies out of the research laboratory and into the market. For example, policy instruments such as investment and production tax credits in the U.S. and feed-in tariff laws in Germany played an instrumental role in the development of and cost reductions in solar photovoltaic (PV) technology in the first decade of the twenty-first century.

The second factor in successful commercialization of new technologies is availability and cost of capital. New technologies go through several phases of development with reducing levels of risk before they are deployed in the market, as shown in Chapter 5 (Figure 5.8). The funding for technology development in these phases is often provided by different types of investors with different appetites for risk.

At the early, high-risk phase of technology development, the cost of capital is high, and funding sources are usually individual (angel) investors, venture capitalists, and the government. This phase corresponds to the concept and feasibility phase of the product development process. The next phase of development (commercialization) comprises full design development, performance qualification, and pilot manufacturing of the product. In this phase, the risk of technology development is moderate and is mostly associated with manufacturing process technology and cost. The amount of capital available for implementation of this phase is significantly larger than in the earlier phase. Acquiring capital to enter this phase is difficult, and it is where companies face the so-called first valley of death (or fad death) in commercializing their new technology. The U.S. government has helped many entrepreneurs cross this chasm by underwriting the investment. For example, in the early 2000s, the government provided loan guarantees in support of selected solar PV start-ups. The third phase of development is the volume manufacturing phase. It requires the largest amount of capital and often represents the second valley of death (or scale death). The sources of low-cost capital for this phase are usually investment banks. These investors are risk averse and invest only if the risk of technology performance and cost of production are sufficiently low.

Return on Investment in New Product Development

The return on investment (ROI) is a cost-benefit rubric and is used to assess the financial viability of developing a new product. Traditional ROI methodologies generally ignore the environmental and social costs and benefits of a product. The cost of environmental protection (such as pollution prevention) is accounted for to the extent required by environmental laws and regulations. And the environmental and social benefits of a *green* product are assumed to be reflected in the market price of the product. The costs of harmful health and environmental impacts are mostly externalized to society, and the social benefits of a sustainable product that are not demanded by customers are not accounted for in the ROI analysis. In this section, the traditional methods of calculating ROI are reviewed, and various approaches to amend the methodology and calculate the triple-bottom-line ROI are discussed.

Traditional ROI

ROI is the ratio of the net value created by a new product to the investment necessary for its development and commercialization. The value is reflected in the price that customers are willing to pay for the product, and it is dependent on the supply and demand profile, product attractiveness, price of competing products (as a reference price), a firm's brand, and the strength of its market assets compared with other actors in the market. The net value or gross profit margin of a product is its price minus the cost of goods sold (COGS) and the cost of warranty coverage. COGS is the total cost of producing and delivering a product to the customer, including costs of manufacturing, distribution, installation, warranty, and post-sales support.

The investment pays for the nonrecurring costs of material, equipment, facilities, and labor required to design, develop, manufacture, and commercialize the new product until the first customer is satisfied. The investment is also inclusive of the cost of money, which is dependent on the discount rate and the investor's perceived risk associated with the product being successful in the market.

A simple indicator of financial success is the return factor (RF), which is the ratio of the net profits accumulated over the planning period to the total investment. The breakeven time is when the net present value (NPV) is zero and the RF equals one. Often the early-phase investors look for an RF of three or more, three years after the introduction of the product into the market.

The ROI measures the rate at which net future profits return the investment and generate a surplus. The common metric of ROI is internal rate of return (IRR). IRR is the interest (or discount) rate at which the NPV of net profits from sales of the product equates with the NPV of investments over the planning period, where net profit for a period is equal to the revenue minus COGS and operating costs. For example, if the total investment made in year zero is I_0, the IRR can be calculated from the following equation:

$$I_0 = \sum_{k=1}^{N} \frac{(Cash\ flow)_k}{(1 + IRR)^k}$$

where N is the planning period in years and k is the year after commercialization starts. According to this equation, IRR is the interest rate that makes the NPV of the project zero. Microsoft Excel calculates IRR for a given cash-flow distribution that includes the investment.

Sustainable Investment and Fully Loaded Cost

The ROI model described in the previous section is the traditional tool for making investment decisions in new technology and product development. However, that model is grossly inadequate for sustainable products. The traditional model does not fully account for the cost of externalities (that is, the life-cycle environmental and social harms of a product), nor does it fully account for the environmental and social benefits of sustainable products. For example, an automobile that burns fossil fuel emits carbon dioxide (CO_2), carbon monoxide (CO), volatile organic compounds (VOCs), nitrogen oxide (NOx), and other pollutants. These pollutants cause short-term and long-term harm to people and the environment. The cost of adapting, mitigating, and correcting these problems is externalized to society and not accounted for in the ROI analysis. Furthermore, the sustainability benefits of a product are not rewarded beyond the price premium that the market is willing to pay. For example, if an automaker designed a more efficient engine and reduced the harmful emissions of a vehicle, it might not capture the value of these benefits (avoided harm) in the market. Customers are either unaware of the avoided harm or unwilling to pay for the benefit of avoiding harm in a distant future. For example, Toyota Motor Corporation designed the Prius to have two times less CO_2 emissions and 20 times less emissions of other pollutants (CO, NOx, VOCs, and particulate matter) in comparison with the average passenger car in the U.S. in 2005.[1] However, most customers in the mainstream market were either unaware or unwilling to pay for the environmental and social benefits of the Prius. Customers rewarded Prius for its higher fuel efficiency and the other customary attributes of a car.

Another shortcoming of the traditional ROI model is its lack of consideration for the diminishing ability of natural and social capitals to be sustained for posterity. Natural capital is made up of nonrenewable resources and renewable resources and ecosystems, and it provides myriad provisioning and sink services for human well-being and for sustaining animal and plant life. Social capital, on the other hand, comprises the institutions of education, health, and government and also society's cultural norms, mutual trust, and other contextual elements that are essential to sustaining society's social cohesion and efficient functioning. In the traditional ROI model, the values of natural and social capitals are represented by the economic costs of access to the services they provide. For example, the economic costs of extracting minerals, cutting and hauling timber, or harvesting fish are included in the analysis. There is no cost or benefit consideration for the preservation and maintenance of natural capital or the development and renewal of social capital for sustainable development.

The new approach—ROI for sustainable development (ROI-SD)—fully accounts for the product's life-cycle impact on society and the environment, internalizes the cost of externalities, and values the attributes of the technology and product that enable sustainable development. Before discussing the ROI-SD for a new product, the requirements of sustainable development on both global and local scales are reviewed, and the challenges of complying with these requirements at the level of a single product or company are examined.

The sources and sinks of the planet (as stock variables) provide the resources and flow of services that support human economic activities. Sustainable development requires that these stocks and their capacity to provide services be maintained in perpetuity. Therefore, human economic activities must be limited by the following sustainability constraints:

- Nonrenewable capital (stocks) must not be exhausted. Nonrenewable stocks cannot be replenished in the time scale of a human generation. Petroleum reserves and ozone stock in the upper atmosphere are examples of nonrenewable capital. Mineral reserves should be categorized as nonrenewable stocks unless they can be recovered economically through (human-made) recycling processes.
- Renewable resources must not be harvested faster than the rate at which they can be replenished by nature. Fisheries, small forests, underground water reserves, rivers, and many ecosystems are examples of renewable resources.
- Social and human capitals must not be diminished.
- Human well-being must not be degraded.

Note that the adverse impacts of a product can be both local and global. The waste disposal from a manufacturing facility to a landfill or a nearby river stresses the earth's reprocessing capacity on a local scale. On the other hand, the greenhouse gases (GHGs) and ozone-depleting substances emitted from a manufacturing facility contribute to global warming and stratospheric ozone depletion on a global scale. Commonly, cost allocation to harmful externalities is done by estimating the cost of eliminating the source or minimizing the impact. The state of California has set a goal for reducing GHG emissions from industrial sources and achieves this goal through a market mechanism called cap and trade, where polluters are incentivized to reduce emissions or pay for pollution allowances that are issued by the state based on allowable levels of emissions that are commensurate to the goal. This methodology sets a price for GHG emissions.

Return on Investment for Sustainable Development

In calculating the ROI-SD, we must estimate the contributed net value of the product to the economy and society; the cost of making, delivering, and using the product; and the cost of internalizing the adverse environmental and social impacts of the product throughout its life cycle. This full cost-accounting method requires valuation of the natural capital, its resources, and its sink services within the previously mentioned sustainability constraints. A valuation framework proposed by the The Economics of Ecosystems and Biodiversity (TEEB) organization[2] is shown in Table 13.1—the cost of externalities would be based on the degradation of the natural capital's value listed in this table.

Table 13.1   A valuation of natural capital

Value type	Meaning
Use values:	
Direct use value	Renewable resources (crops, livestock, fisheries, recreation, knowledge)
	Nonrenewable resources (fossil fuels, minerals)
Indirect use value	Air-quality regulation, water regulation and purification, soil fertility, pest control, pollination, processing effluents from manufacturing, and consumption of products to soil and water
Option value	The future availability of ecosystem services for our personal benefit
Nonuse values:	
Intergenerational equity	The availability of natural capital to future generations
Intragenerational equity	The availability of natural capital to others (at the present time)
Existence value	The knowledge that ecosystems and biodiversity continue to exist, even though we do not understand everything that the system does (for example, the contributions of biodiversity to ecological functions are not understood)
Systems value	The interrelatedness of ecosystems
	The dependence of the biosphere on the integrative functioning of all ecosystems

In ROI calculations, the product cost includes the cost of material and labor for making the product plus the cost of its environmental impact—that is, the impact of effluents from the manufacturing and life-cycle use of the product. The environmental impact of a product is quantified through a life-cycle assessment (as described in Chapter 4). Table 13.1 lists the services that natural capital provides to process product waste. If we can monetize these values, then we will be able to do a full cost accounting of the product for a ROI-SD calculation.

How should we assess the values of the natural capital for ROI calculations? Can all the values of the natural capital be expressed in monetary terms?

Multiple methodologies are used to estimate the monetary values of the natural capital and its services. According to Robert Costanza and Herman E. Daly,[3] ecosystem services are the interest on natural capital. Market-based prices are used when nature's provisioning services of direct use are transacted in the market. Indirect use values (such as water purification services) are estimated based on the cost of human technology that could provide the same service. Current research also is focused on estimating the values of natural services based on their contributions to economic productivity (such as the value of pollination for the production of agriculture products).

The Natural Capital Project[4] has developed a software tool called InVEST (integrated valuation of ecosystem services and trade-offs) to account for nature's contributions to society. According to the Natural Capital Project's website: "InVEST is a suite of free, open-source software models used to map and value the goods and services from nature that sustain and fulfill human life. If properly managed, ecosystems yield a flow of services that are vital to humanity, including the production of goods (e.g., food), life-support processes (e.g., water purification), and life-fulfilling conditions (e.g., beauty, opportunities for recreation), and the conservation of options (e.g., genetic diversity for future use)."

In addition to ecosystem services, natural capital needs to be valued as a stock (asset) that should be maintained for sustainability. The capacity of an ecosystem to maintain its services and its resilience[5] is impacted by human production systems. According to TEEB, resilience is also a natural capital (stock) that provides *insurance* for the continued flow of services. When the natural capital stock is depleted and its capacity for maintaining services is reduced below a critical mass, it is difficult to estimate the value of system resilience. When the system nears a tipping point of going out of equilibrium and small changes amplify, the marginal value of the natural stock rises rapidly. Because in most cases the tipping point of the ecosystems is not known or is hard to estimate, the best approach is to take a precautionary approach and not to reduce the stock of natural capital.

Monetization of the value of natural capital and ecosystem services is based on the assumption that natural capital is a human asset and subject to an economic cost-benefit analysis. This approach leads to misguided conclusions. For example, assuming that natural resources and money are fungible (that is, mutually interchangeable) leads us to substitute an ecosystem with human-made facilities that can provide the desired services at a lower cost. The natural water purification services of a watershed might be substituted with a human-made facility, and the land might be commercialized for housing. This approach is highly problematic because it ignores the value of all other functions that the ecosystem provides (many of which may not be known).

In the ROI-SD analysis, we should refrain from discounting the future values of the natural capital and ecosystem functions, which is the common practice in calculations of the NPV of human-made capital (such as factory machinery). The discounting method contradicts the sustainability requirement for intergenerational equity and legitimizes the depletion of natural stock at the present time, limiting the choice and well-being of future beings.

The methodologies described so far are focused on the valuation (monetary or otherwise) of natural capital, ecosystem services, and biodiversity. However, there is yet another difficulty: how should we apportion the value to a single product?

One approach to overcoming this difficulty is to estimate the costs that would be incurred to have a truly sustainable product whose impact on natural capital and its services would not diminish their sustainability. An example of this approach is discussed in Chapter 12, in the simulation modeling section. The following is a summary of the approach in costing the resources and sink services that a product requires throughout its life cycle. The material requirements are based on the product design and the quantities produced over its life in the market. The environmental impact of the product and hence its demand for sink services (to render them harmless and sustainable) is estimated with an LCA model:

- For nonrenewable resources, the total cost is the sum of two parts: (1) the life-cycle material cost at market price adjusted upward by the rate at which the material is extracted and (2) the cost of pollution prevention and remediation.
- For renewable resources, the total cost is the sum of the following parts: (1) the life-cycle material cost at market price, (2) the capital and operating cost of renewing the natural capital, and (3) the cost of pollution prevention and remediation.
- The costs of the prevention and remediation of pollution come from manufacturing, transport, use, and end-of-life collection and disposal.
- The social costs of using the product should be negligible (and even negative when the social value of the product is not reflected in its market price).

Reporting Cost of Externalities

In this section, a few of the best practices of leading organizations to quantify, minimize, and report the adverse environmental and social impacts of their operations are reviewed. Some firms also attempt to monetize the externalities and create an environmental profit and loss (EP&L) statement.

Puma Corporation is a sport and lifestyle company that initiated the concept of EP&L in 2011. The company aimed to put a monetary value on both the natural services it used and the negative impacts those services had on the environment.[6] Puma's sustainability report for 2015 lists the environmental and social sustainability targets in the company and its suppliers.[7] The following is a summary of the items implemented in the company's sustainability program:

- Track consumption of energy (total and renewables), water, waste creation and recycling, CO_2 generation (Scopes 1, 2, and 3);
- Track environmental key performance indicators at suppliers, including CO_2, energy, and water;
- Track social sustainability factors at suppliers that manufacture Puma's products, including wages, benefits, working hours, health, safety, and forced labor;
- Assign audit rating scores (A to D) to Tier 1, 2, and 3 suppliers;
- Track the health and safety of workplaces and products (for example, the consumption of VOCs was tracked from 2003 to 2015 and was reduced from 66.7 grams per pair of shoes in 2003 to the target value of 24.1 grams per pair in 2015; and
- Track the use of sustainable materials.

The nonprofit B-Lab organization has developed the Global Impact Investing Rating System (GIIRS) to measure the company's impact on society and the environment. The GIIRS rating of a company is generated from weighted answers to questions in an online survey. The questions in the survey cover the categories of accountability, employees, customers, community, and environment.[8]

Conclusion for Sustainable Product Development

A comprehensive ROI-SD model of a product, particularly a model that is not based solely on the monetization of all values and costs, has not yet been developed. The review in this chapter highlights the limitations of the state of the art in calculating ROI-SD. Knowledge about natural capital, ecosystem services, and diversity is limited. It is difficult and even unjustified to monetize all values of nature and their contributions to human well-being. It is difficult to calculate the true cost of resources consumed by a product and account for the social and environmental externalities created by a single product or even a single company. So how should we design a sustainable product and make investment decisions?

The best approach is to try to develop a *zero-impact* product by using the circular economy and supply-loop principles and apply the design-for-sustainability guidelines that are listed in Chapter 8. Although zero impact theoretically is not feasible and, practically, is hard to do, it is the best strategy. We must adopt implementation tactics that get us as close as possible to achieving the zero-impact goal and be stead-fast in practicing kaizen or continuous improvement.

Intellectual Property Protection

Many investors consider competitive insulation as a crucial attribute of a new prod-uct (and technology) and an imperative investment criterion. In other words, they ask if the intellectual property (IP) created by the new product could be protected and if the investors would get exclusive rights to the IP.

The novel ideas and product concepts that are developed during the product development process are IPs, and by law, the inventor is entitled to certain protec-tion rights similar to other property rights. Several legal instruments protect the IP rights of the inventor, including patents, copyrights, trademarks, and trade secrets. IP protection laws are different around the world, and the laws of each country are enforceable only within that country. In the following sections, the IP laws of the U.S. are reviewed.

Patents

Patents are nonrenewable rights granted by the U.S. government to prevent others from making, using, or selling an idea covered by an invention in the U.S. For an invention to be patentable, it must be useful, novel, and not obvious. According to the U.S. Patent Office website,[9] there are three types of patents: "(1) Utility patents may be granted to anyone who invents or discovers any new and useful process, machine, article of manufacture, or composition of matter, or any new and useful improvement thereof; (2) Design patents may be granted to anyone who invents a new, original, and ornamental design for an article of manufacture; and (3) Plant patents may be granted to anyone who invents or discovers and asexually repro-duces any distinct and new variety of plant."

A utility patent expires 20 years after filing, and a design patent expires 14 years after issuance. The preparation and filing of a patent application, including the ser-vices of an experienced attorney (which is often needed), can be costly, and the cost of maintaining and defending a patent after it is issued can be significant.

The inventor has one year to file for a patent after publicly disclosing the inven-tion. U.S. law allows the inventor to apply for a provisional patent that protects the inventor for one year before filing the full application of the claims. The relatively low-cost provisional application allows the inventor to use the term *patent pending* in the description of the invention.

Copyrights

According to the U.S. Patent Office: "Copyright is a form of protection provided to the authors of *original works of authorship* including literary, dramatic, musical, artistic, and certain other intellectual works, both published and unpublished." Copyrights protect the expression of an idea, but not the idea itself (for example, in a novel, a painting, or software). Copyright protection begins automatically when the work is created, and for an individual creator it lasts for a period of 70 years after the author's death. The work can be registered with the U.S. Copyright Office.

Trademarks

According to the U.S. Patent Office: "a trademark (TM) is a word, phrase, symbol, and/or design that identifies and distinguishes the source of the goods of one party from those of others. A service mark (SM) is a word, phrase, symbol, and/or design that identifies and distinguishes the source of a service rather than goods." For example, a brand name or logo is protected by trademark law. A trademark does not exclude others from making the same goods or selling them under a different mark. Trademark rights are established by use, and you can use the symbol TM for goods or SM for services, to indicate the adoption. You can register a trademark with the U.S. Patent and Trademark Office and use the registered trademark symbol ®. A trademark can be registered with states, too, for protection within that state. Trademarks endure until they are abandoned.

Trade Secret

A trade secret is the information that a company considers economically valuable and not known to others and hence, would like to maintain as a secret. Trade secrets might include unpatented technology, business information, or a marketing strategy that may give a company a competitive advantage. For example, the Coca-Cola Company keeps the recipe (formula) of Coke a trade secret. Nondisclosure agreements are used to protect the trade secrets when companies disclose their confidential and proprietary information in business transactions. States (not the federal government) enact trade secret laws, which therefore vary across the United States.

Questions and Exercises

1. What is the risk of monetizing the environmental and social impacts of a product in calculating its ROI-SD?
2. In the standard ROI assessment, the NPV methodology is applied in which the future values and costs are discounted. Can you devise an improved methodology that values preservation of natural and social capitals for posterity?
3. How would you amend the current patent laws to encourage no-cost access to the technologies that solve the social, health and environmental problems of less privileged people in the world?

Endnotes

1. Stacey C. Davis and Susan B. Diegel, *Transportation Energy Data Book*, 25th ed. (Oak Ridge, TN: U.S. Department of Energy, 2006).

2. Adapted from The Economics of Ecosystems and Biodiversity (TEEB), *The Economics of Ecosystems and Biodiversity: Ecological and Economic Foundations*, Pushpam Kumar (Ed.), (Washington, DC: Routledge, 2011), ch. 5, p. 14, table 1. The Economics of Ecosystems and Biodiversity (TEEB) is a global initiative "to mainstream the values of biodiversity and ecosystem services into decision-making at all levels" (http://www.teebweb.org).

3. Robert Costanza and Herman E. Daly, "Natural Capital and Sustainable Development," *Conservation Biology* 6(1) (1992): 37–46.

4. Natural Capital Project, http://www.naturalcapitalproject.org.

5. Resilience is the ability of a system to maintain its functions at an equilibrium state after being subject to a perturbation. In other words, in a resilient system, perturbations damp out and do not grow and move the system to a different operating regime. See also Fredrik Moberg and Sturle Hauge Simonsen, "What Is Resilience? An Introduction to Social-Ecological Research," Stockholm Resilience Centre, Stockholm University, 2011.

6. Simon Beavis, "Puma: Business and the Environment—Counting the Cost," The Guardian, May 30, 2012, https://www.theguardian.com/sustainable-business/best-practice-exchange/puma-impact-environment-counting-cost.

7. Puma, "Puma Training: Annual Report 2015," Herzogenaurich, Germany, http://about.puma.com/damfiles/default/investor-relations/financial-reports/en/2015/GB_2015_ENG_Final_links_low-res-8932dbc11383cd85124e1ba63d86b5cc.pdf.

8. B-Lab, "GIIRS Impact Statement for Primary Solutions," Emerging Markets Company Impact Rating Report, 2010, http://giirs.org/assets/pdf/GIIRS_Sample-Company-Rating.pdf.

9. U.S. Patent Office, http://www.uspto.gov.

Epilogue

REMARKS ON LEADERSHIP AND INNOVATION

Throughout this book, the best practices for developing sustainable products have been discussed. The end goal of the sustainable product development process cannot be reached without excellent organizational leadership and management of the process. New product development and commercialization is an entrepreneurial or interpreneurial endeavor of applying technology to context. Successful entrepreneurs are leaders who have clarity of purpose about what they want to do, are focused, have passion and really care about what they want to do, and build a multidisciplinary team of technologists, managers, business developers, finance experts, legal experts, and people with other skills that are essential to delivering the desired results. Effective leaders create a shared vision and commitment to the organizational objectives, build the necessary competency for doing the job and producing high-quality output, and motivate people for peak performance. This kind of transformational leadership creates commitment and job satisfaction among employees in a positive feedback loop of productivity.

In most circumstances, individuals are part of a team, and their performance is strongly dependent on the working of the team as a unit. The probability of success is greatly enhanced if the team implements business processes that allow freedom of action for creativity and a disciplined focus for producing results. The innovation capacity in an organization is built through purposefulness, looking outward, experimentation, collaboration, and empowerment of people and teams to take initiatives and make decisions.

Effective leaders also pursue organizational excellence through continuous improvement of the competency of people and refinement of business processes. This requires identifying key performance indicators (KPIs) for all organizational units, such as project teams and functional units. Actions for continuous improvement are the outcome of gap analysis between a desired goal versus actual performance for every KPI.

The integration of sustainability requirements in the innovation process and successful implementation of the design for sustainability tools that are discussed in this book require a new corporate leadership, operational strategy, and reward system. Firms must institutionalize sustainability practices by adopting sustainability as a central element of the company's day-to-day operation. In other words, sustainability must be built into all four constituents of the innovation ecosystem—process, organization, management, and culture.

Visionary leaders who channel the creative energy of the organization to develop sustainable products (as we have defined in this book) invent the future that we want.

This book has free material available for download from the
Web Added Value™ resource center at *www.jrosspub.com*

BUSINESS AND ENVIRONMENTAL SUSTAINABILITY AT TOYOTA MOTOR CORPORATION: THE DEVELOPMENT OF THE PRIUS HYBRID VEHICLE[1]

On an unusually warm winter afternoon in 1993, Takeshi Uchiyamada was walking back to his office and thinking about the meeting he had just had with four Toyota Motor Corporation executives. Executive Vice President Akihiro Wada had asked him to serve as chief engineer for the small Toyota group called Project G21, which was charged with creating a twenty-first-century car. Wada was looking for a leader who was open-minded enough to foresee future needs and also experienced enough to lead the team through the many challenges ahead. Uchiyamada was the right person.

Project G21 was established in September of that year by Yoshiro Kinbara, then executive vice president in charge of research and development (R&D) at Toyota, in response to the vision of the honorary chairman, Eiji Toyoda. Kinbara assigned the project leadership to Risuke Kubochi, general manager of the General Engineering Division, who formed the first Project G21 working group; Uchiyamada took over the leadership of Project G21 from Kubochi and held his first project meeting in February 1994.[2]

Uchiyamada was proud to have been chosen as the leader for the team that could shape the future of the auto industry but felt the weight of his new mission on the way back to his office. He was contemplating what the car of the twenty-first century could be.

Exhibit A.1: Toyota History

The Toyota Motor Company, Ltd. was established on August 28, 1937, after the 1936 announcement of the Toyoda Model AA Sedan that was named after the company's founders—Sakichi Toyoda and Kiichiro Toyoda. Toyota exported its first passenger car (and the first Japanese car) to the United States in 1957 and established Toyota Motors Sales, U.S.A., Inc. Toyota was awarded the Deming Application Prize in 1965.

By 1972, Toyota had produced 10 million vehicles in Japan. Toyota expanded its manufacturing base into the U.S. through a joint venture with General Motors Corporation (New United Motor Manufacturing, Inc., NUMMI) and started production in 1984.

By 1990, Toyota had produced 15 million Corolla sedans (its flagship vehicle) 14 years after its market introduction, and in 1999, the company produced its 100 millionth vehicle in Japan. As of 2006, Toyota had 15 domestic plants and 52 overseas companies in 27 countries on all six continents.

Toyota's History of Success and Characteristics of the Auto Industry in 1993

Exhibit A.1 briefly describes the history of Toyota since its inception in 1937. In the 70 years from 1937 to 2007, the company grew into a global manufacturer of motor vehicles that was poised to surpass General Motors Corporation as the industry's leader in 2007. Figure A.1 illustrates the trends in Toyota production and sales in Japan and overseas.

By the early 1990s, the auto industry's competitive playing field had leveled. Detroit had caught up with the quality and production cost-efficiency gains that Toyota had made in the 1980s. The demand for sports utility vehicles was on the rise, particularly in the United States, which represented Toyota's largest market. On the other hand, environmental concerns (such as the depletion of ozone in the upper atmosphere) were widely recognized and had received the attention of the United Nations[3] and many non-governmental organizations.

What Is the Twenty-First-Century Car?

Uchiyamada was looking out from his office window and thinking about Toyota and Toyota City, of which he was proud. More than any other place in Toyota's global landscape, Toyota City and its seven production plants embodied the Toyota way in automobile innovation and manufacturing.[4] Uchiyamada was an expert in noise and vibration reduction and had been at Toyota for 25 years, since his graduation

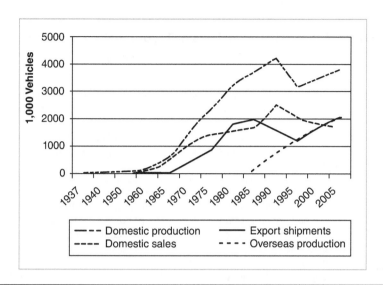

Figure A.1 Trends in Toyota production and sales. Source: Toyota Company Profile, 2006

from the local Nagoya University in applied physics. He was born in Okazaki City along the Yahagi River across from Toyota City and had developed his passion for cars early in life. His father also had worked at Toyota and had been the chief engineer of the third-generation Crown.

How would he define the requirements for the new twenty-first-century vehicle? He knew that he could not focus on any specific market segment and perform the traditional market research because prevalent customer preferences are often lagging indicators and do not reflect future directions. He wanted to develop a car for the market 10 years in the future and for the next century's global use—a car that customers could not envision.

He remembered hearing the company's honorary chairman, Eiji Toyoda, state that "if our activities were not compatible with social and environmental needs, our company could not sustain its success in the future." He also thought of two other sources of inspiration in defining the characteristics of the twenty-first-century car. First, Toyota's fundamental philosophy could point him in the right direction. Toyota's fundamental philosophy was articulated in the *Guiding Principles at Toyota Motor Corporation*, which were adopted in January 1992 (the revised April 1997 version is presented in Exhibit A.2).

Toyota's historical view and organizational learning from six decades of developing and commercializing successive generations of new products were the second source of inspiration for Uchiyamada and his team.

After careful deliberation and several brainstorming sessions, Uchiyamada concluded that the new vehicle had to be convenient and fun for customers and also

---

Exhibit A.2: Guiding Principles at Toyota Motor Corporation

(Source: Toyota Corporation Website)

1) Honor the language and spirit of the law of every nation and undertake open and fair corporate activities to be a good corporate citizen of the world.
2) Respect the culture and customs of every nation and contribute to economic and social development through corporate activities in the communities.
3) Dedicate ourselves to providing clean and safe products and to enhancing the quality of life everywhere through all our activities.
4) Create and develop advanced technologies and provide outstanding products and services that fulfill the needs of customers worldwide.
5) Foster a corporate culture that enhances individual creativity and team-work value, while honoring mutual trust and respect between labor and management.
6) Pursue growth in harmony with the global community through innovative management.

Work with business partners in research and creation to achieve stable, long-term growth and mutual benefits, while keeping ourselves open to new partnerships.

---

had to respond to important societal problems of the twenty-first century. He envisioned that the overarching transportation problems of society in the twenty-first century would be energy costs and environmental impacts. He imagined a world in which population was high and energy was scarce, and he saw China and other developing countries becoming major producers and consumers. Therefore, the twenty-first-century car had to be *highly efficient, small, and light-weight*. Several years later, he said, "I was taking a big risk with this definition of the twenty-first-century product."

Developing a Twenty-First-Century Product: Defining Specifications and the Development Approach

The next step for Uchiyamada and his team was to translate the objectives of highly efficient, small, and lightweight into an engineering specification. The efficiency target for the new vehicle was set at 1.5 times improvement over the most efficient car in 1993 (that was the Toyota Corolla, with 30.8 miles-per-gallon performance). A detailed engineering project plan was developed to identify the necessary improvements in components and subassemblies in order to achieve the overall efficiency target.

Initially, hybrid technology was not considered because the engineering team believed they could achieve the target through continuous improvement of conventional engine efficiency by using such features as direct gasoline injection in a small-displacement-volume engine, lean burn technology, and high-efficiency transmission design.

In the latter half of 1994, two directives by company executives changed the project dramatically. In late 1994, Wada, who was the executive vice president in charge of R&D at Toyota, informed Uchiyamada that management had decided to show a hybrid concept car at the October 1995 motor show in Tokyo and that Uchiyamada was being given the task of developing this concept car in addition to his responsibilities as the chief engineer of Project G21. Uchiyamada's assessment of hybrid technology, which had been in development by R&D for several years, was that various key components, particularly the battery, were not yet fully developed, the infrastructure was not in place for volume production, and the cost of this new technology was too high.

The second management directive came a few months later at a review meeting of Project G21. Wada stated that although the chosen concept for the new vehicle was good, it was not good enough for the twenty-first century. He raised the efficiency target to two times improvement over existing vehicles.

Because the new target surpassed the potential of conventional technologies, Uchiyamada concluded that Project G21 had to be a hybrid car. He was now faced with the daunting challenge of demonstrating the hybrid G21 at the October 1995 motor show and then developing it into a production-worthy vehicle for the mass market. Uchiyamada signed on to Wada's new directive with the condition that the best engineers at Toyota would be assigned to his project. Wada agreed, and Prius was on its way to being born.

Technology Pathfinding

Toyota's standard *new product development methodology* (as illustrated in Figure A.2) had been followed by the G21 team from the outset.[5] At Toyota, R&D centers develop new technologies on an ongoing basis, and product groups, headed by the chief engineer, cherry-pick what they need to meet their goals. At first, when the fuel-efficiency target was set to be 1.5 times that of the Corolla, the project was proposed to adopt a high-efficiency manual transmission and a small-size direct-injection engine. However, to achieve Wada's new directive that the target fuel efficiency should be two times higher than that of the Corolla, there was no alternative other than a hybrid.

On the premise of adopting hybrid technology, development tasks were assigned to the R&D and engineering divisions related to the various components. Several dozen varieties of hybrid vehicle (HV) systems were studied and narrowed down from 80 to 20. Finally, four systems were selected based on performance, physical

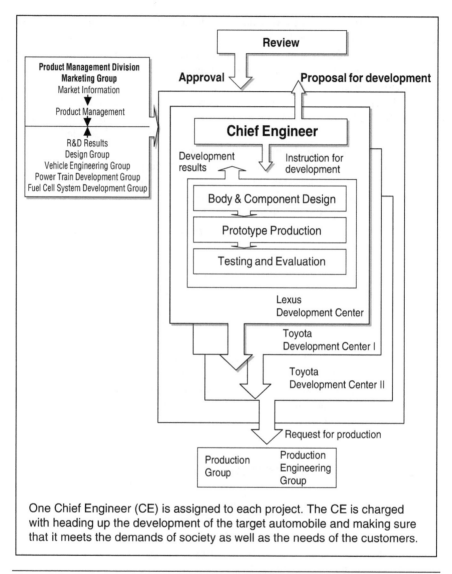

One Chief Engineer (CE) is assigned to each project. The CE is charged with heading up the development of the target automobile and making sure that it meets the demands of society as well as the needs of the customers.

Figure A.2 Toyota's new product development process. Source: Toyota Motor Corporation, Company Profile, 2006

parameters for packaging and assembly, and cost. Detailed parametric studies were made with these four systems, and finally the Toyota hybrid system (THS) was selected for implementation in the first Prius. The final concept was approved by Wada in June 1995, and the final design of components was assigned to various engineering divisions.

Environmental Impact, Platform, and Outsourcing Strategies

The engineering challenge for Uchiyamada was to ensure that the hybrid technology vehicle would become mainstream and affordable. The engineering team knew that in addition to its visionary concept, design quality was the essence of Prius success. Figure A.3 shows the Prius hybrid design configuration and its major subsystems.

The critical areas of technology development included the battery, generator/motor, controls, and inverter. Each of these represented a different degree of engineering risk. Prius technology development was based on meeting the requirements for a small, affordable, and high-performance vehicle and on extending the technology platform to other vehicles.

Size reduction, durability, and reliability were the key design issues throughout the product development cycle. Product cost had to be compatible with customers' price decisions (that is, with what they were willing to pay for the vehicle). And finally, product quality had to meet Toyota's standards, which specified a rigorous testing program (including the type, extent, and length of the tests).

Environmental impact was another prime consideration in the design. The Project G21 team knew that the twenty-first-century car had to be low in emissions and should set the standard in environmental impact. The goal set in 1996 was to reduce nitrogen oxide (NOx), hydrocarbons (HCs), and carbon monoxide (CO) emissions to one-tenth of the level required by then current regulations. Furthermore, carbon dioxide (CO_2) emissions would be halved by doubling the vehicle fuel efficiency. This goal was met by taking advantage of the unique characteristics of the hybrid

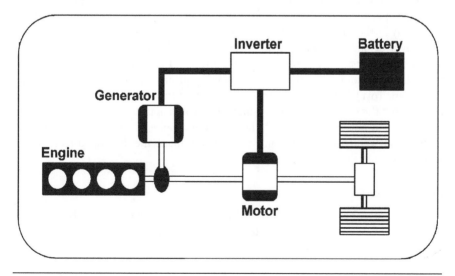

Figure A.3 Prius hybrid design configuration

design that, for instance, enabled running the catalyst warm (at 400°C) during all modes of vehicle operation.

Platform Strategy

The overall goal of Toyota's Prius product group was to develop an economical and environmentally friendly twenty-first-century car. For marketing reasons, the company wanted to introduce a new concept car that had a new name and underscored Toyota's technological leadership. This is why Prius was developed as a new platform.

Furthermore, the Prius team chose a platform strategy that would allow the hybrid technology to be adapted in the future to other product lines (such as Toyota's Camry and Lexus). This adaptation capability posed a significant challenge to the engineers in sizing the hybrid subsystems so that they would fit onto existing product platforms.

Outsourcing Strategy

Toyota's philosophy in technology development is that key technologies must be developed and made by Toyota. In other words, the ability to understand, evaluate, and produce the basic technology should be retained within the company. This strategy was adapted in the following ways by the Prius team as it developed the vehicle's key subsystems.

Nickel Metal Hydride Battery

Toyota did not have exclusive battery technology in-house and in the spring of 1995 decided to partner with Matsushita for Prius battery development and have a prototype ready by the end of the year. Toyota and Matsushita had codeveloped the nickel metal hydride battery technology for an electric vehicle (the RAV4EV) before Prius. In December 1996, Toyota and Matsushita Electric Industrial formed a joint venture called Panasonic EV Energy Co. for developing and manufacturing the battery subsystem. Toyota's president, Hiroshi Okuda, told the executives of the new joint venture that they had to develop products that would appeal to every automaker in the world and not just to Toyota: "The basic philosophy of the company is to first create social value in the Prius and then openly make the developed technology available to society."[6]

Electric Motor

An electric motor also was a critical technology and was developed in-house. Toyota already possessed the necessary technology in this area.

Inverter and Insulated Gate Bipolar Transistor

The inverter and the insulated gate bipolar transistor (IGBT) were the other critical technologies that were developed in-house, although they were not technologies in which Toyota was strong. The inverter is the device that converts the battery's direct-current power into alternating current (AC), enabling the use of an AC electric motor, and the IGBT is the inverter switching device. The Prius design required the IGBT to switch currents of several hundred amps at a much higher speed than the thyristor that had traditionally been used in inverters. The IGBT was one of the critical technologies of Prius, and management wanted to develop it in-house.

By 1985, Toyota had built its own semiconductor manufacturing plant in Hirose, 30 minutes outside of Toyota City. Toyota management had perceived electronics as the area of growth for auto technology, justifying the 15 billion yen investment in the Hirose plant. Many years later, during the Prius development phase, Okuda explained Toyota's reason for investing in electronics technology: "We were afraid of not knowing what was inside the black box. . . . Without that knowledge, we could not accurately calculate cost and had to buy them at the sellers' price."

But Uchiyamada hesitated to develop the inverter and IGBT technologies in-house because of concerns about quality and the fact that Toyota's in-house capability in these areas were much less than that of giant electronics suppliers in Japan and overseas. The Hirose plant developed the IGBT, taking advantage of the IGBT designs that were used in AC motor control devices in Shinkansen trains and in several electric vehicles. Several versions of the IGBT chip were tried before it worked to specifications by the end of 1996. The inverter for the first Prius was manufactured in-house. However, as Prius production volume increased and the hybrid technology also was employed on other vehicle models, a portion of the inverter production was shifted to outsourcing.

Program Execution Challenges

Not until June 1995 was the Prius final concept approved by management, and the development project was kicked off. However, in late 1995, Hiroshi Okuda, who became Toyota's new president in August of that year, asked Wada to accelerate the Project G21 product introduction by one year—to December 1997. This made the engineers, who were already working very hard, extremely nervous.

The engineering team faced a high hurdle to overcome in developing production-worthy components, particularly the inverter and the battery. The different engineering groups responsible for the development of various subsystems thought that theirs was the most challenging. For example, minimizing the inverter size and engineering an efficient cooling system that would maximize its power output density (in 1,000 volt amps per kilogram, kVA/kg) were particularly difficult to achieve. The biggest challenges for battery development were size (it had to be one-tenth the size of a RAV4EV battery), cooling (for long life and performance), and controls (charging and discharging).

Another design challenge was Prius's appearance (shape) and subsystem sizing. These factors interacted and had to be optimized to achieve the best overall system solution. Because Prius was a new platform, however, flexibility in optimization of the system was higher than in other existing vehicles.

The body shape was revisited in early 1996 as a result of a post-1995 auto show concept review. The objective was to address the new trend in consumer preferences that had shifted away from the Corolla shape. Uchiyamada decided to arrive at the best design through a competition among Toyota's four design centers around the world (including the head office in Toyota City, Tokyo, California, and Belgium). A selection committee that included Wada scored the concepts proposed by the design centers based on 20 to 30 criteria and recommended the chosen concept to the president for approval. California's design was selected by a slight margin over that of the head office. Figure A.4 illustrates the product development cycle and key milestones of Project G21.

Management Support

Toyota's executive management ranked Prius development as the company's top priority. Throughout the Prius development cycle, management support was always present and never in doubt. Project G21 was treated as a secret project and from the very beginning received dedicated engineering resources as requested by the chief engineer. As many as 1,000 engineers worked on Prius, and Toyota is estimated to have invested $1 billion in Project G21.[7]

Strong management support was a crucial factor and enabled the Prius team to remain motivated and to achieve its demanding technical and schedule requirements. For example, Okuda drove a Prius several times during its development. After a test drive in December 1995, the company president told team members: "One day everyone will be driving a car like this. You people are working on a great mission. It is probably the most amazing work at Toyota. One day these cars will be needed outside of Japan, especially in India and China."

Every two weeks, a Prius project meeting was held at which the groups reported on their progress. Every six weeks, a meeting was held with the executives in charge of development and production technologies.

Prius Commercialization

The product development plan was to introduce the new vehicle before the beginning of the twenty-first century. However, the timing of the Prius introduction in Japan was moved up by nearly two years to October 1997 to coincide with the

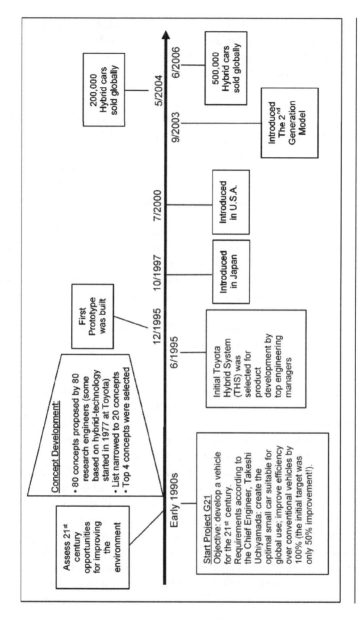

Figure A.4   The product development cycle and key milestones of project G21

signing of the Kyoto Protocol (to the United Nations Framework Convention on Climate Change) and the theme for the 1997 Tokyo Auto Show, which highlighted Toyota's leadership in environmental technology.

Toyota had formulated its strategic environmental initiative at the beginning of the 1990s. In 1992, Toyota founded *Toyota Earth Charter* as an internal index for the company's social and environmental contributions in every stage of business—including design, production, sales, and disposal. At the end of 1996, Toyota's Public Affairs Division launched an environmental project called *Toyota ECO Project* with *Act Today for Tomorrow* as its slogan.

According to the Prius launch plan, a series of events tied the development of the product to the company's environmental strategy. These events started in March 1997 and culminated with the product for sale in dealers' showrooms on December 10, 1997.

Okuda decided to announce the Prius in March 1997 as the flagship of the Toyota ECO Project. In his speech to reporters in Tokyo, he said, "Toyota has developed a hybrid system that is an answer to the environmental problems of the twenty-first century. It achieves twice the fuel economy and half the CO_2 emissions of conventional cars and it reduces CO, HC, and NOx to 1/10th the level of current regulations."

The next launch event was held in July 1997, when Okuda spoke about the Prius again at the Toyota Environmental Forum held in Tokyo. "For the automobile to sustain its position as a useful tool in the twenty-first century, the auto industry must lead society by making environmental efforts. Toyota will position preservation of the global environment as the top priority issue, and will allocate all the necessary resources in our commitment," said Okuda.[8]

After extensive road testing for reliability and endurance, mass production of the Prius was approved through a design review in September 1996, and the sales division requested a production volume of 1,000 units per month. According to the sales group, lower production volume was suitable only for specialized products. For Prius, it wanted to generate the impact of a mass-production model.

Nevertheless, because the initial prerelease reaction to Prius had been very positive in the market and it usually took six months to increase capacity, management of the production division decided to build the capacity beyond the 1,000 units per month that the sales division had requested. They proved to be right in May 1998, when the production target was raised by sales to 2,000 units per month. The first Prius was built in the Takaoka plant, but production was moved to Motomachi for the first-generation Prius and then to the Tsutsumi plant for the second-generation Prius. Figure A.5 shows a photo of a second-generation Prius.

The Prius was introduced to the public in an event in Tokyo in October 1997 as planned. It also was shown at the Tokyo Motor Show on October 22 and at the Kyoto Summit on Global Warming on December 1 of that year. Many reporters from around the world who were present at the Kyoto Summit reported on Prius's birth and Toyota's environmental and technological leadership to the world. On the other hand, the U.S. delegates at the Kyoto Summit refused to accept global warming as

Figure A.5 Second-generation Prius

a scientific fact and refused to agree to a numerical target for CO_2 reduction. They feared that CO_2 reduction would hamper the American economy and auto business, which were booming in 1997.

In December 1997, the same month that Prius was launched in Japan, Toyota received orders for 3,500 cars through the normal distribution channel. The Prius was priced at 2.15 million yen. Buyers were from 30 to 50 years old, and most were buying a car for the first time.

The Chief Engineer's Strategic Dilemma and Most Demanding Challenge

Chief engineer Uchiyamada sat behind his desk in January 1996 and felt good about the development of the Prius hybrid electric car and the progress that his team had made. In spite of many technical challenges, things looked good, and subsystem and component test results were promising, even against the rigorous quality tests of the Toyota Way. In December 1995, the first prototype of Prius, hand-fabricated by the engineers and manufacturing team members, looked like a finished product.

Uchiyamada was concerned that people around him were wondering whether hybrid technology was a fad that would fade away or something that could become a standard (mainstream) product. Another question about the project was its outsourcing approach. Believing that Prius would be a mainstream success, Uchiyamada decided that Toyota should develop and manufacture its key technologies, such as the motor and inverter, in-house. Nevertheless, some team members had reservations about the capability of in-house manufacturing and questioned if they should have partnered with external suppliers, leveraging their technologies for developing the inverter and IGBT technologies, which were not Toyota's traditional strengths.

Although Uchiyamada believed that HVs would someday be a mainstream product, he felt obliged to address the concerns of others regarding their technology, cost, outsourcing, and quality. He knew that some of the anxieties that people had were normal and a common occurrence in the early stages of any new product development. But Prius was different. He could not bring Prius to the world if there was any anxiety about its commercial success. He pondered what the critical success factors for Prius becoming a mainstream product (versus a fad) were and whether he had done enough to mitigate the project risks.

Endnotes

1. Dariush Rafinejad and Robert C. Carlson of the Management Science and Engineering Department at Stanford University prepared this case in collaboration with Toshio Ohashi and with the generous support of Toyota Motor Corporation as the basis for class discussion rather than to illustrate either effective or ineffective handling of an administrative situation.
2. Hideshi Itazaki, The Prius That Shook the World: How Toyota Developed the World's First Mass-Production Hybrid Vehicle, translated by Albert Yamada and Masako Ishikawa (Tokyo: Nikkan Kogyo Shimbun, 1999).
3. World Commission on Environment and Development, Our Common Future (also known as the Brundtland Report, for Gro Harlem Bruntland, WCED chair) (Oxford, UK: Oxford University Press, 1987).
4. Jeffrey K. Liker, "The Toyota Way in Action: New Century, New Fuel, New Design Process—Prius," The Toyota Way: Fourteen Management Principles from the World's Greatest Manufacturer, Chap. 6 (New York: McGraw-Hill, 2004).
5. James M. Morgan and Jeffrey K. Liker, The Toyota Product Development System: Integrating People, Process, and Technology (New York: Productivity Press, 2006).
6. By 1999, Honda had decided to use Panasonic EV Energy's batteries, and other non-Japanese automakers were negotiating deals with the company.
7. Alex Taylor III, "The Birth of the Prius," Fortune, February 24, 2006.
8. Hiroshi Okuda, remarks delivered at the First Toyota Environmental Forum, Tokyo, July 1997.

CHEVROLET VOLT: A DISRUPTIVE INNOVATION BRIDGE TO ELECTRIFIED TRANSPORTATION[1]

Conceived by few and executed by many was the key success factor of Chevrolet's Volt development, recalled Jon Lauckner[2] at a December 2010 event celebrating the vehicle's market launch. It was a long and intricate path from a fateful afternoon discussion with Bob Lutz, vice chair at General Motors (GM), in January 2006 when Lauckner drew the extended-range electric vehicle (E-REV) concept on a piece of paper. Lutz had an *all-electric* dream to regain GM's reputation for technological leadership, which it had lost to Toyota in part because of Toyota's successful Prius hybrid electric vehicle.

Lauckner's argument against a purely electric vehicle was convincing: GM needed to decouple the technological development of an all-electric propulsion system from the development of complementary technologies such as low-cost, high-energy-density batteries and a ubiquitous public/private infrastructure for battery charging. GM needed a revolutionary electric vehicle design that could penetrate the mass market in the short term and bridge the way to realization of the technical potential of all-electric transportation in the long term. The proposed E-REV would be driven by an electric motor that was powered by a rechargeable battery with a 40-mile drive capacity (exceeding the daily commuting range of most American drivers). The propulsion system also would include a combustion engine and generator subsystem that would seamlessly take over when the battery was depleted to generate electricity for longer commutes to avoid *range anxiety* for drivers.

Lauckner was encouraged that Lutz had concurred with his concept and had asked him to initiate a project to develop an E-REV concept car, which was the genesis of Volt. Back in his office after this discussion, Lauckner contemplated the project plan. The dark winter clouds visible from his office window reminded him that the road ahead would be challenging. What is the most effective management approach for developing a disruptive technology in a large company? What is the right mix of skills for the project? What is the right product strategy for integrating business, technology, marketing, and operational strategies for a green new-to-market vehicle concept? He was determined to develop a game-changing product that surpassed the competition and laid the foundation for GM's leadership in the electric propulsion systems of the future.

General Motors Corporation and the Competitive Landscape in 2005

General Motors Corporation was founded on September 16, 1908. At its inception, GM held only the Buick Motor Company but in a matter of years acquired more than 20 companies, including Oldsmobile, Cadillac, and Oakland, which was renamed Pontiac. Currently, GM offers a comprehensive range of vehicles in more than 120 countries around the world. GM's top five markets by sales are China, the U.S., Brazil, the U.K., and Germany. More than 70% of GM sales in 2012 came from outside the U.S. Exhibit B.1 describes GM's vision, technological focus, five guiding principles, and social and environmental commitment.

Exhibit B.1: General Motors Corporation[3]

At the new General Motors, we are passionate about designing, building, and selling the world's best vehicles. This vision unites us as a team each and every day, and is the hallmark of our customer-driven culture.

General Motors continues to develop innovative technologies to shape the future of the automotive industry. We are expanding our leadership in vehicle electrification with advancements in batteries, electric motors, and power controls. The GM team is also working on a range of high-volume, fuel-saving technologies, including direct injection, variable valve timing, turbocharging, six-speed transmissions, diesel engines, and improved aerodynamic designs.

GM's Five Guiding Principles

1) **Safety and Quality First:** Safety will always be a priority at GM. We continue to emphasize our safety-first culture in our facilities and as we grow our business in new markets. Our safety philosophy is at the heart of the development of each vehicle. In addition to safety, delivering the highest-quality vehicles is a major cornerstone of our promise to our customers. That is why our vehicles go through extreme testing procedures in the lab, on the road, and in our production facilities prior to being offered to customers.

2) **Create Lifelong Customers:** We take nothing for granted in our efforts to earn the confidence and loyalty of our customers. We listen to customers to make sure we are meeting their needs and are connecting with them on their terms. Through our relationship with customers, we strive to create passionate brand advocates who love their vehicle and freely tell others about their experience.

3) **Innovate:** We challenge ourselves to be creative and lead in everything we do. From implementing the smallest improvements to executing big ideas, we are constantly increasing our competitive advantage to delight and excite our customers.

4) **Deliver Long-Term Investment Value:** Our shareholders want to feel confident about their decision to invest in our company. By developing the world's best vehicles, building upon our strong financial foundation, growing our business, and operating with the highest level of integrity, we will continue to deliver positive results.

5) **Make a Positive Difference:** We strive to make a difference in our world and in our workplace. Whether finding new ways to improve our business operations, achieving as part of a team, or volunteering in the community, we know that our momentum is tied to positive change.

Commitment

We believe in acting responsibly across the globe and focus our efforts in important areas, including the environment and education. The General Motors Foundation helps us achieve this goal by strengthening communities across the United States through investments in education, health and human services, environment and energy, community development, and worldwide disaster relief efforts. Over the past ten years, the foundation, fully funded by a GM endowment in 2000, has donated more than $350 million to send students to college, keep teen drivers safe, educate parents on child passenger safety, promote diversity, and support vital nonprofit organizations.

Committed to reducing waste and pollutants, General Motors conserves resources and recycles materials at every stage of the vehicle life cycle. We are proud to say that our best practices reduce the impact our vehicles and manufacturing operations have on the environment.

Our commitment to the earth will transcend the here and now through our work with students. We share our knowledge of sustainability with these future engineers, leaders, and problem solvers to help ensure a better future for all.

Although GM led the auto industry for most of the twentieth century, overseas competition, particularly from Japanese automakers, grew strong toward the turn of the millennium and threatened to upset GM's leadership position. GM's revenue history compared to that of Toyota Motor Corporation is depicted in Figure B.1. The financial crisis of 2008 created a major recession in the U.S. economy, particularly in the auto industry. GM, running critically short of operating cash, went

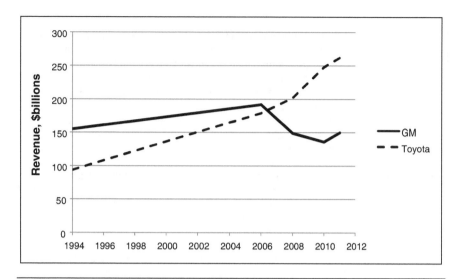

Figure B.1   Revenue Growth History, General Motors and Toyota Motor Corporation

through a severe restructuring of its operations and emerged from bankruptcy in 2009 with strong support from the U.S. government.

With a tradition of technological leadership, GM was the first company to develop the modern all-electric vehicle, the EV-1. In response to a zero emission regulation mandated by the California Air Resources Board in 1996, GM invested an estimated $1 billion to develop and launch the EV-1, a two-seater car with a range of 50 miles between charges. It used a lead-acid battery, which later was upgraded to use a nickel-metal-hydride (NiMH) battery. Low demand, high production costs, and the reversal of the California mandate persuaded GM to discontinue the product in 2003. In addition, GM retrieved the EV-1s from all 1,200 customers (to whom the car had been leased) and crushed them. The latter proved to be a public relations liability for the company.

Toyota's response to the EV-1 was the introduction of the Prius in late 1997. Its hybrid electric technology achieved high fuel efficiency and demonstrated Toyota's technical prowess. The Prius was a mid-sized sedan powered by a hybrid drive system with NiMH batteries that could store regenerative energy during deceleration and braking and achieve 45 miles-per-gallon (mpg) performance. Although other automakers, including GM, had also developed hybrid technology, only Toyota and Honda had commercialized the technology in the late 1990s. Honda's hybrid car, Insight, had limited success, but the Prius became a major success and propelled Toyota into a technological and commercial leadership position, surpassing GM for the first time. Toyota also was recognized for its environmental leadership because of the Prius and its hybrid technology. Conversely, GM was positioned as lagging in technology because of its slow adoption of hybrid technology and as having a poor environmental record by marketing products like the Hummer and *killing* its electric car, the EV-1. In 2007, Toyota replaced GM as the number one automobile manufacturer in the world.

An additional challenge to GM's technological leadership came from an unlikely competitor, Tesla Motors. Tesla Motors was founded in 2003 in Silicon Valley, to develop a high-performing, electric sports vehicle targeted at the high end of the market. The Tesla Roadster, powered by lithium-ion batteries, was launched in early 2008. By the late 2000s, several other companies had introduced all-electric, hybrid electric, or plug-in hybrid electric vehicles (PHEVs),[4] including Nissan's all-electric Leaf and Toyota's PHEV Prius. Chrysler introduced an E-REV concept at the 2009 Detroit Auto Show. GM needed a game changer.

The Society of Automotive Engineers (SAE) definitions of alternative vehicles are shown in Exhibit B.2.

Exhibit B.2: The Society of Automotive Engineers Definitions of Hybrid and Electric Vehicle Technologies

The Society of Automotive Engineers International defines alternate vehicle technologies with electric power capability as follows:

- **Hybrid:** a vehicle with two or more energy storage systems, both of which must provide propulsion power, either together or independently—the two systems are the ICE and a battery charged during braking
- **E-REV:** a vehicle that functions as a full-performance battery electric vehicle when energy is available from an onboard RESS and having an auxiliary energy supply that is only engaged when the RESS energy is not available
- **PHEV:** a hybrid vehicle with the ability to store and use an off-board electrical energy in the RESS

The Driving Force and Product Strategy

The strategic thrust for the development of GM's Chevrolet Volt was the competitive nature of the market in the mid-2000s. The Volt program had three main goals—to regain market and technology leadership by surpassing the Prius, to develop the building blocks of technology for a comparative advantage in the growing electric transportation segment, and to respond to the underlying environmental sustainability and national security concerns about cars' dependence on oil.

GM's chair and chief executive officer, Rick Wagoner, announced the company's strategic outlook in 2006 at the Los Angeles Auto Show and stated that: "Going forward, it is highly unlikely that oil alone is going to supply all of the world's rapidly growing automotive energy requirements. For the global auto industry, this means that we must—as a business necessity—develop alternate sources of propulsion. . . . The key as we see it at GM is energy diversity. We believe that the best way to power the automobile in the years to come is to do so with many different sources of energy."[5]

Since the introduction and rapid penetration of the Prius in the U.S. market in the early 2000s, the idea of developing a competing hybrid car had been raised several times at GM. But the idea had been rejected because the required $300 million research and development (R&D) and $500 million production capital could not be justified. The Prius was deemed to be losing money at the prevailing market price of $22,000 per car and the estimated manufacturing cost of $24,000. However, as Bob Lutz explained, "Toyota's investment criteria was different, they developed the Prius and used it to position the company as ever-attuned to the needs of society rather than for financial gain. . . . one marginally money-losing hybrid car, the Prius, could suddenly prove to be the tide that floated all other Toyota boats."[6]

In addition to the hybrid drive, GM R&D developed other propulsion technologies, such as hydrogen fuel cells, which were showcased at various auto shows. A significant design and manufacturing capability in electric propulsion technology was developed through the EV-1 experience.

Bob Lutz's original idea for a new vehicle that would enable GM to gain competitive advantage over Toyota was a four-seat electric car with lithium-ion (LiOn) batteries. He proposed this idea at several meetings of GM's Automotive Strategy Board in 2005 but could not win the board's approval to proceed. Arguments against a LiOn electric vehicle included the following: the LiOn battery was not ready for automotive applications and was a high risk; GM had to choose electric vehicles over other technologies, such as fuel-cell technology, which were competing for the R&D budget; the EV-1 experience had demonstrated that there was no viable market for an electric vehicle; and GM (at that time) had joined with other car manufacturers in a lawsuit against the State of California's electric vehicle mandate.

The timing for management's decision was critical because Lutz worried that Toyota might soon introduce an all-EV to extend the success it had built with the Prius. The announcement by Tesla Motors that it was developing a LiOn battery-powered electric vehicle gave Lutz the needed ammunition to mitigate concerns over LiOn batteries and to win the approval of GM's Automotive Strategy Boards to develop an electric vehicle concept car. The Volt was born!

In subsequent brainstorming sessions, Jon Lauckner's idea, which persuaded Bob Lutz that an all-electric vehicle was not viable for the mass market (in spite of its attractive technological purity), was further developed into an E-REV with a 16 kilowatt hour battery pack and a 1.4-liter internal combustion engine (ICE). The battery would power the vehicle for the first 40 miles,[7] and the ICE would power an electric generator to drive the propulsion system for an additional 300 miles (see Figure B.2 for a diagram of the Volt powertrain).

In 2011, a year after Volt was introduced to the market, Lutz reflected on the strategic impetus for its development: "The Volt means a lot to GM and to the industry

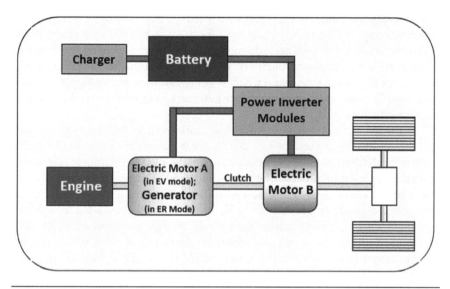

Figure B.2 Volt powertrain

on a variety of levels. First of all, this is a solid technology that is going to be proven reliable. It's a practical way that we can electrify the automobile and drastically reduce our dependency on imported petroleum. It's also important to GM to help reinforce and continue its proud history of technological innovation, and to help restore the image of leadership that accompanied that history. . . . Volt is a shining testimonial to the company's vision and willingness to accept large risk. . . . Volt is the future."[8]

Disruptive Innovation in a Large Company

Jon Lauckner argued that the E-REV concept had many benefits. On the one hand, it removed the range anxiety that customers felt about a pure electric vehicle, and on the other hand, it did not require excessive battery capacity for a 100- to 200-mile range, which, with the current state of battery development, meant excessive weight and cost. Furthermore, the E-REV decoupled the vehicle's success from the availability of public infrastructure for charging the battery, which was a problem that EV-1 faced. And finally, E-REV was an optimal transitional concept to a pure electric vehicle because the drive system was electric and the onboard internal combustion engine was merely another source of generating electrical energy. The future road map for the vehicle could readily adopt a variety of engine technologies, including alternate fuel engines (bioethanol, diesel, hydrogen, or natural gas), fuel cells, or no engine at all for a pure electric configuration.

Volt's extended-range concept represents a disruptive technology that can transform the transportation industry and its infrastructure by creating a bridge to an all-electric system. Volt also has a disruptive potential for society by enabling environmental sustainability through replacing oil with electricity from renewable sources. For the end users, however, Volt is not a disruptive technology as defined by Clayton Christensen;[9] it does not create new markets or new users via affordable and accessible functions.

The E-REV concept was inspired by the innovations of lead users at General Motors.[10] A similar powertrain was used in 1994 during the EV-1 development. Andrew Farah (the Volt chief engineer and one of the EV-1 development engineers) recalled the innovation process when he and other EV-1 engineers converted EV-1 prototypes into an E-REV out of necessity: "We were driving the EV-1 back and forth across the state on a regular basis. Because the engineers needed more miles to do their work than the batteries alone would provide, they devised small trailers equipped with gasoline-powered generators that their EV-1 test vehicles towed along behind. Push a button and it generated electricity, and as long as you were not driving faster than sixty miles per hour, you could keep driving until the gas ran out."[11] Developing a disruptive technology in a large company is a mixed blessing. Although a large company has superior capabilities in marketing, technology, operations, business processes, and financial management, it often lacks decision-making agility, and there is aversion to risk. This creates a unique environment that is both supportive and challenging for disruptive technologies in which they can thrive and come to fruition. In contrast to a disruptive technology, sustaining technologies aim to improve existing products continuously and hence are maintained by the status quo inertia. Sustaining technologies enjoy the support of the incumbents and are reinforced by existing business processes, which are robust and risk averse. The disruptive technology, on the other hand, requires a new strategy and business model whose outcome is uncertain.

Lauckner could count on GM's deep knowledge of the auto industry, world-class design, and manufacturing technology to lead the Volt project through all phases of the product-development process—including market launch. However, he had to navigate within a complex network of stakeholders with disparate experiences, interests, and strategic and tactical objectives. The stakeholders represented multiple vertical and lateral levels of the organization following entrenched business processes—from the CEO to functional managers and management review committees.

Even though the Volt champions, Bob Lutz and Jon Lauckner, held senior executive positions at GM, the complexities of the product-development process in the large company and the forces of sustaining technologies abated their power and influence. But as Lauckner pointed out, leaders must have the necessary skills to persevere through courage of conviction, a strong will to overcome objections, and a profound knowledge of the product and technology. They also must be able to articulate the long-term benefits to the company, including the benefit of being first.

After the E-REV concept was communicated to the Automotive Strategy Board and received its tacit approval to proceed, the *institutional forces* of sustaining technologies kicked in, citing all kinds of problems. Many colorful discussions ensued between *them* and Lutz and Lauckner, who had to persuade the naysayers across the company who stated that *it cannot be done*. According to Andrew Farah, "GM's culture creates defensive antibodies against development of radically new technologies like Volt! Antibodies attack innovations like Volt and argue that we cannot do that."[12] However, strong executive support from the beginning of the project provided the necessary shelter against the organizational antibodies.

Lauckner, believing that successful innovations are *conceived by few and executed by many*, was mindful of the people versus process trade-offs. Individual initiatives are often undervalued when processes take over and the company becomes *process-oriented*—believing that the best ideas come from well-oiled processes rather than individual ingenuity. He remained committed to the original E-REV design concept (of an electric car that had 40 miles of electric battery range plus an engine for the extended range) throughout the program. When Lauckner and Lutz faced political, management, and technical challenges during the project execution, they did not compromise in bringing the initial vision to market. To win, the project leadership team had to make the organization accept the inherent risks and challenges (of the new technology and unconventional approach) and to execute the program successfully in solving the technology problems to maintain management support. To ensure quick decision making, they also formed a unique leadership board for the program, established a dedicated team in each product development area, and assigned project leadership roles to people with technical expertise and creative vision.

Although the development of the Chevrolet Volt—a disruptive technology in a large company—proved challenging, significant organizational learning ensued at GM. Volt proved to GM what was possible and how important it was to embrace inventions. Many members of the Volt team were promoted to higher levels and took their product development lessons to other parts of the organization.

The Project Team

The organizational structure of GM's Chevrolet Volt project is depicted at three levels in Figures B.3, B.4, and B.5—showing executive management, the concept phase, and the production vehicle phase. The executive management structure was composed of two review boards—the Automotive Strategy Board (ASB) and the Automotive Product Board (APB), whose membership included Rick Wagoner (CEO), Bob Lutz (vice chair), Tom Stephens (group vice president of global powertrain), Ed Welburn (vice president of global design), Jim Queen (vice president of global engineering), and Jon Lauckner (vice president of global program management). These two boards oversaw the strategic direction and execution of the program and made recommendations to the GM board of directors for funding R&D and strategic investments in supply chain partnerships and production facilities.

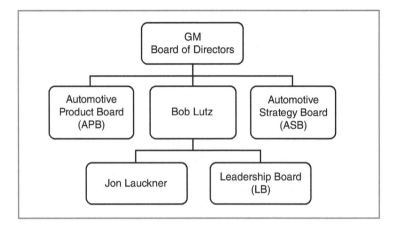

Figure B.3   Program organization: executive management

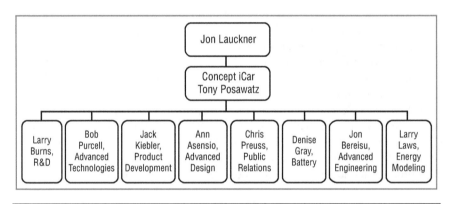

Figure B.4   Program organization: concept phase

GM's standard product development process also included reviews by the GM Global Product Development Council (GPDC). In the case of the Volt, the APB agreed with Lauckner's recommendation to form a leadership board of senior executives to oversee the program in lieu of the GPDC. The leadership board had 12 high-level U.S.-based executives (including Lutz, Stevens, and Lauckner) and met with the development team on a monthly basis, which was indicative of what Lauckner saw as the more active involvement of senior leadership in today's climate.

From the onset, the formation of the project team by Lutz and Lauckner was different from GM's traditional product development team and management structures, perhaps because of the characteristics of the program leaders themselves. Lauckner noted that Bob Lutz was wired differently than other executives; and so

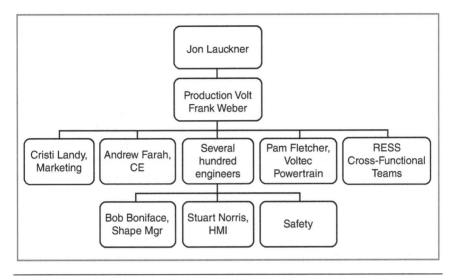

Figure B.5   Program organization: production vehicle phase

was he. Lutz's choice for the program's leadership was Lauckner because he *was an engineer and a brilliant schemer* and could be counted on to produce results. Jon was the VP of global program management (for vehicle development) with a B.S. in mechanical engineering from the University of Michigan and an M.S. in management from the Sloan Fellows program at the Stanford Graduate School of Business. He had also attended the GM-Harvard Senior Executive Program.

In taking a disruptive technology to a high-volume vehicle for the mainstream mass market, "you need the right mix of quant and poet types of people," said Lauckner. At the initiation of the concept and feasibility phase, he gathered a small team of unconventional thinkers to create technological breakthroughs that were both affordable in production and met global safety standards on an accelerated schedule. He knew who the likely candidates were and unofficially recruited them, warning that the project had many technological challenges and required a lot of hard work. The characteristics and sources of motivation among the team members varied. Many were passionate about the electric vehicle concept and knew a lot about the technology. EV-1 people knew its flaws, too, and wanted to fix them. Others had technological capabilities and experience in related technologies, like the fuel-cell and hybrid vehicles. They liked the technical challenges of Volt and wanted to work on the project (even part-time).

The concept vehicle was named iCar, and the team's charter during the concept development phase was to verify the feasibility and viability of the proposed E-REV concept. Tony Posawatz was assigned as the project manager to produce the concept car for the Detroit Auto Show in January 2007 (Figure B.4). Although initially he was the only full-time engineer assigned to the project, Posawatz was motivated by the innovation and technological challenges of the iCar and strived to develop it not just as a concept car for the show, but with the design capabilities necessary for volume production and commercialization.

Cristi Landy, who was a *Chevrolet person*, was assigned to the project as the product marketing manager from the beginning during the iCar planning stage in 2006. This was unusual because GM concept cars often are created to stimulate thinking about future designs and technologies and not to target commercialization. Landy represented the Chevrolet marketing department and was responsible for knowing the customer requirements (as the voice of the customer) and for working with the product design team to ensure compliance to the maximum possible extent.

Battery development was assigned to Denise Gray, who in the summer of 2006 had been promoted to be GM's first global director of rechargeable energy storage systems, responsible for all hybrid vehicles and future storage technologies.

After the 2007 Detroit Auto Show, where the concept was unveiled, the initial concept and feasibility team was folded into a larger, formal Volt program team for the development of the production car. This team comprised the best talent at GM and numbered several hundred (Figure B.5). The team leader was Frank Weber, who was brought in from the Opel division in Europe in February 2007. Weber's role and responsibilities as the Volt program leader were different than those of the leaders of other vehicle development projects in the standard GM process.

In GM's standard process, the product development organization was headed by two leaders—a vehicle line executive in charge of program management (including schedule, budget, and product commercialization) and a chief engineer responsible for delivering a vehicle that met all design and engineering requirements. Volt's product development organization combined these two functions into one position that was assigned to Frank Weber. He was a hands-on system engineer who liked to create the future and had the right mix of technical and business experience. He was technologically savvy and could navigate the unchartered territory of creating Volt's new technologies. He also had extensive product planning, production, marketing, and project management experience at GM. Frank was motivated to take on the project because he cared about the environment and saw Volt as an opportunity to make a difference for society and to reduce the environmental footprint of transportation.

The other members of the production vehicle development team included several EV-1 veterans, fuel-cell engineers (who brought with them knowledge of power electronics and high-voltage energy management systems), hybrid engineers (with knowledge of regenerative braking systems and electric motors), the gasoline engine team (representing a century of expertise in combustion engine vehicles), and many new engineering hires. The notable late additions were Andrew Farah, who was the EV-1 chief engineer and came from GM Europe in August 2007 as the chief engineer for Volt, and Pam Fletcher, who was the global Voltec and plug-in hybrid electric powertrain chief engineer. According to Fletcher, she was not one of the early team members but was brought on board at the reality check-in time.

Several cross-functional teams were created to carry out the development of critical subsystems of the product. For example, the cross-functional team for developing the rechargeable energy storage system (RESS) was responsible for systems engineering, controls, heat transfer, electronics, high-voltage wiring, manufacturing, quality, purchasing, and project management. The RESS team was segmented into product development teams that would design, manufacture, test, and validate prototypes of components and subassemblies of the RESS. The product development teams were coordinated by a RESS system integration team and a RESS integration team. The system integration team ensured that RESS met the requirements for mass, cost, quality, and manufacturability, and the RESS integration team managed the physical integration of the RESS and controlled the interface control documents. The other key subsystem managers were the design director, who was responsible for development of the Volt's appearance during both the concept and production design phases; the interior and exterior design managers, who led the development of the interior and exterior appearance themes; a human-machine interface (HMI) manager, who designed the controls and displays; and the safety and crash managers, who tested the safety of the vehicles.

The project team members came from GM offices around the world, including Germany, the United Kingdom, New York, Michigan, and California. Some of the software was done in India. However, because subsystem integration was a critical task of the product development, most of the development engineers were co-located.

The Volt development team went through tough times, including the global financial meltdown (2008), GM's bankruptcy (2009), GM's government-funded resurgence, CEO turnover, and the loss of some key engineering executives. Some team members went to Germany to develop the European version of Volt, the Opel Ampera. In spite of the difficulties, the Volt management team under the leadership of Jon Lauckner maintained the project's momentum and the focus on the original program objectives. Furthermore, the resources of the program were not reduced, and the executive management support continued unabated.

Project Execution: Invention on the Critical Path

The Volt product development timeline with manufacturing milestones is depicted in Figure B.6. The vehicle development program documents and the approval gates to production release are also listed. The product development process is described in Exhibit B.3.

In June 2008, 17 months after the concept car debut at the Detroit Auto Show, GM's board of directors approved a budget of several hundred million dollars for development of the Volt as a production vehicle. The engineering budget for the program has not been disclosed, but GM's investment was over $800 million in Michigan alone, including the Detroit-Hamtramck plant where Volt is assembled

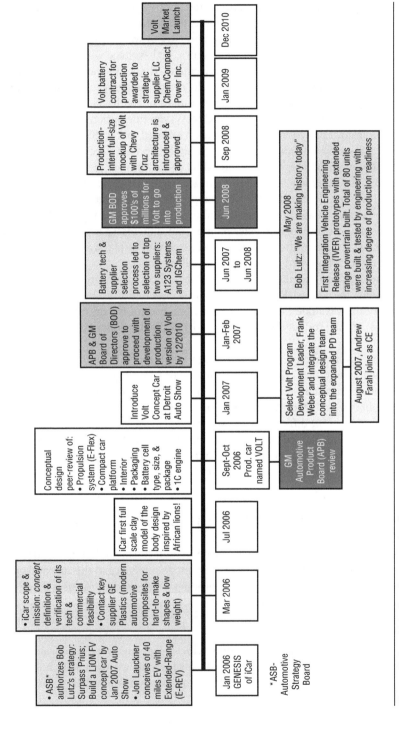

Figure B.6a   Volt development timeline

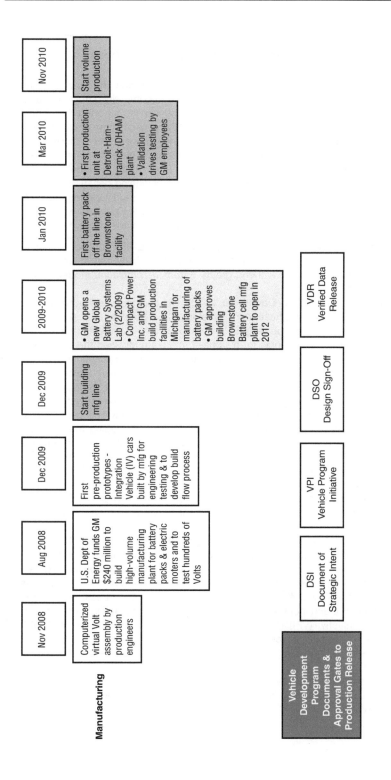

Figure B.6b Volt development timeline

Exhibit B.3: Product Development Process

GM's standard product development process has gone through many revisions over the years to improve efficiency and to respond to competitive market needs. For example, in July 2012, GM's News and Stories website reported that a new product program structure had been adopted at GM, consolidating the leadership of each program under one executive chief engineer who would be totally responsible for her or his vehicles from inception to production. These changes removed a layer of management and approximately 20 executive positions globally.

The Volt project was under the spotlight from the beginning because of the internal politics in the company and extensive media exposure. Therefore, the leadership team decided to have an *open* product development process with ample reviews. The Volt product development cycle went through five phases:

- **Phase 0 (January 2006):** Strategic approach and E-REV concept definition.
- **Phase 1 (January to March 2006):** Concept viability and feasibility verification by the initial working group. Extensive simulation modeling was used in this phase.
- **Phase 2 (March to December 2006):** Concept car development. The early tasks of this phase were developing the body exterior design and evaluating alternate powertrain (propulsion system) concepts that met the 40-mile EV performance. In this phase, the team followed the company's peer-review process to ensure that the proposed technical concepts and associated risk assessment approach were sound. Design reviews were conducted by the experts from across the company. For example, a peer review by the powertrain experts validated the propulsion system modeling and integration approach. Several other peer reviews were held at various stages of the design throughout 2006, concluding the technical feasibility of the iCar's propulsion system in meeting the performance targets. Several executive review meetings were also held in this phase. Jon Lauckner presented the iCar's concept design to the APB and underscored the extendability of its platform and powertrain designs to future all-electric and fuel-cell-powered vehicles. Phase 2 was concluded with the detail design and manufacturing of the concept car for the Detroit Auto Show in January 2007.
- **Phase 3 (January 2007 to December 2010):** Production Volt development. This phase went through several go/no-go gates at critical milestones before the first full-scale prototype (IVER) could be built and driven on the test tracks. These milestones and associated sign off documents (as defined by GM's standard vehicle development process) are listed in Figure B.6 and include the document of strategic intent (DSI), vehicle program initiative (VPI), design sign-off (DSO), and verified data release (VDR). The road-testing milestones in this phase were designated as *x-percent drive tests*, indicating that the test vehicles were at the x-percent production readiness state. The drive tests were carried out with prototypes that were at increasing levels of production readiness from 65% to 100%.
- **Phase 4 (January 2011 to 2013):** Market launch and early market surveillance.

and $43 million in the Brownstown battery plant facility for manufacturing of the battery pack. In addition, as part of the American Recovery and Reinvestment Act of 2009 (the Recovery Act), the U.S. Department of Energy awarded GM over $240 million for the high-volume assembly of the battery pack and electric motors and for testing of hundreds of preproduction units.[13] The initial Volt battery cell manufacturing plant was built in Holland, Michigan, by Compact Power, Inc., a subsidiary of LG Chem, with $150 million (50% cost share) funding from the U.S. government.

To keep the project team focused through the upheavals of the external environment, the leadership team established three guiding principles in managing the project and making choices among conflicting requirements:

- Design for 40 miles of electric vehicle range;
- Create Volt for all customers everywhere globally, including those operating in different climates, and satisfy both early adopters and mainstream users; and
- Start volume production in November 2010.

Pam Fletcher required her team members to sign up to three credos—"I cannot fail. I am responsible. No sacrifice is too big."—and this meant many long days, weeks, and months.

Marketing was involved in the project from the beginning in 2006, but customer research did not get into high gear until early 2007, after the concept car was unveiled at the Detroit Auto Show. During the concept car phase, the product manager, Cristi Landy, developed the product content by listing the unique features that had to be designed in the vehicle.

Marketing held focus groups with owners of various types of cars, including midsize hybrids, electric vehicles (including EV-1), and the Toyota RAV4EV. These focus groups provided valuable information about what they liked and did not like about their cars and made suggestions for the Volt. A representative from GM's Opel subsidiary in Germany assisted in defining the user interface requirements, including the two seven-inch display screens with coordinated motion and sound. The focus groups also performed evaluative research on multiple design concepts and features, including four or five seats, manual or powered seat adjustment, 24-hour Internet connectivity, ease of plug-in and recharging, and design of the two display screens for navigation map and advanced electronics capabilities. Marketing pushed to maximize the standard features on the vehicle commensurate with its target price.

Engineers wrote the requirement specifications for all subsystems, although many of the requirements, particularly those of the controls and software, evolved during the program. A significant challenge brought about by the newness of the extended-range EV technology was identifying the new and nontraditional regulatory requirements of the Environmental Protection Agency (EPA), Underwriters Laboratory (UL), electric utilities (represented by the Electric Power Research Institute), and various municipalities. For example, the standards for EPA certification that were necessary for product commercialization did not exist for Volt as a new class of vehicle. A dedicated Volt team helped skeptical EPA regulators develop a new labeling method and test procedures for the vehicle according to the EPA's timeline, which was not always aligned with the project's tight schedule. Figure B.7 shows the EPA-Department of Transportation (DOT) Fuel Economy and Environment label for a 2013 Volt. Another Volt team worked with the International Society of Automotive Engineers to revise the J1772 standard for Volt's plug-in charging equipment, which also met UL safety requirements.

The standard GM vehicle development process required all technologies to be proven to the *readiness* point before adopting them in the product design. However, the Volt development process deviated from this rule and consequently created a few process challenges in the GM system. Bob Lutz characterized the Volt process as *decoupled development*—decoupling the *most engineering-intense subsystems* from the development path of the rest of the vehicle. For example, the RESS development followed a nonstandard process practiced in advanced technology R&D. The RESS development cycle started with definition of the requirements and went through five preplanned design and test iterations.

The tight project schedule placed the battery and propulsion system innovations on the critical path to production, requiring the managers to be knowledgeable about the details and available for timely decision making on a short notice. The project's guiding principles helped prioritize alternate choices.

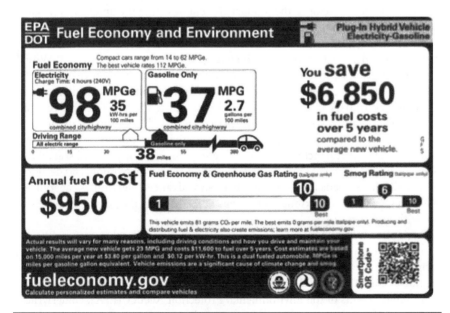

Figure B.7   EPA-DOT Label for the 2013 Volt

Volt's new and more stringent design requirements led the engineers to take a more cautionary design approach than was customary in the standard product development practice. For example, the team decided to overengineer everything in vehicle electrification to ensure safety, arguing that future generations of the product would provide the opportunity to refine and optimize the design. State-of-the art-simulation and testing tools were also used extensively to accelerate the design-optimization process and meet the time-to-market goal.

On September 16, 2008, the centennial of GM—a full-size mockup of the production-intent Volt based on the Chevy Cruz architecture—was revealed to the public by Bob Lutz and Fritz Henderson, the GM CEO. Some Volt enthusiasts and journalists at the event were surprised and disappointed by the extent that the production vehicle's proportions had deviated from the original concept car's *daring* design, as shown in Figure B.8.

Concept iCar

Production Volt

Figure B.8   Volt Concept and Production Designs

The first integration vehicle engineering release prototype was built in the summer of 2009, and 80 Volt prototypes were built and tested during the product development cycle at the Pre-Production Operation (PPO) facilities at the Tech Center in Warren, Michigan.

The Volt team created a high-performance E-REV on a tight schedule, but an important marketing challenge loomed as the product went to production in November of 2010: how should the technology and the car be communicated to mainstream customers?

Volt Design Requirements and Features

According to the Volt product manager, Cristi Landy, "Volt must be an electric car for the masses, as the Chevrolet brand is. This above all means affordability." However, design for affordability became a significant challenge because of the extensive new technology content that had to be built into Volt to satisfy its performance requirements. In the traditional vehicle development process at GM, a cost target is set for the vehicle based on the marketing price target and vehicle business model. The cost target drives the design specifications and vehicle manufacturing process. For the Volt, the development team felt that *beating the competition* was the number one priority and the business case was second. This change in the strategic outlook in vehicle development seemed to transcend Volt and extended across GM in 2006.

In 2006, Toyota owned the hybrid market, so GM's iCar had to go beyond. According to the list of requirements that was given to the Volt team (Exhibit B.4), the Volt had to be *a vehicle that is more accessible, more environmentally acceptable and significantly 'cooler' than the Prius could ever be.* Although the initial code name of iCar was intentionally associated with electronics products like iPod, an outside agency eventually came up with Volt as the name of the production car.

Exhibit B.4: iCar Vision, 2006

According to GM's vision,[14] an iCar is:

- A global vehicle that will launch a paradigm shift for GM.
- A vehicle based on the same marketing ethic that makes iPod so popular—style fashion, practicality, and freedom—making the car a seamless part of one's personal lifestyle and technology portfolio.
- An electric vehicle with plug-in hybrid (E85 and biodiesel) and pure electric (battery and fuel-cell) capability.
- An affordable four-place vehicle with high sales-volume potential.
- A lightweight, highly styled, and highly functional vehicle about the size of an Astra/Cruz.

- A vehicle that is more accessible, more environmentally acceptable, and significantly *cooler* than the Prius could ever be.
- A vehicle that is efficient in terms of energy, space, and time.
- A vehicle that is fun to own and use with no worries and no excuses.
- A vehicle that is a platform for passion, fashion, driving, riding, connecting, communicating, socializing, and powering.
- A vehicle for the twenty-first century that redefines mobility for mass markets, being *connected* to everything and transcending transportation.
- A vehicle wherein traditional comfort features are exchanged for high utility and functionality, low cost, and *fun to drive*. (This does not mean an unrefined vehicle. It means rethinking aspects of the vehicle that have become commonplace with respect to creature comforts and occupant interfaces.)
- A vehicle with elegant simplicity providing meaningful value and avoiding extraneous technology that adds complexity and confusion.
- A vehicle marketed to high influencers globally.
- A vehicle that prompts the response: "Why didn't I think of that?"

The marketing group conducted user research and updated the competitive landscape throughout the Volt development cycle. Exhibit B.5 summarizes user characteristics, needs, and wants—and Figure B.9 depicts the competitive outlook in 2009.

Both the market requirements specification (MRS) and the engineering requirements specification (ERS) for Volt were influenced by the EV-1 experience. The Volt team wanted to overcome the limitations of EV-1 that contributed to its demise, including limited range, limited passenger and luggage space, and rapid battery depletion driving uphill. The MRS for the EV range (in the battery-discharge mode) was 40 miles based on market information that 80% of American and European car owners commuted 40 miles or less in a day. The battery power and energy capacity had to deliver a 40-mile performance for a compact sedan comfortably carrying four people with luggage through a wide range of road and weather conditions, including extreme climate conditions from $-40°C$ to $+40°C$. Safety was also a major MRS item and drove the cell chemistry and manufacturing selection process because impurities in cell manufacturing could result in cell overheating—a potential fire hazard. The battery energy capacity for powering the vehicle in the EV mode and also for powering all auxiliary energy consumption such as heating, ventilation, and air conditioning was calculated to be 16 kilowatt hours (kWh). The battery pack life and size were the next two critical specifications.

The MRS called for a 10-year warranty for the electric propulsion system, including the batteries, based on consumer expectations set by the competitive hybrid vehicles in the market. Therefore, the battery life had to be designed for 10 years and 150,000 miles, and individual battery cells had to be liquid cooled to control the cell temperature under all operating conditions. The battery pack size was established

Exhibit B.5: User Characteristics and Needs-and-Wants Analysis, 2009

	Mid-car	Hybrid	Electric vehicles
Psychographics	Conservative Risk averse Very practical Worried about battery charging time and where to plug in	Draw attention to me	Early adopters Motivated by technology and the environment We are special, so we enter the bubble of the EV world. Use solar panels on their homes
	Concerned about global warming, the environment (clean air—asthma, animal health), future generations Recycle, change light bulbs, walk rather than drive		
Wants	Reduce their dependence on petroleum Environmentally friendly materials To do the right thing		Doubt that hydrogen-EV is the answer. Want an all-EV vehicle Plug-in hybrid EV most immediate promise in furthering technology, a solution for society Politically correct materials
Willing to pay	Did the math and the hybrid price is not better than paying for gas. Price deterred me. When it is the same price as gas, I will buy.	I didn't do any calculation—just assumed it would be worth it.	Willing to pay the most
Purchase mindset	Rational: calculated that other things can help the environment just as much (walking, recycling, conserving energy)	Emotional: not just about saving money, more about the environment	Obsessive: energy conservation always on their mind, part of their identity Society is not ready to go all electric; I am ahead of the curve.
Other	My car is an appliance, so I want the one that does the best job for me.	I love the attention I get from driving a hybrid. I am proud that my car makes a statement about me.	My car is part of my identity. Obsessive desire to appear green and have the latest products

Source: Cristy Landy, Chevrolet marketing director, 2009.

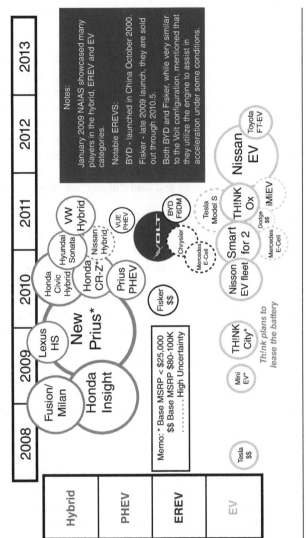

Figure B.9   Competitive Outlook for Electric Vehicles, 2009

based on the overall vehicle dimensions, the size of other subsystems, and the number of battery cells needed for the 16 kWh capacity.

Additional MRS and ERS requirements included vehicle acceleration of 0 to 60 miles per hour (mph) in 9 seconds or less. The top speed was set at 99 mph. Although these specifications were the nominal performance requirements, the product design was often driven by the requirements in extreme conditions. For example, customers would expect to drive the Volt at 70 mph speed on a 6% grade at high elevations. Andrew Farah estimated that 60 kW of power was needed for this level of performance, which he called the lunatic fringe requirement. The control system had to be designed for the vehicle response to be intuitive to the driver and seamless in both pure EV mode and the engine-charging mode at all driving conditions (including steep roads, high and cold climates, and vehicle acceleration/deceleration).

The product marketing strategy set by corporate executives established Volt's platform strategy and drove many aspects of its design. The length, width, and wheelbase of the global compact car architecture were felt to be the suitable design specifications for Volt. The leadership team argued that starting from scratch with an all-new chassis made no sense. Completely new vehicle architecture would have required significantly more production capital and engineering expense and would have adversely impacted the product launch schedule. Rick Wagoner, GM's CEO, insisted that the Volt must be a Chevy product rather than an entirely new brand (60% of GM business in the mid-2000s was in Chevy sales, and it was up to 70% in 2012). However, Chevy was not a technology leader, and Rick Wagoner wanted to strengthen its brand.

The platform choice and the required energy efficiency created significant constraints on the Volt body design. The sleek design of the concept car that had received rave reviews could not be used. Using computational fluid dynamics modeling and extensive wind tunnel testing, the body shape was redesigned to meet the target drag coefficient of 0.28.

The user interface and interior design requirements were defined mostly based on the company's internal knowledge about the wants and preferences of mainstream customers. Customers were believed to want *an electric aesthetic* and an interior that reflected the Chevrolet brand character as represented by the latest models of Malibu or Camaro. Marketing believed that Volt buyers were tech savvy and comfortable with Xboxes and Twitter. However, different customers had different reasons for wanting to buy a Volt—it would be: the coolest thing on the block, powered by E-REV technology, getting the country off petroleum, or a smart purchase because it saved money on gasoline consumption.

A 9.3-gallon fuel tank was specified to achieve the 300-mile extended range. The vehicle was designed to use premium instead of regular unleaded fuel. Although this was contrary to the affordability requirement preferred by marketing, it was needed to achieve the desired miles-per-gallon performance. Another feature that was preferred by marketing was having a spare tire, which was voted down based on engineering's desire to reduce weight and packaging constraints.

Sustainability and environmental friendliness were not specific design requirements. However, Volt designers were aware of the positive environmental potential of an electric car and maximized the use of renewable and recycled materials in the product, even though it was not easy to find materials that met automotive-grade durability requirements. Product design and manufacturing methodology and details are described in Exhibit B.6.

Exhibit B.6: Volt Product Design and Manufacturing

Powertrain

The Volt design benefited greatly from GM's core expertise in automotive design and manufacturing. The EV-1 experience helped Volt engineers in the development of the electric powertrain, software, and controls system, even though the EV-1 design was a one-motor single-speed drive that could not meet the E-REV requirements of Volt.

The Volt was an E-REV. Its powertrain system was formally renamed Voltec (Figure B.2) and was designed to enable Volt's operation over the entire range of speed and acceleration. The Voltec powertrain has two operational modes: the electric-vehicle or charge-depletion mode runs 40 miles on the battery, and an extended-range or charge-sustaining mode is powered by the ICE. Voltec's electric transaxle enables the patented operation of two motors and one generator during all operational modes of the vehicle. Voltec designers reused many components and tooling that had been previously developed for GM's front-wheel-drive hybrid electric vehicles to improve product reliability and to reduce the development schedule and manufacturing cost. Volt was also designed with an off-the-shelf 1.4 liter gasoline-powered ICE. Although a more efficient and customized engine or an unconventional power unit could have been designed, the task was deferred to the next-generation product for cost and schedule reasons.

Three modes of operational control were designed for the vehicle, which the driver could select by a switch mounted on the center console—normal mode, sport mode (for more spirited driving), and mountain mode (when the ICE is turned on sooner to ensure there is adequate battery charge for maintaining the cruise speed while climbing up a steep road or at high elevations).

Battery Pack

The 16-kWh LiOn battery pack comprises 288 cells that must work flawlessly because failure of one cell can cause failure of the entire pack. A large design-of-experiments study was carried out to gather data for battery management calibration and to develop a battery life model.

The battery cell temperature is actively controlled by a liquid cooling/heating system that is integrated in the battery pack with the thermal management and power control subsystem. The 5.5-foot long, 140-cubic decimeter (dm^3, about half a cubic meter) battery pack weighs 198.1 kilograms (kg) and supplies energy to the 111 kW (149 horsepower) electric drive unit. The T-shaped housing of the battery pack serves as a semi-structural member of the car and is secured properly to eliminate any movement of the batteries during shock, vibration, and impact.

The LiOn battery cells, liquid thermal management, and battery pack assembly posed the biggest technical risks of the program and presented many R&D and manufacturing challenges, including cell chemistry stability (for safety and efficiency) and cost. When the program started, there was extensive battery research at leading universities and companies in Japan, the U.S., France, Germany, Korea, and China. Taking advantage of these research activities, GM's battery team conducted an analysis of two dozen battery cell chemistries and suppliers and selected the Korean company LG Chem for its advanced technology, responsiveness, and manufacturing capabilities. The LG Chem battery cell electrolyte used nano-phosphate, a benign and ultrastable compound instead of cobalt that was used in LiOn batteries of computers and portable devices. Compact Power, Inc., a U.S. subsidiary of LG Chem, was contracted to build the battery pack and thermal management system.

The development of battery cells by LG Chem engineers and the design of the battery pack by Compact Power and GM engineers were tightly integrated to overcome the technology and integration issues on the tight project schedule. The initial manufacturing cost of the batteries was estimated to be $10,000, and it was expected to go down to $5,000 (or $312 per kWh) at 40,000 cumulative production units.

The battery charging equipment was designed according to UL and SAE J1772 standards, which were developed with the active participation of Volt engineers.[15] The EV-1 experience provided valuable information about customer expectations and the technical issues. For example, EV-1 charging was inductive, which proved to be a mistake. Volt batteries can be charged at regular household power outlets at 120 volts, although it takes roughly 10 to 16 hours to charge the batteries fully from a depleted state. With a 240-volt power supply, the charge time is reduced to four hours. Charge stations with a 240-volt supply are increasing at public locations across the country, and many businesses are installing charge stations in employee parking lots.

Software and Controls

Volt software has 10 million lines of code to operate 100 electronic controllers. In contrast, a Boeing 787 has 6.5 million lines of code, and an average GM car in 1990 used one million lines of code. Developing defect-free software was a challenging undertaking. In software development, it is a rule of thumb that there will be 0.1 to 1 software defects per 1,000 lines of code (not counting comments) and that the cost of fixing bugs rises exponentially in subsequent phases of product development.

Volt's rapid product development was enabled by deploying a model-based design approach and automatic code generation. Nearly 100% of software was generated automatically, which is believed to have improved software engineers' efficiency by 30%. In the model-based design approach, engineers model the system dynamics and control algorithm, including diagnostics, while the hardware is being developed instead of waiting for completion of the hardware design and prototyping of new components and technologies.

The OnStar team at GM developed several features and remote apps for Volt. It also partnered with Volt engineers to work with utility companies and government agencies in the development of *smart-grid technology* to program Volt software for charging at the lowest possible electric rates and to guide drivers to public charging stations. The OnStar team also helped in product development by designing diagnostics and monitoring electronics for testing Volt prototypes.

The Body

The body (exterior) design was one of the first tasks of the vehicle design during the concept development phase. Multiple design sketches and subscale models were proposed by GM's design studios around the world in Warren, Michigan; London, England; and North Hollywood, California. The proposed designs were reviewed in April 2006 by the project leadership team, including Bob Lutz, Jon Lauckner, and Ed Welburn—who was the global design vice president. The selected concept was conceived by the exterior designer, Jelani Aliyu.

During the production vehicle development phase, the product exterior (shape) and interior deviated substantially from the concept car design. Through 500 hours of wind tunnel testing on one-third-scale and full-scale models and analytical computational fluid dynamics modeling, the final body design was developed. The production Volt body shape achieved a coefficient of drag of 0.28, in contrast with EV-1 and the Prius, which had a coefficient of drag of 0.19 and 0.30, respectively.

Another design criterion for the body was crash safety of the high-voltage electrical system. This was new to the safety experts at GM and needed special attention. Volt crash safety was evaluated by both computer simulation and the testing of full-scale prototypes.

Interior Design

A rich mix of state-of-the-art technologies from GM and GE were used for a cool, affordable, light, strong, and recyclable interior design. A state-of-the-art graphical user interface was designed to display the battery storage level, fuel level, propulsion system data, and other standard vehicle information. The instrument panel displays were tested in a GM driving simulator to make sure that the high-tech displays would not distract drivers.

Manufacturing

The Volt was intended to be manufactured in Michigan to the maximum extent possible—to turn Detroit into an Electric Motor City. The final assembly began at GM's Detroit Hamtramck Assembly Plant (DHAM) concurrently with other GM vehicles like Cadillac DTS and Buick Lucerne. DHAM workers were trained in building the Volt and its unique electric propulsion system through involvement with the prototype manufacturing team and assembling the prototypes in the PPO shop at the GM Tech center in Warren. In turn, the manufacturing involvement in the prototype phase helped the design engineers improve manufacturability of the product and its manufacturing process flow. GM production engineers started to develop a computer model of the vehicle assembly process as early as November 2008 and started to build the assembly line at the DHAM plant in late 2009, one year before the Volt went into production.

Originally, GM planned to have Compact Power manufacture the battery pack assembly with cells coming from LG Chem in Korea. That strategy changed later in the program, and GM decided to manufacture the battery pack assembly in Brownstown's new LiOn battery pack manufacturing facility, which went online in 2012. This change in the manufacturing strategy was motivated by the desire to control the system integration and battery pack design intellectual property. Furthermore, GM wanted to use Volt's power train design in other vehicle lines, too.

A new high-speed battery pack assembly process was developed to achieve the desired precision and throughput. The takt time of the battery pack assembly process was 60 seconds. The process was a combination of conventional car assembly techniques and manufacturing processes of medical and electrical products.

Key Suppliers

GE Plastics, Compact Power, Inc. (CPI), and its Korean parent, LG Chem Ltd., were the key suppliers in the program. In early 2006, after the initial concept was born out of the brainstorming discussions with Bob Lutz and Jon Lauckner, Lauckner contacted GE Plastics to partner in creating the concept car. GM would design the propulsion system and the vehicle design (shape), and GE Plastics would supply lightweight advanced composite plastics for the body and the interior. GE Plastics' composite materials also could support exterior shapes that were hard to manufacture in metal, and because they were lighter, they could further help the drive range.

Battery development had the biggest supplier involvement in the program. Immediately after the ASB's approval following the introduction of the concept car in January 2007, the battery development work got into high gear, including technology-360 and the supplier and partner selection process. The battery supplier selection went through a three-phase process. In Phase 1, 155 chemistries proposed by various makers and technologists were prescreened. In Phase 2, 60 potential candidates were evaluated during multiple workshops, resulting in the selection of 16 different suppliers. The battery proposals from these suppliers were assessed using a Pugh decision matrix comprising multiple parameters including power, energy, abuse tolerance, packaging layout, temperature capability, software and control, life, technology maturity, mass, and part count (representing complexity). In Phase 3, two finalist suppliers were selected. The first supplier group was CPI of Michigan, which developed the battery pack, and its parent company, LG Chem of Korea, which supplied the battery cells. The second supplier group was A123 Systems of Massachusetts for cells and Continental Automotive Systems of Germany for the battery pack. The dual-supplier path development was chosen to mitigate risks in the critical battery system development. The finalists were evaluated throughout

2008 before CPI was announced as the Volt battery production supplier of choice based on LG Chem's superior cell architecture and chemistry and its manufacturing readiness. The LG Chem cell design is prismatic (flat package) and uses a carbon graphite anode and a lithium-manganese-oxide cathode.

Another important supplier was dSPACE Inc., which provided rapid controls prototyping and hardware in the loop systems for control software development and performance validation of various subsystems during vehicle dynamics, safety, and integration testing.

Pricing Strategy

There was a disagreement in the company about where to set the list price. Marketing felt that early buyers were technology adopters and therefore, would be willing to pay a modest premium for the new technology. Company executives, on the other hand, felt that marketing did not know the right price because Volt was a *game changer* and a new-to-market invention. In the summer of 2010, the standard vehicle price was announced at approximately $40,000 dollars or a $350 per month lease with a $2,500 down payment. The retail price was believed to be too high by some automotive analysts, although the lease financing seemed competitive.

The pricing decision was not based on competitive reference pricing, particularly against the Prius, which was selling in the $25,000 to $30,000 range. Instead, the price was based on the Volt being a new class of product in the market that delivered benefits (40-mile electric vehicle capability) that the Prius did not offer. Even with a $40,000 price tag, executives believed that GM was demonstrating a willingness to commercialize Volt at an initial loss in order to establish technology leadership in the market. Although the relatively high initial consumer price had been a deterrent to rapid market penetration, rising gasoline prices and anticipated changes in greenhouse gas emission regulations favored Volt and were believed to drive the future demand.

Product Launch and Market Penetration

When GM's iCar was unveiled at the Detroit Auto Show in January 2007, Toyota labeled it a public relations exercise and questioned the safety of LiON batteries. Volt had been under the spotlight throughout its development. Newspaper headlines had created buzz around the technology and awareness about the product, and this proved to be a blessing at the product launch in December 2010.

Before a new product is released to market, GM gives early units from manufacturing to employees to drive and provide feedback to engineering and marketing. Because Volt was new to GM employees, it was decided to give it to a group of "EV-advocate" customers. Ten such customers were selected from target market regions near the service locations in New York, Los Angeles, and Washington, DC.

In the first year after launch, customers were *fighting over the product*, said Cristi Landry, and customer satisfaction with Volt was highest, based on a Consumer Reports analysis. The marketing team held monthly web communications with a selected group of buyers (10 to 12) to receive feedback. These customers were treated as a trusted confidant focus group. Marketing prepared a *market launch assessment* document six months after launch in October 2011.

Beyond the initial momentum with technology enthusiasts, selling the car at the desired rate became a challenge. Dealers did not know the product and its technology, and marketing feared that they might discourage customers who came to showrooms. To mitigate this risk, marketing set up a dedicated Volt advisory team to help customers and educate them about the *optimal way of using Volt*. Figure B.10 shows the unit sales history of the Volt from December 2010 to June 2013.

"Our challenge is how to communicate to the mass market the extended range of 300+ miles and the 40 EV miles," said Cristi Landy. The tag line in early TV commercials was "More car than electric," and it did not help viewers understand the car. The challenge was to answer fundamental questions: "What is a Volt? How can we define it, differentiate it, and justify its price?" The commentaries by investigating reporters and even by GM developers about the car revealed some of the underlying issues. Andrew Farah was pleased with the Volt but "wondered if those who write about it will really understand just what the car is all about." Larry Edsall concluded his experience with Volt by noting that "driving it is so unremarkable . . . Volt is not a different experience. It is simply a means to an end, a way to get from Point A to Point B, safely, comfortably, enjoyably, but without needing much, if any, imported petroleum. It is, after all, a car, just as it was meant to be." Landy thought

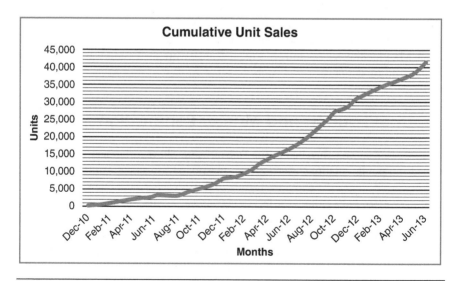

Figure B.10   Volt Sales History

that electrification of transportation was the driving force and paced the market penetration momentum.

Retrospect and Looking Forward

Two years after the product launch, the Volt team felt they had done a good job. The 40-mile range had been the right choice and was market-tested. Customer experience, various consumer reports, and EPA data were positive.

Volt has done many things for GM, beyond being the first E-REV in the market and paving the way to electric transportation. Volt demonstrated the will and technical prowess of GM in the face of considerable risks, including developing a revolutionary technology, being in a market that was not yet ready for Volt as a new class of electric vehicle, and meeting the regulatory fuel economy labeling criteria. The investment in developing Volt created several building blocks of future success for GM, including the design and manufacturing technologies for LiON batteries, high-capacity traction electric motors and power electronics,[16] and EV software and controls technology. The technology building blocks are being used in upcoming product lines, such as the Cadillac Converj coupe (which was put on hold during the company's financial crisis in 2008) and the new Chevy Spark all-electric car (which shares a significant amount of its battery and propulsion system concept with Volt).

As marketing focused on improving Volt's market share in 2012, GM's product planners were contemplating the strategy for developing the second-generation Volt. How should GM respond to the lessons learned in the first two years of Volt in the market and to the changes in the market conditions? Was it time to set an aggressive manufacturing cost target for the second-generation product to enhance its pricing flexibility? Should the 40-mile electric vehicle range be increased to blunt the market momentum of pure-EV competitors like Nissan's Leaf, which has 75 miles EV range? How should the battery cost (dollars per kWh), energy density (watt hours per kilogram), and charging speed be significantly improved? Should GM participate in the development of the charge-station infrastructure across the country?

Endnotes

1. Dariush Rafinejad prepared this August 27, 2013 case with the generous support of General Motors Corporation as the basis for class discussion, rather than to illustrate either effective or ineffective handling of an administrative situation.
2. Jon Lauckner is currently General Motor's chief technology officer, vice president of research and development, and president of GM Ventures.
3. This exhibit was taken from the General Motors website at http://www.gm.com in 2013.

4. See Exhibit B.2 for definitions of various technologies according to the Society of Automotive Engineers (SAE), International.

5. Rick Wagoner, General Motors chair and chief executive officer—remarks delivered at the media preview at the Los Angeles Auto Show, November 2006.

6. Bob Lutz, *Car Guys vs. Bean Counters: The Battle for the Soul of American Business* (New York: Portfolio/Penguin, 2011).

7. The 40-mile range was chosen (over the initial 10-mile estimate) based on a marketing study that showed that the daily trips of 80% of American drivers were 40 miles or less.

8. Lindsay Brook, (Ed.), "Chevrolet Volt—Development Story of the Pioneering Electrified Vehicle," Published by the International Society of Automotive Engineers (SAE), 2011.

9. Clayton M. Christensen, *The Innovator's Dilemma: The Revolutionary Book That Will Change the Way You Do Business* (New York: HarperCollins, 1997).

10. Eric von Hippel, *The Sources of Innovation* (Oxford, UK: Oxford University Press, 1988).

11. Larry Edsall, *Chevrolet Volt: Charging the Course*, foreword by Bob Lutz (Minneapolis, MN: Motorbooks, 2010).

12. Lindsay Brook, (Ed.), "Chevrolet Volt—Development Story of the Pioneering Electrified Vehicle", Published by the International Society of Automotive Engineers (SAE), 2011.

13. Perry Chiaramonte, "Plant That Got $150 Million to Make Volt Batteries in Michigan Furloughs Workers," Foxnews.com, October 8, 2012, http://www.foxnews.com/us/2012/10/08/lg-plant-that-got-150m-to-make-volt-batteries-in-michigan-puts-workers-on.html.

14. Chris Preuss, GM Advanced Technology Communications, 2006.

15. Charging levels are defined as level 1, 120 V AC and 16 A (= 1.92 kW); level 2, 208–240 V AC and 12–80 A (= 2.5–19.2 kW); level 3, high voltages (300–600 V DC) and high currents (hundreds of amperes).

16. In 2013, GM opened a new electric motor plant in White Marsh, Maryland, near Baltimore. It was the first plant that a major U.S. automaker dedicated to making the critical components for vehicle electrification. http://media.gm.com/content/media/us/en/gm/news.detail.html/content/Pages/news/us/en/2011/May/0517_baltimore.html.

INDEX

Page numbers followed by *"f"* and *"t"* indicate figures and tables respectively.